THE RAINBOW COMES AND GOES

BORN Lady Diana Manners, the youngest child of the 8th Duke of Rutland, Lady Diana Cooper became famous as a great socialite between the wars and during her marriage to Duff Cooper—the politician, writer and first Viscount Norwich—whose wife she became in 1919.

This is the first of her three-volume autobiography, in which she writes fluently of her early life—from her Edwardian upbringing as one of the 'Quality', to her presentation at Court in 1911 and the years during which she earned a reputation as a 'scalp-collector' of 'eligibles'—though the 'ineligibles' were always more to her taste. Before her engagement and marriage to Duff Cooper, she also describes her period as 'Nurse Manners' at Guy's Hospital during the 1914–18 war.

The reader of this memoir enters both the life of an exceptional individual, and the fascinating world of the aristocracy before and during the First World War.

Lady Diana Cooper's autobiography is continued in two further volumes, *The Light of Common Day* and *Trumpets from the Steep* and is available as a boxed set. The author lives in London in the aristocratic bohemia of Little Venice; her son is John Julius Norwich.

The Rainbow Comes and Goes

AUTOBIOGRAPHY

DIANA COOPER

CENTURY PUBLISHING
LONDON

LESTER & ORPEN DENNYS DENEAU
MARKETING SERVICES LTD
TORONTO

First published in Great Britain in 1958 by
Rupert Hart-Davis Ltd

This edition published in 1984 by
Century Publishing Co., Ltd,
Portland House, 12–13 Greek Street, London WIV 5LE

ISBN 0 7126 0452 9

Published in Canada by
Lester & Orpen Dennys Deneau Marketing Services Ltd,
78 Sullivan Street, Ontario, Canada

The cover shows a detail of the workroom of
the Gerrards Cross War Depôt by J. Barnard Davis

Reprinted in Great Britain by
Richard Clay (The Chaucer Press) Ltd,
Bungay, Suffolk

The Rainbow comes and goes,
And lovely is the Rose . . .

At length the Man perceives it die away,
And fade into the light of common day . . .

The Cataracts blow their trumpets from the steep,
No more shall grief of mine the season wrong . . .

WORDSWORTH
*Ode (Intimations of Immortality from
Recollections of Early Childhood)*

Contents

The Rainbow Comes and Goes

CHAPTER ONE

No Shadows

THE celestial light shone most brightly at Cockayne Hatley,
a house in Bedfordshire that must always be remembered
as the place where the clouds cast no shadows but were always
fleecy white, where grass was greener and taller, strawberries
bigger and more plentiful, and above all where garden and
woods, the house and the family, the servants and villagers,
would never change. It was a rather ugly house, verandahed
and ivied, which my father had taken, not as I thought for
eternity but for perhaps ten years, to house his family of two
sons and three daughters. We had grown too big for our
London house, 23a Bruton Street, where I was born. (It still
stands, unrecognisable with its discreet front door replaced by
blatant shop-windows. Not long ago, walking home after
dinner in Hill Street, I followed a fire-engine for the first
time in my life. It led me to the house of my birth burning
brightly, and in the crowd I came shoulder to shoulder with
my brother.)

Hatley was an unpretentious house and my mother, I think,
did nothing much to improve it. There were assegais in the
hall and a gong to say that meals were ready, and a dark dining-
room with the Marly horses in black bronze on the chimneypiece. It was a room into which I scarcely went except to say
good morning to my father eating his breakfast alone, and to
be given a minute tidbit of his roll spread with butter and

marmalade, and on "occasions" such as snapdragon at Christmas or when my father showed his magic lantern. Two or three times a year the children and household were given this double treat of magic and *contretemps*—the burnt finger, the appalling smell of multiple substances burning, the upsidedown pictures, the reliable sameness of the slides. These never changed, any more than did the servants, who must have wearied of the programme. All fathers of the nineties had magic lanterns and slides of the Zoo and the Houses of Parliament and Niagara, but we thought ourselves unique and superior by having one—only one—of Father himself and my eldest sister Marjorie, taken in Scotland, with a background of moors.

The drawing-room had a palm and a draped grand piano and three big windows, whose blue curtains were seldom hung in the summer, as they had to be laid out on the lawn to get their inartistic brightness faded by the eternal Hatley sunshine. There were screens and faded red chintz-covered sofas and down-at-castor chairs and an ottoman, and pictures of Cust ancestors and children (the house was owned by Lord Brownlow). There were white fur rugs in profusion, my mother's touch and a happy one, for children to roll upon, with a more interesting smell than the common knee-excoriating carpet. There was a little room, used only for the Christmas tree, and there was my father's study, well lined with books and giving on to the garden, into which jutted a glass palm-filled bubble. Today we can admire a Victorian conservatory, but my Pre-Raphaelite mother would have none of it.

Upstairs the house wandered without sense through passages and baize swing-doors, different levels and wings, with no symmetry or plan but to my child's reason the true design. There was the schoolroom wing and the nurseries. The schoolroom was ruled by Deborah Metzker, a squat, flat-slippered, manly woman, severe and orderly, with no give, few smiles and no caresses, but "Debby" was loved by Marjorie and our brothers Haddon and John. When I was three they were respectively fourteen, eleven and nine. There was an age-bar that allowed us to mix only very occasionally, although the next child, my sister Letty, was already seven. Sometimes the nursery would visit the schoolroom and be impressed by its age and intelligence, its aviary of canaries and bullfinches and its many pugs, the only breed of dog considered "safe with children." Sitting there one day at tea, high in my mother's arms, I remember looking down on the sad fair face of my brother Haddon. Soon after he was to die and cause my mother such an anguish of grief that she withdrew into a studio in London, where in her dreadful pain she was able to sculpt a recumbent figure of her dead son. Cut in marble it now lies in the chapel at Haddon Hall, and the plaster cast, which I think more beautiful as being the work of her own hand, is in the Tate Gallery. All her artistic soul went into this tomb, and critics of fifty years later, their vision, values and perspective deformed or reformed by Henry Moore, have bowed to the truth and beauty of what she created. My mother did not live to mourn the death of her other children. She used to tell me at eighty how the thought of this dead child could hurt her as keenly as ever, but that the thought grew ever rarer.

The schoolroom visited the nursery only when they were dressed as musketeers or Romans or clowns and were desperate for an audience. The nursery did not have pets. It had Nanny, who was all and everything. She looked like a little dried-up monkey. I thought her most lovely. Her eyes were blue and almost met, the pink of her cheeks was broken veins; her hair she dealt with once a week with a sponge and some dark liquid in a saucer which resulted in an unsuccessful brown-black; her teeth were long by nature, her body a mummy's bones. She took her bath every morning behind the nursery screen on which Walter Crane's Sleeping Beauty, Yellow Dwarf, Beauty and the Beast, etc. were pasted. I was given a Marie biscuit to allay my curiosity and never did I peer through the screen chinks. Nanny always wore black, winter and summer—a bodice and skirt made of "stuff." On her head she wore for the Park a minute black bonnet that just covered the top of her dear head, moored down with strong black velvet ribbons tied beneath her chin. I loved her dearly, because I was an affectionate, incurious, unenquiring child, so that it seemed only natural that I should not be allowed to take a toy in my perambulator to the Park, or my doll to the garden, and that Nanny would never cuddle or comfort me. Nor did she ever play with me. She sat always at the plain deal nursery table mending our clothes and darning her own stockings on an egg.

It was a leisured life. I do not think that Nanny did the children's washing (the laundrymaid saw to that), and she had a nurserymaid to lay the table and dust and make our beds and dress my sister Letty and push the perambulator when in London. Strapped into my navy-blue pram, a crescent balanced on sensitive springs, a wide *moufflon* cape leaving nothing exposed but my white woollen hands, coifed in a so-called "Dutch" bonnet tied like Nanny's under the chin, I would be wheeled, long-haired tam-o'-shantered sister Letty walking alongside, to the Nannies' fashion centre, Rotten Row, where Nanny would meet Nanny Benson and Nanny Poynder to talk of their charges in dark undertones, spelling out the flattering p-r-e-t-t-y, or the ominous d-e-n-t-i-s-t, or to discuss disloyally the "enamelled" Princess of Wales or my Nanny's unreasonable dislike of the Duke of York. We wheeled along

Rotten Row and ladies and gentlemen on tall horses would stop and ask whose children we were. Later, when I was always dressed in black satin, more riders stopped. I was taken out of the pram for leg-stretching, but no romping was allowed. The grass was too dirty, hoops too dangerous, so I walked demurely with Letty and Daisy Benson talking of Christmas and birthdays. On muddy days the one-legged crossing-sweeper always got a penny for the channel he had cleaned, and would grin and touch his cap, passing the time of day with Nanny, whom he called "Mrs Whatmore." My aunts called her "Whatmore." Mother said "Nanny" and the aunts thought this as wrong as saying "Cook" or "your master." I realised life's monotony and accepted it as one of the natural laws, but it was a great delight to go out, as I sometimes did, with my mother in a hansom cab, even though she did once drop me on the pavement when stepping out on that precarious little foothold —an event that I do not remember but heard tell of a hundred times.

And so back to dinner at one o'clock. I was the baby and in consequence Nanny's special charge and favourite. As I sat perched high in my baby's chair, strapped in with a tray for my food that, attached to the chair, came whirling over my head and imprisoned me safely, Nanny would feed me bread and milk, teach me to use my right hand, give me a crust to suck and later a chicken drumstick to gnaw—a bone I see to this day as the symbol of the soul. On my feeder in red cross-stitch was written "Don't be dainty" and I wasn't, but poor Letty, like so many children, while not dainty, could not swallow her food. Round and round it went in her mouth, colder and more congealed grew the mutton-fat, further away receded the promising pudding, and very often I saw her unfinished plate put cold into the cupboard for tea. Nanny, typical of her date and dryness, trained us by punishment only, never by reasoning and persuasion. I was so rarely naughty that I came in for very little chastisement: occasionally a "bed for the rest of the day" like life-sentences that never finish their term, so that by teatime I was picked up and given a treat—a paintbox perhaps with magazine pictures to colour and instructions not to lick my brush like grown-ups, who if they licked green paint, known to be arsenic, would surely die. But Letty, although a good child too, got boxed on the ears and, cruellest and most humiliating, a "dose" as a punishment. What seemed dreadful favouritism may have been due to our difference in age. Letty was given rhubarb, an obnoxious yellow powder to be taken in water, milk or jam (Letty chose jam through her tears), while I had a glass of cheerful tinkling citrate of magnesia. I used to cry for Letty's tears and occasionally bought her a reprieve.

Letty was my be-all, my dayspring, my elder, my accomplice. Hers was the invention. I do not remember having any myself. Hers was the daily "strip" whispered from her bed to mine in darkness—long sagas, no fairy stuff, more family life with my aunts and grandmother or the Dan Leno family, a sort of normal background of home with quite dreadful happenings and tortures predominating. Then Letty could draw well, and Letty rode side-saddle on Cobweb, and Marjorie galloped on Trilby, while I sat in a padded worked chair-saddle, like a howdah, on Shetland. Letty was graceful, I was a blunderbuss. Letty picked up a lot and brought the news to the nursery— tremendous news—that Aunt Kitty had not died of a chill but had drowned herself in the lake at Belvoir, that she had seen our mother sobbing, and that Nanny, said to be on her holiday, was never to return. In argument Letty would gain the point by reminding me that she was four and a half years older, but

I thought of us as twins with her as the clever one. She said older prayers—"Our Fathers"—at Nanny's bath-aproned knee while I, my face glowing from the fire and glistening with lanoline, mumbled "Please God bless Papa and Mama" and "Gentle Jesus meek and mild."

Nanny taught me my letters on building-blocks and taught me to read without tears by the ripe age of four. I learnt that E was like a little carriage with a little seat for the driver, that G looked like a monkey eating a cake, and later that the pig was in the gig and how ten men met in a den. By five or six I was on to *Line upon Line* and *Lines Left Out*, which dealt un-expectedly enough with Abraham and Lot's wife. The first book I read to myself was *Stumps*, which on finishing I began again. I resolved to do this for ever. The next was *Little Christian's Pilgrim's Progress*, as a serial story in a bound copy of *Sunday*. I knew Pliable and Obstinate and Faithful (I don't suppose that Carnal Cogitation figured) as I knew ordinary surnames—Nixon the butler, or Searle or Durrance. They car-ried no allegorical sense any more than Marderveen, in its fluted pyramidal bottle sealed in scarlet, meant Pommade Divine, sovereign for bumps. I learnt my tables (early ones), and strokes and pothooks came easily, I imagine, since I remember making and enjoying them. Nanny sat and I stood by her side reading aloud, as I followed her guiding pencil, from *Little Arthur's England*.

I knew a lot of poems by heart, but never funny ones. My mother did not mind nursery rhymes. She liked only the beautiful in everything. Tolerant of toys, she was unsym-pathetic to any that were conventional or comic. Japanese dolls and Japanese crinkly-paper books were encouraged. She ab-horred anything in the fashionable golliwog style. I am not capable of describing the extraordinary beauty and flavour that emanated from my mother. She had ethereal iridescence, passionate but not over-demonstrative love for her children, and a certain mysterious detachment. I never knew her tired or sad or very gay. Crossness was out of her ken. She would rock me and I would press my face into her cream (never white) silks and laces, and shut my eyes to smell more clearly the faint orris-root that scented them. I hope that as this story moves on she will here and there be seen as she was, but it is too much to expect.

When I was about six the world-shattering news that Hatley was to be sold overwhelmed us all. Shades of the prison-house had begun to close very early for me. I knew that "things didn't last for ever," that Nanny had once been a child and would die. Already at five I would tell myself that I too was to be a victim of death. I would say "You are only a child. It is too far ahead to think of." I suppose that subconsciously it was my brother's death that had instructed me, although I do not remember the happening, nor my mother's misery, nor talk among servants and villagers, but there it was, I knew that we were moving on, and superimposed on this little shadow of instability came a black thundering ejecting cloud. Hatley and Bruton Street were to be sold, and a new house bought in London. It was to be goodbye to the known world. A fig for Bruton Street! but Hatley . . .

The grown-ups too were very sad (in itself disconcerting)— Nanny and Debby and Miss Tritton, and Rose the nursery-maid and the gardeners who were to watch us go, and the groom who was to go but not with us, and Miss Laxton and her old mother in the house across the field, and the clergyman and the washerwoman, and the Peels, the only neighbours. All seemed to be part of this tragedy. Goodbye to the tall grass and the hay, the pond with the island and the little boat, and the frogs in the gruesome pit that pyramided themselves until they toppled over, to the garden and the sun-hot fruit on the kitchen-garden walls. What would go with us? What would be jettisoned? Was the toy-cupboard going as it stood? Yes—a relief but not enough. Funnily, though, I do not remember the last day. I suppose that it was benignantly camouflaged. Shetland went to Belvoir, so did the carriage-horse Svengali. The pugs and canaries came to London, and the excitement of the huge house boasting of electric light and two bathrooms swept us into a new world that dazzled our eyes, putting the past into a shade that now has become the nostalgic fountain-light of being.

The new life in Arlington Street ended babyhood. Taps and electric switches gave one a certain adult power. It was a vast house of exquisite proportions, now half-obliterated and totally deformed by the Overseas League, which has suppressed the William Kent decorations, torn up and roofed over the eighteenth-century cobbled courtyard and built a lot of new rooms. In our day the cab-horse (we never had a carriage of our own) was driven beneath an archway built into the lodge house, in one hutch of which lived Mrs Seed, the white-haired lodge-lady. The horse would slither and slide and panic on the slippery outsize cobblestones, the bells would ring an alarm and we would dash to the third-floor nursery window in the hope of seeing him fall.

The Quality, when the front door opened, found themselves in a darkish pillared hall, to the right of which was a wide and shallow-stepped staircase of stone, beautifully balustraded in wrought iron. Tradesmen darted down a stairway in the lodge and followed a subterranean passage that ran the long length of the courtyard. Huge kitchens were beneath the lodge, so that the food had a long cold journey before it reached the house. On the passage level was a fine big room looking on to Green Park, known as the "basement," in which stood my brother's unplaced tomb. There was also a servants' hall where the nine servants ate and laughed uproariously. Never to-day are children told to shut the door against the deafening laughter of the staff. The narrow back stairs went up five stone flights with an iron banister curved outwards to give place to ladies' hooped skirts—a pre-crinoline line. Between these banisters there just fitted a labour-saving letter-box slung between two leather straps and worked by a top-floor wheel and a basement handle. The procedure was to communicate from the upper floors by an echo-age telephone, saying to the cave-dweller "I've put some letters in the box," and he would rush to manipulate the handle. Another device was a small electric gadget on the wall by the front door which, when a little lever was pulled down, would produce in a short time a child of nine dressed in heavy blue serge uniform, a pillbox hiding one ear, who would for sixpence encircle like Puck any distance in forty minutes, bearing letters or parcels.

Giving on to the Park on the courtyard level, connected by an outside stairway to a mangy garden below, was a Kent-decorated dining-room painted cream, a colour now much condemned as a background because it lasted too long as the artistic fashion, and a library for my father, with the *Encyclopaedia Britannica*, bound copies of the *Badminton Magazine*, current works of Conan Doyle and Kipling, Hansards, Blue Books, Red Books, *Who's Whos*, *Burke's Peerage*, Turf Guides and a large writing-table at which he wrote letters to Drummond's Bank, the Leicestershire Agricultural Club, the Sun Insurance Co., occasional articles on dry-fly fishing for the *Badminton Magazine* and a blue-moon letter to *The Times*. I remember the dear man scratching away with his J-nib in an exquisite legible hand. He would lay down his pen to give me a pink sweetie called Otto of Rose against the doubtful breath of smokers, or to dab my nose and chin with a drop of *cèdre* (a manly scent) from a bottle on his table. No secretary and no typewriter gave a householder two good hours of tiresome work every morning, and the new income tax was another irritating complication. Years later, I remember, it rose to elevenpence in the pound. We all thought Papa would die. He looked too ashen to recover.

My own anxieties had begun. Ruin stared us in the face—everything sold, beggars in the street. This real fear must have come from my father's perpetual threat of bankruptcy. Another great and yearly dread was the divorce of my parents. Never was such a thing in question. They lived exceedingly happily together, adored their children and were fully conscious of their happy condition. My father had a wayward temper that sometimes ran away with him, and once he threw a napkin at my mother because she had asked Princess Beatrice of Battenberg to luncheon without telling him. This must have started my fears. Heaven no longer lay about me.

To return to the house. There was, looking on to the cobbles, a large morning-room—my mother's. Had she been less unselfish she would have put my father on the yard side of the house, to be disturbed by the clop-clopping of the horses, and taken for herself the sunny Park-side room, completely noiseless except on Sunday evenings in summer when the military band played *Pinafore* in the Park bandstand. True, the morning-room had the Kent plasterwork of fruit and flowery swags. It was densely packed with furniture and loved objects, all of sentiment, or things of a colour that she could not resist, such as blue-green Chinese jars or the dead straw of the palm-leaf fan that she used to protect her cheek from the fire. A great many of her drawings hung on the walls. Every room boasted an elaborate chimneypiece of carved wood or marble with an open steel grate.

On the next floor there was a vast ballroom on the court side, generally used as a studio, music and play room, with a piano littered with opera-scores and often an unfinished bust of one of us mobled in wet cloths, a centre-skylit drawing-room elaborately decorated, and two rooms on the Park side with iron balconies. One was a gilded drawing-room (later to become my nursery) and the other my mother's bedroom, with next door under the stairs a slip of a bathroom with a narrow tin bath like the one in which the brides were drowned. The rooms were enormously high on these three floors and the stairs were very exhausting, especially for the ever-changing seventeen-year-old nurserymaid who carried our trays up the last flight of four, and for the "boy" who carried them up the other three storeys. Many a time did we hear with joy the interminable clatter of a whole tray's fall, with its horrid mutton and cabbage and tapioca pudding.

On the third floor a passage, the only one above stairs, led from my father's bedroom and a spare room to the schoolroom, Marjorie's room and Mrs Page's, who had now replaced Deborah. On this floor was the special bathroom-cum-box-and-lumber room. My father was very pleased. A six-foot-two man, he had never had but a hip-bath and now he could soak at full length and have a very big sponge. I remember how shocked I was when he told me that he never used soap in his bath. He had Windsor soap, we had Vinolia and Pears (a choice at Belvoir) and drearily innocent Cimolite at home. Above this floor two wooden flights of stairs led to the three-roomed nursery wing and the four-roomed maids' wing. God knows where the other servants slept—in the basement or lodge presumably.

So much for 16 Arlington Street, one of the most unspoilt eighteenth-century houses in London, built at the end of a cul-de-sac, where daily lingered a hope of a barrel organ (to whose now lost music the clumsy-booted children danced, holding wide their skirts with more graceful fingers), wrapped in its inevitable overalling of patterned green baize complete with Italian grinder, corseted, mortar-boarded wife and the soliciting monkey in regimental red, equipped to present arms. Or very rarely the dramas of Punch's life, and Judy's death, and Toby's indifference, ringed round with a knot of smaller children, cabbies, and flocks of pigeons and sparrows squabbling for the grain that fell from the poor horses' nosebag, horses that in cul-de-sacs never found the straw to deaden their hoof-fall for dying ears.

Here my mother drew, and entertained very occasionally. Here my father wrote his letters, laced on his boots at mid-day and walked down Bond Street, taking off his top hat to bow to acquaintances at every other step. Here we all had our meals at one and two o'clock respectively on different floors. From here Marjorie went for casual education to Miss Wolff's classes in South Street, Mayfair, and to art schools in Kensington, and Letty too later on, and brother John came and went to school.

I became a good little girl, affectionate and, Nanny said, "well built." No one thought me pretty but my mother. My hair was put into curl-papers every night since memory starts. It was all a pale yellow fuzz in the morning and at parties, but fell lankily at the end of the day or when it rained. I wore scarlet shoes with rosettes like Harriet's (and the Matches), and for best a black satin Vandyck dress with collar, cuffs, and apron of lawn and real lace. I also had a short sensible black satin coat for the Park. I was a happy trusting child, a little frightened of the dark and never allowed the chink of open door that would have helped me. Spitting out cod-liver oil in the "place" was my only deceit I remember.

My mother spent the mornings in bed. I see her sitting cross-legged in her bed writing endless letters with a flowing quill pen. On her knee was balanced a green morocco folding letter-case, with blotting paper and a pot of ink which, curiously enough, never got splashed on the Irish linen sheets. It had a bristled penwiper and pockets for letters written and unwritten. Having no telephone, in urgency she would give a stylised scream to attract her maid Tritton, to whom she would hand a letter marked "Messenger Boy" to be put in the box. My mother would not take long to get up or to wash in soft sterilised water poured out of high stone bottles bought from the chemist. She used very little powder (Fuller's Earth) and a speck of Roger & Gallet's pink lip-salve (the same that she would surreptitiously smear on my resisting mouth for fancy balls).

My mother entertained occasionally at two o'clock luncheon. Very beautiful women were always round the table. Lady Westmorland was the most lovely in my eyes, perhaps because she painted her face. I would come down in my embroidered-with-wheat-ears lawn frock and scarlet shoes and stand by my mother's chair while she plucked admiringly at my hair and let it flutter slowly through her fingers. No one saw me with her eyes. The gentlemen were kind. I was told particularly to remember Cecil Rhodes, a thick square man who stared at me and did not know what to say either. Later on I remember the bearded Lord Salisbury (Prime Minister on and off), to whom my father was secretary. I remember him chiefly because I dropped a valued sixpence behind a bookcase in the drawing-room and half-crying told him, so he gave me another. I was scolded for asking gentlemen for money.

My father went down to the House of Lords in the afternoon. My mother would etherealise Cecil Rhodes, Paderewski, Arthur Balfour or George Meredith with her skilled pencil. Queen Victoria she drew, but with only one sitting (Deborah Metzker, a pudding-basin and mantilla on her head, had to pose for the accessories). She was a justly renowned artist. In 1902 at the Grosvenor Gallery, in collaboration with Benjamin Constant, she gave an exhibition of 192 pencil portraits. Two were bought by the Luxembourg. All the celebrities of politics, literature or the stage, all the beauties of their day, were pleased to sit to her and see themselves through her beatifying eyes. We were often her models, statue-still for hours at a time. Lessons went forward with Nanny, and I would go every morning to the schoolroom for piano lessons from Mrs Page. This idyllic life was varied by visits to Belvoir, my grandfather's castle in Leicestershire, and to Sussex, where my mother rented cottages beside the summer sea.

CHAPTER TWO

The Castle on the Hill

THE Castle stands high on a hill overlooking the vale of Belvoir, then a contented vale of solid farms and farmers who followed foxhounds and thought of their acres in terms of "runs," "jumps" and "coverts." The Duchess who had built this Valhalla was a Howard from Castle Howard and as a bride had been grievously disappointed at the low wandering Charles II house built on the foundations of a Norman strong- hold. She had expected better, so her kind rich husband allowed her to raze it to the ground and to build on the old foundations a real castle, neo-Norman, neo-Gothic, neo- everything. Scarcely had she got it up than it was burnt almost out, with many of its prized treasures. Undaunted she built it up again. So steep was its hill that she made a cyclopic causeway to link it to a neighbouring mound. She furnished it lavishly. She hung it with the family *chefs d'œuvre* and a respectable collection of Italian and Dutch Masters, with Gobelin tapestries and all the stained glass, the dogtooth, the red and the gold of the day. This second castle was opened by the Prince Regent in 1820.

The Duchess bore about ten children and died of what must have been an appendicitis at forty. She had prepared her mausoleum on the further mound, where in statuary she floats heavenward towards her recovered marble-winged babies. Blue and yellow hidden windows light her flight. Her sorrowing husband did not re-marry, and at his death his son succeeded him—Uncle Granby to my ears but not to my eyes, for he died before my birth, and his brother John, my grandfather, inherited the estate. The fortunes had been sadly depleted by the castle-building.

Lord John (now the Duke) was a beautiful bent old man. I can see him very clearly, walking down the endless corridors of Belvoir, wrapped warmly in a thick black cape buttoned down the front, for these passages in winter were arctic—no stoves, no hot pipes, no heating at all. He would unbutton his cape at the drawing-room door and hang it on a long brass bar with many others. He joined his large family at lunch, but I do not remember his talking very often. I would sit on his bony knees when the meal was over, and be allowed to blow open his gold hunter watch, and ask for a comical poem that he and I both liked to hear recited in a sing-song tone that has stayed with me until now. A strange choice for a child of six, it was about a cuckolded Roundhead whose wife was hiding an escaped Cavalier:

> I went into the dairy to see what I could see,
> And there I saw a gentleman's boot
> Where a gentleman's boot ought never to be.
> So I called to my wife and I said "My dear,
> Pray what is this gentleman's boot doing here?"
> "Why, you old goose, you blind old goose,
> And can't you very well see
> That it is a milking-pail
> My granny has sent to me?"
> "Hobs bobs, here's fun!
> Milking-pails with spurs on."
>
> I went into the kitchen to see what I could see,
> And there I saw a gentleman's sword
> Where a gentleman's sword ought never to be.

So I called to my wife and I said "My dear,
Pray what is this gentleman's sword doing here?"
"Why, you old goose, you blind old goose,
And can't you very well see
That it is a toasting-fork
My granny has sent to me?"
"Hobs bobs, here's fun!
Toasting-forks with scabbards on."

I went into the chamber to see what I could see,
And there I saw a gentleman
Where a gentleman ought never to be.
So I called to my wife and I said "My dear,
Pray what is this gentleman doing here?"
"Why, you old goose, you blind old goose,
And can't you very well see
That it is a waiting-maid
My granny has sent to me?"
"Hobs bobs, here's fun!
Waiting-maids with breeches on."

After this poem, or another starting "O that my lips might bleat like buttered peas," lisping Aunt Queenie would say "Tingaly the bingaly, Farver," and he would let me ring the gold bell on the table. The groom of the chambers, thus summoned, would ask what orders for the stables. Some days the answer was "Perfection round at a quarter before three, if you please." These were the good days for me and Letty. We would watch my grandfather mount Perfection from the mounting-stone against the castle wall. Perfection was snow-white, very fat and quiet. Either one of his sons or Mr Knox, his private chaplain, would ride beside him, while a smart old groom, liveried in blue and buttoned in silver, top-hatted and cock-aded, jogged behind.

The Rev. Knox, our private chaplain, was "extra-parochial."

I have never heard of another ordained clergyman being extra-parochial. My grandfather was his bishop. He could, I suppose, have celebrated Black Mass in the little white plaster gothic chapel, and nothing said. But Mr Knox was not a Black Masser. He was a black Irish Protestant with a brogue, who played a jig on the fiddle and had the hands and legs of a man who thinks of horses even in the pulpit. We had prayers every morning, and church, morning and evening, on Sunday. We said our prayers and sung our canticles out of morocco-bound, octavo books printed with f's for s's, and prayers for the eternal health of Queen Adelaide. How well we knew, by the speed of the morning prayers, if Mr Knox was hunting that day or not, and how far off the meet was. We used to believe that he wore his spurs under his cassock and surplice.

He was, among other unclerical activities, Captain of the Belvoir Fire Brigade. That was a magnificent turn-out. The alarm would ring and the brigade would muster, some of them from a mile away with a precipitous hill to climb. They had axes and Britannia helmets. The engine was hand-pumped and went out for real business, in my recollection, but once—to a burning stately home of a neighbour eight miles away. I think that its going was more in the nature of a gesture than anything else. The house was burnt to the ground.

But the days when my grandfather did not ride were not so free for us. A lengthy discussion would be carried on between him, some aunts and the groom of the chambers as to whether it was to be the landau, the victoria or the barouche that should be used for the drive. I never understood what the issue was—the size of the vehicle, the state of the roads or the condition of the horses. Anyhow, the decision was made and the children were dressed for the afternoon drive. I remember genuinely hating it, I don't know why. It was not more boring than the pram and the walks holding Nanny's hand, never for one second being allowed to relinquish it. Perhaps it was because I, for one, always felt sick and dreaded the smell of the blue leather padding and the hot horses, and sitting backward, sometimes on the vast landau seat, sometimes on the minute stool of the victoria. Whatever it was, I hated it. I would be dressed, as usual, in a black satin coat, black satin bonnet and scarlet shoes with rosettes. We would drive for an hour and a half through country roads of very little interest. There was no town within eight miles and scarcely any neighbours to leave cards upon. So round and round the muddy lanes of the estate we splashed, with an immense apoplectic coachman on the box and an alert footman in a fawn boxcloth liveried coat, check-lined and almost to the ground, who sprang up and down to open the too many gates.

When we reached home, a large crowd of tourists would have collected on each side of the last hundred yards of the approach, and my grandfather would uncover his head and bow very slightly with a look of pleasure and welcome on his delicate old face. He loved his tourists. They represented to him England and liberty and the feudal system, and were a link between the nobility and the people. The house was open to them three times a week and on all bank holidays. They would arrive in four-in-hand charabancs from all over the country. Bedrooms and one drawing-room, one study and a dining-room were excluded from their tour. Otherwise, from morning to dark, armies of sightseers tramped through that welcoming house. No efforts were made to improve it for them. There were no signed photographs of royalty or of the family, no special flowers or Coronation robes draped casually over a chair, coronet to hand, no tables laid or crumpled newspapers. Nor could they have any idea of how we really lived. In the summer my mother arranged for us children to picnic out and not to return until the hordes had departed, for in truth the atmosphere—the smell—was asphyxiating. Not that one could get away with one's picnic—they all brought picnics too and were encouraged to eat and sleep and take their boots off and comb their hair in the garden, on the terraces, all about and everywhere. They paid no admittance and two or three elderly ladies in black dresses—Lena the head housemaid, the controller of a regiment of maids and the terror of our chapel choir (she sang loud and false to poor Miss Thursby's pedal-sore harmonium), and Mrs Smith the housekeeper, sparkling with jet arabesques, or a pensioned retainer—would shepherd them round.

On Sundays the family, its guests, its governesses and nurses, my grandfather's gentlemen secretaries, his chaplain, Mrs Knox and their child, made a tour of the demesne. Soon after lunch church clothes were changed for equally long close-fitting costumes. The pony chaise was ordered for my grand-father, and a groom to lead it. We would make first for the stables. Mr Durrance, the head groom, would be standing there in blue and silver, carrots in hand, to receive us. The gigantic Princes, Belvoirs and Wellingtons that drew the carriages, lined up hind-end foremost, were given a pat on the withers by my grandfather's withered hand, and a carrot was proffered to each twitching muzzle. Next the sore backs of the hunters were looked at reprovingly. An apple for my Shetland pony, and the doors closed on the champing, the ammonia smell and the exquisitely-plaited selvedge of straw. A minute's glance at the harness-room's gleaming crests of peacocks on blinkers, another at the carriages, dog- and tub-carts and the sleigh. I never knew a great house that did not sport a sleigh, and yet I never saw one used in England. How did they ever

come to the coach-houses and where are they sliding to
now? Did Russian princes present them, or were they mascots
to ward off the hunter's dread of ice and snow?

After the stables came the gardens. Mr Divers, the head
gardener, had a black W. G. Grace beard covering his chest, a
black cut-away coat, Homburg hat and a bunch of Bluebeard
keys. It was impossible to imagine a spade in his hands. He
would cut us off a fine bunch of white grapes from the thousand
hanging clusters in the vinery, pick us a camellia apiece and
offer some not-up-to-much apples to munch on the walk. My
grandfather would congratulate him on his last-won horti-
cultural medal and pretend to understand the Latin names of
his flowers. I liked the poultry yard better because there was
a muster of peacocks, and best perhaps the dairy and Miss
Saddlebridge the dairymaid (whose face was not her fortune),
who filled the dishes with creamy milk and churned yellow
butter-pats crested with peacocks. The kennels next, but they
smelt of dead horse, and hounds are not trained to know the
difference between men and doorposts, so ladies often weakened on this last call. It was an exhausting walk and my legs
were very short. I got a lift sometimes on my grandfather's
lap in his chaise, but it was hard on the polite and reluctant
men and women who trudged a good three miles, the ladies
gathering up their long skirts in their little frozen hands.

My grandfather would come to London for the season.
He had a house in Cambridge Gate, the only ugly row of
Regent's Park. He would send the carriage and pair to fetch us
to tea occasionally. It was no fun.

We were not very fond of our aunts and uncles who lived
with him at Belvoir. There was poor Aunt Kitty who drowned
herself. Unarmed for life, artistic and frustrated, she sought
and never found relief, neither by joining the Church of Rome

nor by becoming a nurse at Guy's—a highly-commended move in 1914 when I followed her to that great hospital, but in her day condemnable. These departures exasperated her eccentric mother (my grandfather's second wife), so Aunt Kitty, decked in what jewellery she possessed and marking the fatal brink with her parasol, found peace in the deep Belvoir lake. When his Duchess died, Aunt Queenie kept house for my grandfather. She painted water colours and wrote about art for the *Connoisseur*. Aunt Elsie, the youngest and our favourite, married Lord George Scott, who came over the Border like Young Lochinvar to court her. She scarcely knew him when they were married in the Belvoir chapel. I was bridesmaid in a Vandyck dress (cream satin this time). She died alas! too young.

Uncle Cecil was a big success with children, being always on all fours. He went to the Boer War as a reporter. He quarrelled with the family. He suffered from spy-fever and at the age of eighty, I am sorry to say, could no longer endure life itself so ended it beneath a train at Crowborough. Uncle Billy died young of fits, and Uncle Edward, the eldest of my father's half-brothers, died of tuberculosis and other dread diseases. Uncle Bobby, the youngest, had all the strength and health and character that the others seemed to lack. A gallant soldier in the Boer War, with a D.S.O. for us to admire, he became Master of the Belvoir Hounds. He wore an eyeglass and had a drawl, though he very rarely spoke. I remember his man asking us when or where some event was to happen, adding "I've asked His Lordship, and all His Lordship says is 'Aw'." He was forty-five in 1915 and on the reserve of the Sixtieth Rifles, so the war took him and killed him.

We were chiefly at Belvoir in winter, I suppose, for I think of the tobogganing down slopes worthy of a world's fair, and my fear of the horse-pond ice breaking and drowning Letty, and of day-and-night prayers for snow. The elders outprayed me in their petitions for thaw and for the Meet of the Belvoir Hounds at the Castle door. Bright and beautiful as meets were, I would rather have had snow. Meets were two a penny, and following the hunt in a pony-cart frankly bored me. The ladies wore top hats or billycocks with very black veils drawn taut across their cold noses, and fringes and buns. The men were in pink, with glossy white "leathers," swigging down cherry brandy from their saddles to keep out the cold. Hounds making a faint music of excitement were dexterously and mercilessly being whipped into a pack by Ben Capel and his underlings. The Master, Sir Gilbert Greenall, was popular though seldom seen, and in his place would be his redoubtable wife surrounded by the horses pawing and twitching and foaming at the mouth, some incorrigibles sporting red bows on their tails that said "I kick." Then they would be off, with a flinty clatter of hooves and suppressed oaths and the language horses are thought to understand, through the bare woods to the open Vale, the second horsemen following demurely. They would hack home cold, weary and fulfilled in the twilight, generally caked in mud and smelling of horse, and fall upon the tea and boiled eggs, and discuss the runs and falls and scandals until the gong rang for dressing-time, getting louder and louder as it approached down the unending passages.

The gong man was an old retainer, one of those numberless ranks of domestic servants which have completely disappeared and today seem fabulous. He was admittedly very old. He wore a white beard to his waist. Three times a day he rang the gong—for luncheon, for dressing-time, for dinner. He would walk down the interminable passages, his livery hanging a little loosely on his bent old bones, clutching his gong with one hand and with the other feebly brandishing the padded-knobbed stick with which he struck it. Every corridor had to be warned and the towers too, so I suppose he banged on and off for ten minutes, thrice daily.

Then there were the lamp-and-candle men, at least three of them, for there was no other form of lighting. Gas was despised, I forget why—vulgar, I think. They polished and scraped the wax off the candelabra, cut wicks, poured paraffin oil and unblackened glass chimneys all day long. After dark they were busy turning wicks up or down, snuffing candles, and de-waxing extinguishers. It was not a department we liked much to visit. It smelt disgusting and the lamp-men were too busy. But the upholsterer's room was a great treat. He was exactly like a Hans Andersen tailor. Crosslegged he sat in a tremendous confusion of curtains and covers, fringes, buttons, rags and carpets, bolsters, scraps (that could be begged off him), huge curved needles like scimitars, bodkins, hunks of beeswax to strengthen thread, and hundreds of flags. The flags on the tower-top, I suppose, got punished by the winds and were constantly in need of repair. I never saw him actually at work on anything else. There were slim flags for wind, little ones for rain, huge ones for sunshine, hunting flags, and many others.

The water-men are difficult to believe in today. They seemed to me to belong to another clay. They were the biggest people I had ever seen, much bigger than any of the men of the family, who were remarkable for their height. They had stubbly beards and a general Bill Sikes appearance. They wore brown clothes, no collars and thick green baize aprons from chin to knee. On their shoulders they carried a wooden yoke from which hung two gigantic cans of water. They moved on a perpetual round. Above the ground floor there was not a drop of hot water and not one bath, so their job was to keep all jugs, cans and kettles full in the bedrooms, and morning or evening to bring the hot water for the hip-baths. We were always a little frightened of the water-men. They seemed of another element and never spoke but one word, "Water-man," to account for themselves.

If anyone had the nerve to lie abed until eleven o'clock, which can seldom have happened, there were many strange callers at the door. First the housemaid, scouring the steel grate and encouraging the fire of the night before, which always burned until morning, and refilling the kettle on the hob until it sang again. Next the unearthly water-giants. Then a muffled knock given by a knee, for the coal-man's hands were too dirty and too full. He was a sinister man, much like his brothers of the water, but blacker far and generally more mineral. He growled the single word "Coal-man" and refilled one's bin with pieces the size of ice-blocks.

The carpenter's shop was an excitement. It smelt good. One could use the lathes and coax Mr Ricketts to frame a picture or make a box with one's name fretted into it. Then too there was Betsy, the little old stillroom help. She was ninety when I first remember her. She had been born in the Castle, no one quite knew how, and for seventy-five years she washed and dried the plates for the lesser meals. She was felt to be one of the Castle's treasures, together with the Benvenuto Cellini ewer and basin. The visitors were always shown her. She had never learned to read or write—no disgrace, I think, to the family, as what child of her class did learn to read before Waterloo? But maybe she was the happier for her ignorance, for she was always laughing, lived to over a hundred and had a grand funeral.

Lastly there were the watchmen, who frightened many a

newcomer to death. There was a little of the water-men about them, but they were dreadfully silent and they padded. All night they walked the passages, terraces and battlements, yet no one really saw them. One would leave a paper with a request (as one put a letter to Father Christmas in the grate) on the floor of the passage. The paper would disappear and the request would be granted by this remote, unseen power. Always if one woke in the night, as the fire flickered to its death, one would hear a padded foot on the gravel outside and a voice, not loud enough to waken but strong enough to reassure, saying "Past twelve o'clock. All's well."

Nothing changed until my grandfather died. He was well over eighty and had lived a life devoted to ideals. His heart had been broken when his lovely young wife, Miss Marley from Ireland, had died bearing him his second child (the first was my father). Twenty years later he had married again the "Grandmama" I knew, who bore him about eight sons and daughters. His political leader was Benjamin Disraeli. If anyone still reads Disraeli's books, they will find Belvoir described in *Coningsby* as Beaumanoir and Lord John Manners, as he was then called, in the character of Henry Sidney. He became Postmaster-General and Chancellor of the Duchy of Lancaster without aspiring to office. His biography was written by Charles Whibley.*

As soon as the Castle became my father's property the old order began to change. Bathrooms were carved out of the deep walls, rooms and passages were warm without the coal-man's knock, the water-men faded away into the elements. Forty strong horses turned to the power of one motor-car. Only the kettles remained, singing night and day on the hobs. The

* *Lord John Manners and his Friends*, 1925.

watchmen still guarded the fort, but no longer cried "All's well."

The children at Belvoir became the Castle guides for the Quality. The unfortunate guests, after the Sunday walk and a tremendous tea, were handed over to Letty and me (the novice) to be instructed about our family history and heirlooms and any legend we had picked up, or the facts about the authenticity of the Benvenuto Cellini ewer, or the strange panel representing Henry VII and his minions Empson and Dudley. I cannot tell how irritating or disarming we were, babbling and embroidering truths and suppressing nasty rumours about the Gainsborough being a replica.

My father was frankly philistine. He was wise and knew about dry-fly fishing and how to be loved, but very little about the possessions which he inherited late in life. If we were not to be found and he was forced to show them himself he would, with a gesture, wave a whole wall away—a wall studded with the finest Nicholas Hilliard miniatures (pronounced in those days "minnychers")—with a "Don't worry about those: they're all fakes." Running in late on our duties, we would blush for him and lovingly shield him. I remember with what solicitude we tried to save his dear face when he discovered to his humiliation that the massive gold snuffbox embossed with Rs and coronets and presented to him with "A Happy Christmas from Harry" (my uncle) had been taken out of his own show-case. The castle tour took hours and its victims were spared nothing. There was the Regent's Gallery, endlessly long with blue-and-white Chinese bowls the size of vats, filled with Belvoir potpourri, in each of its twelve windows. Marble busts of Caesars and of our own Dukes lined its walls, hung with Gobelin Don Quixote tapestries, and a carpet of arum lilies on a scarlet ground covered its acreage. There was the Elizabeth Salon, with a Canova-ish marble Duchess presiding, hand on heart. She had commemorated herself in the painted ceiling as Juno enthroned beside her good friend the Duke of York (undressed) as Jupiter. Light from the great bow-window was all but blotted out by two over-life-sized easelled pictures of her and her legitimate Duke, looking as though they were alive and might, when the fancy took them, step out of their golden frames on to the huge velvet footstools placed at their feet. The final lap of the ordeal was the hardest and meant their climbing the highest tower (the last hundred feet by ladders), to be battered by the wind like the flag above them.

Sussex by the sea was wonderfully different—a cottage for a castle. I never went there until I was six, and I was disappointed by the beach. It was middle tide when I first saw the sea, with rows and rows of little long white waves. I had imagined something generally bigger with occasional breakers the size of hills, but the sand was a delight that I had not been told to expect. We took every year rather squalid cottages at Aldwick near Bognor, at Rustington, at Angmering—all of them villages scarcely marked on the map. Finally we got to the outskirts of Aldwick and stayed there. There was a four-roomed thatched cottage called Prior's Farm, from which one walked through acres of waving corn to the tamarisk hedge that protected it from the sea. A tired old dear cooked and cleaned and heated water for washing. The earth closet we disapproved of but bore with resignation.

The last cottage found was an early nineteenth-century sailor's house and lodge. In the house, which still belongs to my son, lived Mrs Fisher, a woman in her eighties, six foot high with white plaits framing her ears like Queen Victoria's on the florin. On two sticks under a black straw mushroom hat she would sail haltingly round her garden and orchard of an evening, complaining always of her groins (we learnt later that these were breakwaters, not parts of her body) and rating poor Maria, her adopted daughter, who cooked and cleaned and mowed and chopped and dug and harvested and nursed the tyrannical old beauty. She never went to bed, but slept in her clothes in the dark kitchen. They said that sixty years before, on a white horse, she had galloped down the narrow lane to the sea with her husband-to-be, and seeing the little house had vowed she would live in no other.

The lodge, where we lived, was a Regency bungalow. Nanny and we children undressed for bathing in a little coppice at the sea end of the garden. There would be murmurs of "Turn your back" and lo! Nanny was dressed in bloomers and tunic of shocking-pink. The Tree children were with us and Iris, the youngest of us all, was tethered by a rope to her drunken Nanny. There was never a question of learning to swim, but we splashed in the waves or crab-dabbled wearing waders and picking up cuttlefish or decorating our sand-castles with tamarisk. In my earliest days at Bognor I remember being in a bathing-machine drawn into four feet of water by a carthorse, and dipped head and all into the sea by the old bathing-woman, her long skirt billowing in the water.

My mother, coming for Sundays with Maud Tree, and many a pampered sybaritic man from the Great World, unused to pallet beds and earth closets, would take rooms at Mrs Fisher's. One of these dandies, Claude Lowther, a poet and a wit, who always wore a gardenia and with whom I was furiously in love, once sent on bed and bedding in advance, saying that it was "hideous but comfortable and without fleas." When Mrs Fisher died my mother, with borrowed money (she had none of her own), bought the little property and twenty years later gave it to me. The cornfields that isolated it are harvested for ever. King George V gave Bognor a Regis to its name and made Aldwick the Royal Road to Health. The Bay Estate now replaces the waving wheat. Dorothy Perkins ramblers and scarlet salvias have driven out the poppies and cornflowers and binding convolvulus with which we trimmed our straw hats, with a cabbage leaf in the crown to protect us from sunstroke (which I got). In the middle of the Tudor canker of Manor Ways and dinky villas, we are still the three-acre blot, the undeveloped waste-land.

CHAPTER THREE

Shades of the Prison-House

I WAS becoming burdened by my apprehensions. They weighed against my happiness. At three I had feared prison bars when one went where trespassers will be prosecuted. I was learning anxiety. No one was teaching me. My mother concealed all her fears and sorrows, but the consciousness of destruction by disaster was defined and obsessive. Yet what might have frightened me with reason left me quite unapprehensive.

Uncle Edward went to Sweden (one wonders why) and returned to Belvoir jerking with new exercises. Young and old were lined up in the drawing-room to be taught by the new addict the secret of physical well-being. Up and out and down swung their arms and round like cartwheels, touching toes and stretching for the stars. I did my best but not well because my arms would not be raised higher than my shoulders. It was noticed at last and caused consternation. So that was why I bent my head over my cup when drinking, and why I could not turn over the music page on the piano-rack. Was it why I was labelled "blunderbuss" and always tumbled and therefore had permanently scabs on nose and chin and knees? From that day I went to doctors, in memory it seems daily, and never to the same one twice. It was during this time that Letty saw my mother crying without restraint and reported it to me, telling me that she thought I was the cause. I do not remember having any fuss or fear about my health. I took it as children take most things, for normal, but then I did not know what the specialists were presaging—a sure and steady degeneration of muscles that would take me through paralysis to early death. My mother's tears cannot have been of despair or resignation. Visiting doctors increased, dark consulting-rooms became part of the day's progress and ended in a grand and embarrassing climax. A crowd of consultants sat in a ring of elders, crowding the gilded drawing-room, while I walked round the arena, naked as a worm and suffering. I was brought up to be a modest child. Those were the days of clothes and hats, three petticoats and no somersaults, and bathing in bathing-costumes. Exposing full nudity to these gentlemen made me unhappy enough still to remember it.

Life changed from that hour. The fifth-floor nursery came down to the gilded drawing-room. No more was I to stagger up the stairs, very slowly and bent. In fact there were to be no more stairs at all, but instead a little chair in which I could be carried to the first floor. No more walks in the Park, only drives. No more lessons (I had had very few after Nanny's cramming), but Mademoiselle must read more *Bibliothèque Rose*. The minimum exercise, no getting up in the morning, and Dr Coleman to come every day when the family was in London to treat me with galvanism. For several years I had treatment—a big box of plugs and wires and Ons and Offs and wet pads clamped upon me that I might tingle and jerk. I was never to be gainsaid and spoiling was the order. Suppose this treatment, devised by the great Professor Herb of Hamburg, did not work and my life were to end before my twentieth year, let it be the happiest of lives, crammed with indulgences and treats. It was fortunate that, having a nature that took everything as normal, I did not become unduly spoilt. I was given every encouragement. The grown-ups became slaves to my demands, fetching and carrying and rarely saying No.

Since the age of two when I was taken to see Marie Tempest in *The Geisha* we went a lot to the theatre. We went to the pantomime too, at Christmas, to see Dan Leno and Herbert Campbell as very old Babes in the Wood, and fairies invisibly wired on tiptoe for flights through transformation gauzes. This was my father's treat. My mother's love of the beautiful in everything took us to Her Majesty's Theatre for every production and repeatedly to all Shakespeare's plays. We were a family brought up on both sides of the Beerbohm Trees' velvet curtain. For ten years they ruled that theatre with a rod of magic. We were taken with the three Tree children—Viola, Felicity and Iris—to performances and rehearsals, as often as we liked, and were allowed to pester the actor-manager Tree (Mr Daddy to us) in his dressing-room. I do not think that he minded, though he had great occasion when we motley children plastered our faces with his grease-paint and bearded our baby chins with Henry VIII's hair, slashed our arms with great Caesar's blood and hee-hawed through Bottom's head. Often we threw on cloaks and elbowed our way into the Forum to lend our ears, or found ourselves Ancients among the tents pitying gentlemen in England still abed.

Even without these favours, like all children, we would have been inveterate dressers-up. At home we had the feather-and-flower box, the ribbon-and-lace drawer, the fur chest (very mothy), the stuffs—yard upon yard of dress-lengths for all times and seasons, plushes and chiffons, sprigged muslin and cloth of gold. All these precious reserves in time found their gay end in the dressing-up box, a huge wicker hamper, a cornucopia spilling out skirts and hats, a few yellow plaits for Wagner, helmets, swords, ballet-shoes, deer-stalkers, boas, Ophelia's straws and flowers, jackboots, wimples and wigs.

Musical comedies were allowed, if unvulgar. I remember being too young for *The Belle of New York*, though I could sing "Follow On." Since my beatific infirmity I could command twice as many outings. I liked the thrill of night better than a matinée and so we went in the evenings. It meant extra sleep from tea to 7.30 and sometimes (before *Henry V*, I remember) being sick from excitement.

Galvanism revived my muscles. It took several years of care and spoiling and dear Dr Coleman's bribing presents. He came every morning to treat me. Mademoiselle whom I loved so well left, and horrid Fräulein Meminger came in her place. I wonder to this day how my mother set about finding those extraordinary people to whom she entrusted her children. In those days, unlike these, it was better to be good than beautiful. In fact in certain walks it was necessary to be ugly, with nothing more than dyed hair or a gold brooch to attract. Deborah Metzker was merciless and very unprepossessing. Nanny was both hard and hideous. Mademoiselle came to us, without one word of English or any recommendation, from a family in Toulouse via a situation in Tiflis. She actually had a passport, perpetually brought out as a curiosity to show children and even adults. Her nose had been broken across her face, so she did not look at all like other people. Who can have recommended her? She was a lovable woman of thirty. She loved us and read to us and weathered our loyalty to a lost Nanny, with no language to help her. She was proud of her figure and, after pressure, showed us her breasts. They were a great surprise to me. She would stroke her long well-shaped feet, saying "*Ils sont très fins.*" She had stories of Prince Dimitri and sleighs. She had a fur cap, and for best she used *poudre de riz*. She never had a holiday (Nanny did not have *one* in the seven years she was with us). She had no friend except the household. She left ostensibly to see the Paris Exhibition, promising to bring us back individual flying wings which she sincerely, I think, believed were on sale. She never came back. It must have been preconcerted, as my mother cried when she said goodbye to her at the garden gate. Why did she go?

Where was Fräulein found? She was a criminal type, filthily dirty, with a monstrous greasy appearance. Letty was old enough at twelve to discriminate. There was no love between them, but I gave her all my affection. My mother disliked her. Why did she ever engage her? She had no idea of teaching or any accomplishment. She worked only at a pink silk blouse for herself with lace insertions, all the two years she was with us, and at making pink flannel nightdresses. She slept in the gilded drawing-room with what was then called the "article" drawn out from its modest underbed and stood between us. Into it she spat through the nights. If food was spilt at meals she mopped it up with our bath-sponges. A vile woman, she did her utmost to undermine our trust in our parents and the schoolroom. It all came to a bad end, for when at long last dismissed she barricaded herself in the disused nurseries. Three months' notice was her right, so there was nothing to be done to evict her. Alone in the house, she cooked for herself on a spirit-lamp and wrote a scurrilous pamphlet about my mother. With her savings she had it privately printed and distributed all over London. I learnt this story when grown up (I never saw a copy of the libel) but thirty years later I found a thick packet of condolences and comfort addressed to my mother by friends and strangers to whom the despicable German had sent her venomous outpourings.

So Fräulein went, and Mrs Page ("Podgie") took us two into

the schoolroom. Podgie made sense and very good sense. She was known to my mother as having brought up the beautiful Pamela Plowden and her sister. Pamela had lost her mother in India, where her father was a magistrate, and coming to London at eighteen almost lived in our house. My mother was to be a second mother to her. The South African war must have taken a bitter toll of Pamela's admirers, for I can remember her often in tears and my mother saying "Someone has been killed in the war." She afterwards married Lord Lytton (I was her bridesmaid, dressed as usual as a Vandyck) and she will, I hope, read on this page how in my young and therefore critical eyes she was the most beautiful creature on earth.

So Podgie was known and Podgie was very pretty, prematurely white with a winsome sensitive face, a forceful character and a cultured adventurous mind. Browning she loved, and Bernard Shaw and the Fabians, and *The Dream of Gerontius*. She had ideas of right and wrong. Although Mademoiselle and Fräulein had considered her a hypocritical fiend, it had made no difference to our acceptance of translation to the schoolroom.

The Boer War was over. It had meant nothing to me except learning to knit and crochet Balaclava helmets and comforters. I watched the C.I.V.s march back to London, sitting high on my father's shoulder and being swept down St James's Street to Mr Willie Milligan's room in Pall Mall. I think that Queen Victoria was receiving them under my very eyes but I can't see where. I saw her receive General Buller too in the courtyard of Buckingham Palace, and we often saw the little black bundle, with its minute black parasol against sun or drizzle, driving through the Park in a victoria. I saw her Diamond Jubilee from the same room in Pall Mall, as always a black bundle, but that day set in a glorious panoply of Life Guards and Gurkhas and drawn by her flesh-coloured horses ornate with caparisons. I did not see her funeral. We must have been at Belvoir and—worse—we were not allowed black, a great disappointment as many other children were plunged into it. We had to wait nine years to don Court mourning.

Nothing much was done about my education. Mademoiselle had left me with a smattering of French, on which unimproved I have managed to keep talking for ten years in France. She only *tutoyéd* me, so that when I came to the diplomatic life in Algiers and Paris I talked to General de Gaulle and the Government and the Académie Française as though they were intimates, children or inferiors.

In Nanny's day I learnt a ridiculous poem which started:

> He lifted the golden cup from the board;
>   It sparkled with purple wealth.
> He pressed the brim her lip had kissed
>   And drank to his lady's health.

My mother thought it common, so my next poem was in her better taste but equally unsuitable from my lisping lips:

> Come live with me and be my love
> And we will all the pleasures prove.

When I was seven and Nanny was on her first and eternal holiday I slept in my mother's room and in the early mornings she would teach me by heart the easy "Road to Mandalay," the difficult "How they brought the Good News" and the dirgeful "Fear no more the heat o' the sun." But the poetic rot set in again when Mademoiselle came. She taught me:

> *O petit doigt de ma maman,*
> *Je t'aime bien—va!*
> *Mais de grâce ne lui dit pas ce que se passe.*

My mother thought it appalling. After Shakespeare she loved Browning (naturally not the complete works) and a lot of Tennyson. Our Christmas presents were always a volume of a Shakespeare series of little books illustrated by Byam Shaw, or a slim illustrated volume of *The Idylls of the King*.

There was a lot of reading aloud and to oneself too. After *Stumps* and the *Pilgrim's Progress* there were fairy books in all their colours of red and blue, violet, yellow and even brown, with the imaginative Ford illustrations which I thought the world of, as I do still. They were probably my first artistic appreciation. Next came stories from Spenser's *Faerie Queene* and a book of Flaxman's drawings for the *Odyssey*, followed by Church's Homer and Kingsley's *Heroes*. These gave me romance and names to drop. Historical stories were in demand. In *The Little Duke* I remember always crying over the death of Carloman. Comedy was never encouraged by my mother and I believed utterly in her, my oracle. We did not care for *Alice*. The *Just-So Stories* passed muster. My father's reading aloud *The Jungle Book* was a little beyond me, but being by a long way the youngest I was used to treading water and pretending to be cleverer than I was. This lack of confidence, this clear-eyed assessment of myself, and worse this hunted feeling of being discovered and exposed, was certainly one of the shadows closing in.

Everything we read aloud was too old for me, but I struggled and gave an impression of understanding. Reading was really all the education I was given. Arithmetic faded out with my muscles and to this day I do not know the process of division. Subtraction and multiplication are fearful obstacles. Adding is all right, I think. We had learnt no word of German from the loathsome Fräulein Meminger. Geography was considered as unnecessary as Exports and Industries. Latin, the use of the globes, the acquiring of algebra, ancient or modern philosophy —all such branches of learning were undreamed of in our curriculum; so were domestic science, cooking, preserving, and the rest. The piano was practised, drawing and clay-modelling were encouraged as a game, and we would sew and embroider in wools and silks and ribbons, making our dreadful Christmas presents of sachets and velvet holders of shot to act as my father's paperweights.

My sister Marjorie was undoubtedly a genius, and now that we were schoolroom children and the feuds over, I could begin to realise her gifts. Nothing was artistically denied her. She could draw like Holbein, and sing like no other amateur of her generation. She embroidered as artists painted. She imitated with professional brilliance and her taste was of surprising originality. So gradually she came to be my exemplar. Any feeling I have for art or taste in colour and form, in music and in literature, was given me first by my mother and with more abundance by Marjorie. Humour came from Marjorie—my mother, while appreciating fun, did not depend upon it. She could do without. She loathed the ugly, the comic caricatures, the grotesque toys, the red noses. A cap-and-bells jester must be an exquisite, not a hunchback. She would have hated Groucho Marx and perhaps loved Harpo for a wistfulness or a line of jaw or neck. No knockabouts or jack-in-the-boxes for her. "Nasty common things," she would say detachedly.

A great many things were "common," even tomatoes and lemon as flavouring, and dyed fur, holding hands or grown-ups being seasick, and kissing with one's mouth instead of cheek to cheek like a symbolic accolade. She hated funny books. Fairy stories must be ogreless and not German. Germany on the whole (Prussia rather) was common, except its music and Wagner in particular. Our cradles were rocked to

Wagner motifs. An often-evoked scene is that of my mother sitting at a very large "grand," puzzling out scores of *The Ring* or *Tristan* (*Lohengrin* and *Tannhäuser* were verging on the common). She was no virtuoso but could read from sight adequately and derive a world of joy for herself and for me, and as a girl (as I was told by musical faddists like Mr Arthur Balfour) she could sing *Lieder* and old songs and ballads like no other.

My mother had great beauty. She was tall and frail with a complexion as delicate as the palest anemone. Her hair was just auburn and she wore a cloudy fringe like Sarah Bernhardt and a classical handle of hair pinned where the Grecians pinned theirs. Once she cut it short to be like Ellen Terry. Her dressing had, I imagine, never changed. She was forty when my eyes first realised her. She had in her day despised fashionable bustles. She was greenery-yallery rather than the Duchess of Towers, with very high-heeled pointed shoes, with buckles, to increase her height, beautiful slim legs and ankles, a small waist drawn tightly into a silver-buckled petersham belt, a creamy flimsy open-necked shirt, free-wristed, with numberless little cream lace scarves draped round her neck and elbows. Always a sprig of bay was pinned high up to her neck by a green enamel tortoise. In London for out-of-doors there were faced-cloth clothes (greenish-greyish-bluish-fawnish) with tabs and smoky flat pearl buttons, and three-cornered hats with panaches of cocks' feathers.

For the big evenings, great balls or dinners I would be taken, wrapped in an eiderdown, to see her. I remember black tulle over moonlight-blue, and flesh-pink satin stuck over with sequins or bunches of rosebuds, always the creation of some little dressmaker, never Paquin or Worth. The noble family tiara was worn back to front, holding up the Grecian handle of hair. Nothing was used for its true purpose. The diamond eighteen-inch waistbelt that had sparkled at great London houses, when the beautiful Duchesses of Devonshire and Rutland laced themselves mercilessly to achieve the smallest waist, was divided into two pieces and formed her shoulder-straps. Nell Gwynn's Lely pearl necklace hung in a festoon between two sensational diamond drop ear-rings from her shoulder. Diamond butterflies, bows, dragonflies and daggers sparkled about her bosom. Many fell and were lost and found, or not found. There was the diamond Garter star convertible into a necklace, which was worn on the nape of her neck, and the diamond words *Honi soit qui mal y pense* she pinned where the fancy prompted her. My father was not at that time a Knight of that Order.

She looked most beautiful at parties, they said, but familiarity did not allow me to see her as so different, even dressed for the Court, from the person I saw when I slipped into her bed for my breakfast and she coaxed me with buttered English *croissants*. Her silk frilled nightdress was worn under a cream flannel kimono-shaped garment, and her beautiful head was bound, I cannot say how, seemingly in a knitted vest, the long sleeves of which wound round her chin and head in a mediaeval way. Podgie would say "Her bones can never grow old." Nature she loved far less than art—carved alleys, statues in groves, stone seats everywhere, never moors or wild hills; rather symmetrical cypresses, classical lore, nothing wind-swept or primaeval.

How can I hope to show her? I never saw her cross. Sulkiness was unknown to the whole family and quarrels too, after the childish days of "I'll never speak to you again." I have seen her anxious, impatient with trifles and exasperated with children, friends and servants if they concealed colds in their heads. She believed in the prophylactic powers of Dr Mackenzie's

Black Smelling Bottle and a carbolic throat-spray, and in saucers dotted over the house holding old scraps of blotting-paper mirror-written, saturated in eucalyptus oil, and in the agonised swallowing of twenty drops of spirits of camphor on a lump of sugar. Naturally we hid our colds until they over-flowed, dreading these consequences, and so the circle became vicious.

She had no respect for time or time-tables, regularity of bed-time or for going out or lessons—she thought them all unneces-sary. The children must lie flat to keep their backs straight and hold themselves and their heads up. Holly pinned to one's frock beneath one's chin was threatened but not used. She had no sympathy with punishment or with any teaching but his-tory, poetry, the piano and art.

Our schoolroom walls, papered in William Morris's olive leaves, were half-covered with photographs framed in arty green wood of Italian Masters—not familiar Raphaels but Crivellis, Mantegnas, Fra Lippo Lippis, Primitives, Botticellis and details of Botticellis, such as Primavera's flower-scattered dress and the Graces' pearl-threaded plaits, or the round-cheeked Wind blowing Venus to the shore and fluttering her daisy-strewn cloak. There were also macabre death-masks of Napoleon, Beethoven and *L'Inconnue de la Seine*, and casts of the hands and feet of Pauline Borghese and Lady Shrewsbury.

We pored over *The Hundred Best Pictures*, a curious collec-tion of Millais, Lord Leighton, Holman Hunt, Burne-Jones and Turner, and became picture-perfect in those schools. My mother had been painted by Watts and had sat to Millais for the nun in *St Bartholomew's Day*. Many of the figures in the Burne-Jones pictures were portraits of our friends the Horners. It made us feel proud and part of it all. I was taken to see Watts, a memorable old figure in a white smock and black skull-cap.

In his studio was a naked man on a horse, snow-white and too big for perspective. It must have been the cast of *Physical Energy*. I was often the artist's model. The first picture by J. J. Shannon, when I was two, I do not remember sitting for; but another painting, when I was eight, I well remember, and the huge studio in Holland Park, Shannon himself, whom everyone loved, darting backwards and forwards with palette and mahlstick, delicious smells of paint and turps, a mirror behind the painter in which I could watch the picture grow, while my mother's gentle voice read aloud stories of musicians. She was a more exacting pose-master; besides, when the drawing was finished a new one was begun at once, and there was a not very successful bust of me as Joan of Arc that lingered on and on unfinished. We had to be statue-still while my mother, with her Waterman's block held firm by a cushion on her lap, peered up at her model and down at her hard 3H pencil for hours at a time.

I can see very distinctly a typical morning in the white-panelled drawing-room at The Woodhouse, Rowsley, an old manor house on a Derbyshire hill not a stone's throw from Haddon Hall, where I yearly spent three summer months, after babyhood on the beach. If I was the model, my mother and Marjorie and Letty would all be drawing me perched on a cushion on a hard oak settle, while Podgie would be reading aloud a book a bit above my head, generally historical. The even voice would be broken into by my mother saying "Right ear a little down" or "Nose towards the window." At twelve there was a break, curiously enough, for port and biscuits brought by a liveried footman on a silver tray. Then perhaps Marjorie would open the piano and play and practise some songs by Liza Lehmann or Gounod or from the new Puccini opera. Viola Tree, so often there, would sing too, and their clear young voices would merge in a duet and transport me. A short run among roses, and dahlias on stakes with a flower-pot on top to snare the earwigs and other pests, jumping to loosen my statued limbs, I crunched the diamond quartz gravel peculiar to the Woodhouse garden, and doubled back to a lunch of trout and grouse and garden peas and pudding. Meals were very gay. Viola and Marjorie, I had come to realise, were excruciatingly funny, imitating friends and stage people, inventing characters and acting them. I would have to run out of the room with my mouth full to avoid choking with laughter. Idleness was a crime—sew, knit, draw or read, but "Don't do nothing."

The few letters I find of those days written to my father are wonderfully illiterate, generally sympathising with him over his health (he was an extremely healthy man) and overflowing with protestations of love, and always "We are so *so* happy— you've no idea how happy we are."

So these happy years passed, but anxieties grew. If my mother was late or not to be found I would imagine her dead, murdered even. Motors had accidents and I could hardly bear Letty to be in one without me lest it killed her. My prayers became like an insurance policy. "Please God, don't let there be a famine or a drought (I had seen pictures of starving Indians and Chinese), or train or motor or carriage accidents. Don't let any of us be ill or have operations. Don't let the house burn, and don't let Father or Mother die before I do, and let me live until I'm eighty or ninety." I always felt that I did not know how to pray, but I persevered. For years I prayed that Bimbash Stuart, a man I hardly knew but one who had died in our street, might be in Heaven. I was in love with him for dying.

My next love was for Fridtjof Nansen. He was a Norwegian giant who called me "Viking," and I loved him obsessedly. At eleven years old I read the two-volume work on his expedition to the Pole. Only true love could have carried me through the unintelligible scientific data. I think I must have been a snob in those days. All my loves were celebrities and generally very old ones. I must have been flirtatious too. I wanted passionately to be loved. When Letty reported that someone had said I was pretty or amusing or clever for my age, I would make her repeat it a hundred times while my face glowed with pleasure. After the old gentlemen, it was Marjorie's admirers that I gave my heart to. They took pains with the young sisters and sent us presents and feigned an interest in us. I would get up at dawn and comb my hair becomingly and meet them at the door to wave them goodbye and beg them to return. I hoped that they would realise my feelings for them. Our cousin Ruby Lindsay practically lived with us in those days. She also did not lack for swains, being very beautiful and spirited, and her admirers too I loved to distraction.

I was growing tall and rather fat, very dissatisfied with my appearance and myself. I felt that I wasn't clever, which I so longed to be. I felt that people over-estimated me and that I should be found out and cause disillusion. It haunted me and yet I could not help showing off, a surface glitter, wanting and trying to shine through thick miasmas of shyness. I saw no one of my own age except the two younger Tree children, and another little girl with long wavy hair and smart dresses, called Irene Lawley. She had come from India, where her father was a Governor, and had been, according to Nanny, "spoilt by the ayah." She came often to tea, and Letty and I yearly stayed with her in Yorkshire, where together we wrote a thriller about the French Revolution. She still lives in Yorkshire and I love her as I loved her then. Whatever house we were in was packed with friends of my grown-up sisters and Viola, or notables of my mother's generation. Looking back I wonder how such men as Lord Curzon, Alfred Lyttelton or Arthur Balfour could have endured a night at The Woodhouse. True, it broke their journey to or from Scotland in the summer, and this fact must account for their facing more than once a small damp house loud with children, with one bathroom, generally locked and blacked out because of its use as a developing room. When they did get in, it would smell of the hot red oil-light or of developer and hypo, and into the bath dripped negatives pinned to a festooned tape. There would be four candles to a room (no electric light), plenty of servants, deafening prac-tising of scales from 8 a.m., and snap patience after dinner. No one played real cards except my father, who therefore never got a game. When I was fourteen, a turning date for me, every-thing changed. Another bathroom was added, electric light was installed and one could better understand these notables coming to a house and family that had something unlike other establish-ments.

CHAPTER FOUR

Brave New World

Mᵧ fourteenth year changed everything. My grandfather
died of old age. My father succeeded him. There was
more money but no less talk of ruin. Income tax had reached
elevenpence. Every successive penny rise plunged us again into
fear of the workhouse. Letty "came out." Her long hair went
up. I was alone at home, so allowed to stay away. That year
the Tree family had a house at Brancaster and I went to stay
with my dearest friends for perhaps three weeks. The Dormy
House in the village and also another hired house were filled
with Oxford boys on a reading party. There I met on equal
terms (I was tall, precocious and on my own) people who
were to be my friends until their death—too soon it came—
Charles Lister, Alan Parsons, Patrick Shaw-Stewart, Edward
Horner, Bunt Goschen and many others. Never was I so
happy.

There were also Lady Ribblesdale and her two Lister daughters, now Laura Lovat and Diana Westmorland. No one could
hold a candle to Laura. A little older in years, much our elder
in experience and ways of the world, she was someone to emu-
late. I bought secretly a bottle of peroxide. I had heard that it
made hair golder. I experimented and denied the experiment,
declaring that the sun had bleached my hair. Our days were
spent in bathing and crabbing and picnicking and practising
the piano and butterflying and sleeping out on the "Enchanted

Island," and for me in exulting over this brave new world. The evenings were always musical. A German governess in the house was a fair pianist and Viola and Marjorie would sing. Tennyson's *Maud* set to music by Arthur Somervell was sung through pretty well every evening. I knew that the young men saw Maud like Laura and not like me.

> Maud is not seventeen,
> But she is tall and stately.

I was not tall enough. I was curiously ignorant and innocent compared with today's fourteen-year-olds, but now all knowledge and all anticipation and the excitement of being myself a part of romance and adventure, and not only hearing and reading about it, intoxicated me. I was showing off madly with my new gold hair and knowing about Browning and Meredith and lots of erudition that other children had not got, and concealing the nine-tenths of the iceberg of total ignorance. Iris Tree, four years younger, told me many unbelievable facts. I cannot think that I should have liked myself, but I must have had something appealing and enthusiastic and affectionate.

I was in love with Alan Parsons, naturally, because he loved Viola Tree and later married her, but some others I really thought loved me and promised to write and to find me again wherever I went. So I returned home grown up, with friends of my own, to find the old world as I had left it—my mother remaking Belvoir and my father "pottering" on the terraces, Letty and Marjorie hunting and going to winter shooting-parties and hunt balls, both of them and my cousin Ruby occupied with suitors and philanderers. I hugged my secrets and had no envy whatever of their boring parties and eligible eldest sons. I had my own intellectuals and I would lie in secret wait for the postman, and then, with my letters, lock myself into that small closet which can temporarily be one's own, and read and re-read the little protestations I was hungry for.

Each year now enriched me. The original few at Brancaster became part of all our lives. Edward Horner was a son of great family friends. His sister Cicely was a close companion of Marjorie's, and another sister, Katharine, became my dearest friend. She married Raymond Asquith, who, though older, was part of that haloed band who were to die in the war and leave us, our generation and England, woebegone and maimed—Julian and Billy Grenfell, George Vernon, Edward Horner, John Manners, Patrick Shaw-Stewart, Ego and Ivo Charteris, and many many others.

Greek—everything must be Greek. I must draw a bow and have a crescent in my hair, draperies, sandalled or bare feet (dragging at the second toe to make it longer than the big one), peplums, archaic smiles, shining white limbs of the godlike youths in the river, Pan pipes, Butcher and Lang's Homer readings, and human statues photographed on pedestals. There is a bust that Mackennal made of me with Grecian curls and a crescent and the rest of it.

Fashion had come round to us. Gone were the buttoned boots, the curves, the boned collars, the straight-fronted stays, the hennaed hair and hair-nets. We subscribed to a fashion paper called *L'Art et la Mode*, with drawings by a then little-known artist called Drian. It was everything my mother had always stood for—"*le vague*" and lines of the body slinkily followed into the feet, loosely knotted hair, willowy and dependent, not armed for merciless conquest. I became an inspired dressmaker. A "fit" was no longer necessary. I suppose I made a guy of myself, and soon worse was to come.

Henry Bernstein came to Belvoir. He was, I suppose, young
and very noble-looking. He smothered my mother in red
roses, which we thought was a French custom. With him
came Princess Murat, a fascinating surprise and totally different from anything we knew. She brought to us, Gentiles
where fashion was concerned, the glad tidings of the rising star
Poiret, an eccentricity, a new word and a new mania. She herself wore the first of those tanagra-esque garments, later sold
by thousands (many to me over twenty years), made by
Fortuni of Venice—timeless dresses of pure thin silk cut
severely straight from shoulder to toe, and kept wrung like
a skein of wool. In every crude and subtle colour, they clung
like mermaid's scales. I think she must have had in her luggage a Poiret invention. It was a chiffon shirt worn in the
evening over a skirt. It was cut like an Eastern djibbah and
edged at hem and Eastern neckline with braid. I elaborated the
design, even to putting fur instead of braid, and made them by
the dozen for friends and friends' friends. They cost me about
fifteen shillings and I charged two guineas. I made over a hundred pounds, all of which I spent on books—*éditions de luxe*
and first editions, the Edinburgh Stevenson, Meredith, Wilde,
Conrad and Maupassant. I owed a lot to Poiret and made him
ridiculous, no doubt, by my base imitations.

When I was fifteen came our first trip abroad. My mother
took us three girls, Ruby Lindsay and white-haired Louise
Piers to Florence. My father, unsympathetic to travel, gave
her a hundred pounds to cover tickets and all expenses. The
Villa Palmieri in Fiesole had been lent to my mother by her
cousin Lady Crawford, so the fortune stitched into her stays
would not have to pay a Florentine hotel. Our luggage and
paraphernalia were prodigious. Little was trusted abroad, so
everything must be taken from home—a pharmacopoeia, a

clinical thermometer (French ones being unusable) with spares in case of breakage, umbrellas rolled in rugs, sunshades of natural-coloured cotton lined with dark blue or green. We were armed with a *laissez-passer* by favour of the French Ambassador, Monsieur Cambon, so that no luggage should be searched. It did not stop a desperate struggle at Dover, and at Calais a free fight. Guards and porters from London to Dover were questioned about the state of the sea. My mother took an opium pill but I, on a steamer for the first time, was determined to feel like a figurehead. While the train dragged round its *ceinture de Paris* we piled into a *fiacre* to see in eighty minutes the main monuments. I had never before seen a meter on a cab, and watching its changes interfered with my sight-seeing. At the Gare de Lyon we hired a tartan rug and a pillow apiece (*wagons-lit* were not dreamed of) and sat well-tucked through the long night in the lurid light of a blue bulblet. I saw the Alps through the chink of smoke-caked blinds. Clouds *below* the peaks were unhoped-for. Daylight came and the remains of our station dinner were brought out for breakfast—rolls not eaten the night before, stuffed with fragments of meat and salad and cheese and butter. These with bowls of steaming coffee bought at a stop in Switzerland made a good change from porridge and eggs and milk (milk was not safe abroad, or water either).

We followed Baedeker from left to right of the train windows. The opening sentence rings still: "Over all the movements of the traveller the weather exercises its despotic sway." Baedeker's warnings of what not to eat were well digested and his suggestions for clothing disregarded. The third-best hotel was chosen on principle, which meant two to a room and fairly dirty. We stopped at Genoa to be taught about Vandyck and for me to discover the beauties of clothes-lines slung across the narrow mountain-built streets, and at Pisa to dread the tower falling upon us.

At Fiesole the Villa Palmieri was interiorly disappointing. I had expected a Capulet *sala* as designed for His Majesty's Theatre. Instead it was stuffy plush with a bust of Queen Victoria, but the garden had Juliet's balcony overlooking all I expected of Italy—little pointed hills, cypresses, lemons in flower, oranges to pick. We were always hungry in Florence. There were days of gruelling sight-seeing, churches and pictures, with a spaghetti lunch at Le Sport for 1.50 lire a head, chianti included, which went a little to Marjorie's and Ruby's heads, and led them to make eyes at the uniformed officers at other tables. At least my mother attributed it to the wine. There would be no tea, but a lot of buying at antique shops. My mother, though limited to her hundred pounds, seemed to have *carte blanche* with the Belvoir Clerk of the Works, so she bought unstintingly big Bolognese cupboards and tables, gilded frames and Forum-sized marble pillars for her Italian garden at Belvoir. They were sent *petite vitesse* and arrived months later. Estate expenses are not gone into. My money, collected for months, went on church candlesticks (cheap because the gilt had come off, which I could later home-gild myself with gesso, size, gold leaf and a burnisher), tassels and braids, anything to make my new room at Belvoir more like Carpaccio's idea of St Ursula's.

From 1907 until my coming out in 1911 were years of galloping expansion and happiness. Puppy-fat was being dropped by hard effort of running and banting, urged on by vanity. I must learn Greek to be worthy of Oxford. I strode along well enough until I sought and found a teacher who killed my ambitions by bewildering me. I had no experience of teachers and they (the Greek one and a music one) tore my nerves to shreds.

I had at one period been taken to Miss Wolff's classes for young ladies, but my autocratic spoiltness made so many provisos—no German, no mathematics, no essays particularly—that fetching and carrying me became impossible and undermined the morale of the class.

We had our first motor-car about now, a blue-green Renault limousine with a peacock crest on the door. The Trees had been pioneers with Panhards, into which one climbed from the back under the hood and sat on the door's *strapontin* which made the third back seat. A wicker umbrella-holder was attached to the outside of the car, which gleamed with brass. We were goggled, dust-coated and hatted with peaked motor-caps, attached with a six-inch safety-pin. There was a fearful smell and dense clouds of dust, causing the horses to shy and the adventurers to be jeered and scoffed at. The cars always broke down, but by 1907 they had become adult and except for occasional breakdowns we travelled in style all over Derbyshire. This widened the pony-cart's periphery. My mother had been enterprising and in infant days we had explored new roads, churches, manors, farms and curiosity shops. We drove in turn. We covered a lot of ground, returning after dark behind the steaming pony, everyone but delicate me getting out of the tub when the hill was steep. The Renault now took us to Midland towns to look for Haddon's lost furniture in the old antique shops of Sheffield, Manchester and Derby. (When the family built the new Belvoir they abandoned Haddon Hall, and stacked its furniture in an unguarded barn, from which it was gradually stolen. From then until my father's death the sad shell was untenanted save for hordes of tourists. My brother John realised his life's ambition when, for his wife and five children, Haddon again became a roof-tree, invisibly modernised and furnished with purest taste.)

MR FRANK

Now at last we had a telephone, and a neighbour to telephone to. He was called Mr Green ("Mr Frank" to us). He was our fairy godfather, and we, during those years at The Woodhouse, were his chief interest in life. He gave my sisters hunters. To me he gave antiques, Battersea snuffboxes and paste brooches. He sported a large Daimler and would take us to run with his beagles at Beresford Dale. I watched from a hilltop. He was a big-fortuned eccentric who taught us about furniture and architecture and ornament. He owned the Traveller's House in York, decorated as a house of its period. He gave me a narrow four-poster bed for my new room at Belvoir, which was to be painted black. The bed was upholstered in red damask. An alcove was scooped out of the wall for my jug and basin and painted by me with stylised seawaves. A stone shell, once a holy-water stoup, held the soap. The black walls were hung with swags of everlasting flowers *à la* Crivelli. The table and chair were Savonarola-esque and the window, granite fireplace and coalbox solid Victorian. There were coloured reproductions of Madonnas in gold Italian frames and the candlesticks from Florence, regilded and burnished as planned. I thought it beyond compare, but greatly feared criticism. My mother never damped our taste— she who had so influenced it. An unexpected addition to this strange room was a removable punch-ball attached to two hooks in the ceiling and floor. This I would batter until I weakened from exhaustion, dressed in a jockey's rubber jacket and light boxing-gloves.

Mr Frank took us to cathedrals and old houses, and we thought he was as sound as a bell until one day he admitted to veering towards Victorian taste. We stopped our ears. We had not yet come to Regency, though Belvoir was converting us to its elegance. What a dear man he was! We lost sight of him forever in the first war when everything broke up, although he died but two years ago at an immense age.

The Woodhouse months became our favourite in the year. The express trains to the North would be stopped especially for us at Rowsley station. We tumbled out, laden with the paraphernalia of art and sport, into two or three flies and a pony cart: the tumbling had to be at full speed as the engine was screaming to be off. This could not happen today, but we thought it quite as natural a privilege as when we went to Belvoir the Flying Scotsman, if not scheduled to stop, also threw us out at Grantham to oblige. The guns, rods, cameras, easels, books and opera-scores were trotted through the village where the children, pouring *en masse* out of school, would cheer and wave us home as though from a long and precarious absence. Shooting parties and picnics on the moors, fishing for trout with worms on the Lathkill river, photographing, printing, squeegeeing, casting our own hands and feet and those of visitors in plaster of Paris, with always the danger of a boot or glove of solid plaster hanging like a prisoner's ball and chain, that had to be chiselled off. There too we had our first gramophone. Another of my idols, Melba, to whom I must have declared my love, gave me a gramophone and all her records. It had a mahogany megaphone three feet across and we had the same concert nightly for six weeks, unless it was a fine warm night. Only then would the young ones leave Melba and Caruso and Kubelik and Kreisler and wander up to the Great Elm swing. Girls were swung high by the boys and we would sit on moonlit grass reciting Keats's odes and sonnets in turn, and revel rustically on the way home. We would go to empty Haddon Hall most afternoons for water-colour sketching and gardening and, best of all, at full moon for an after-dinner drive in brother John's open screenless racing-car packed with young men and girls—fears and excitements, cries and claspings. My mother was strongly against these expeditions, perhaps more from fear of cold and the fast car than from disapproval of escapade, but my brother invariably had his way. There too was my first election at Bakewell, a Derbyshire constituency. It sounded surprisingly bloodthirsty. I wrote:

"Booh! Suffragette!" is the taunt. They say "Why should you have such pretty furs?" and the Liberals' refrain is:

Up with your spears,
Into the Peers.
Up with your swords,
Into the Lords.

I must have been wonderfully happy at fifteen or sixteen. I did not know it, having no yardstick, but the proof was there. I wanted time to stop. What could be better, even with the shades and inner glooms thrown in? I marvelled that I could run downstairs as unconscious of doom as a spring lamb, and climb up half an hour later slow with care and apprehensions of all kinds. I felt unfitted to be independent, when I would be without help, when I would have no pilots, no moorings, no one to ask, no one to comfort me. My ugliness weighed upon me, and indeed with reason—a cauliflower ("a bled pig," said Margot Asquith), not tall enough for a goddess, so I must hang on a trapeze—but I could not, having weak muscles. I was dressed curiously unbecomingly by my mother (who recognised that I had outgrown Vandyck) in Rumanian peasant shirts and ill-fitting skirts hung on a pinched-in waist, and black stockings of course. As to my hair, I hate to say how dreadful it was.

There was a craze in our family for the fabulously beautiful Cavalieri, the luscious Italian who was to become a successful opera singer. Marjorie bought all her pictures. There being then no stage postcards, one would cut out one's favourites from magazines or buy in the Royal Arcade glossy photographs mounted on cards of stage celebrities and even of society beauties. Cavalieri became Marjorie's mirror of fashion. We only saw her once in the flesh (I must have been fifteen) when my mother asked her to a ball and was criticised for exposing her daughters to this Babylonian beauty. Cavalieri's raven hair was parted in the middle and waved symmetrically round her face, low as the lobes of her pearled ears, to be gathered in a shining knot behind. She wore a riband like a wreath (would it be a snood?) to keep this neatness intact. So all three of us wore ribands round our hair. They are to be seen in our three drawings by Sargent. But at sixteen my shortish ashen hair was still by convention hanging down my back, so though from the front this band only looked unnecessary, from the side and the back it looked absurd. To make things worse I back-combed my hair to thicken it. I could not rely on my adolescent complexion and would steal Marjorie's rouge, which she kept from scrutiny in a hidden dressing-case. My mother pointing her finger to her cheek once said in a whisper, "Do you think Marjorie . . .?" She could not use the word "rouges." Lady Helen Vincent, the most beautiful of her generation, we believed to have had her mouth tattooed by her mother's orders and to have slept in stays since childhood.

My mother was disappointed only in my hair. She had wisely wanted to keep it Joan of Arc length, but I had insisted that it must grow into long golden plaits to the knee like Isolde or Guinevere. I meant to thread them with pearls for best. It had not grown, in spite of endless hair-brushings and massage with Harlene.

All things considered, my position at that time of a grown-up child was a favoured one. I did not want to grow up. Things could only worsen, my melancholy voices told me. I could lie down or go to bed with *The Egoist* or talk to the servants until I appeared after dinner to accompany my sister's songs and dance to Strauss waltzes pedalled out on the pianola in the ballroom at Belvoir. I was not very proficient but with practice and enthusiasm somehow got away with it. She sang German *Lieder*, Fauré, Reynaldo Hahn, César Franck, Debussy, Puccini and Mozart. I even managed the *Liebestod*. I loved and feared the performance. Dread led me to give myself a voluntary wound in my thumb when the great teacher and composer Paolo Tosti came to stay.

I could take as much or as little of the young men's company as I wanted. I didn't want much alone with them. I needed support. At bedtime we used to have hair-brushing beside the fire in Marjorie's drawing-room-sized bedroom. The favoured men were allowed to join the throng. This was criticised a lot by staider friends of my mother's, but she liked the look of it. If one allowed the eligible ones to join, one must perforce admit the riff-raff, and the riff-raff were mine. My mother must have been a little alarmed at my precocity, for in 1908 I wrote to a swain, as usual extravagantly:

I cried all last night without a break. It's too depressing things coming to an end—such a summer too of my happy-go-lucky life, which the authorities say must be stopped. The new régime is schoolroom tea, no Oxford friends—instead music and French from snobbish masters and perhaps even solitary confinement at Belvoir.

This régime was not stillborn but died very young. Life at Belvoir was unrecognisably changed since childhood days. It was warm and one could wash and live like other people and eat less and dance and sing. Still my father kept some *tenue*—morning prayers in the chapel, feudal Christmases with the waits and bellringers, bells and gongs to warn and announce meals, crowds of servants, the silver tray of "sprays" and button-holes carried round for dressing guests to choose from, *jardinières* of flowers, a different decoration nightly for the dinner table of gold or silver ornaments trimmed with orchids and cyclamen. There was the Marine service, all crabs and lobsters with Neptune surmounting the shells and tridents (it was made to commemorate our Westminster Abbey hero, Lord Robert Manners, who in the eighteenth century died fighting the French in the West Indies), and there was the Charles II oriental silver, and the Charles II gold, and the Charles I rosebowl, filled with floating camellias, and for great occasions the Cellini ewer and basin. We knew all their styles and dates from showing them off and we have forgotten them all now. The ladies dressed for tea in trailing chiffon and lace, and changed again for dinner into something less limp, and all the men wore white ties and drank sherry, then champagne (pink, called *œil-de-perdrix*) and then port and then brandy. In the daytime the men wore stiff collars except for shooting. My father did not like the relaxation of this rule. There would be about twelve people staying for a shooting party, all with maids and valets and large "dress baskets." So it made a long table-load, with two parents, one son, three daughters, Uncle Charlie Lindsay and Ruby, and probably Mr Knox the chaplain—about twenty-four or so.

The guests would arrive on Monday and my father would expect them, so that would be all right, but when they left on Friday, and a new dozen arrived, not expected by my father and generally of a much younger generation, he would greet them ashen in the face with: "What train are you taking on Monday?" It was the shock: once recovered he was happy with them all and sad to see them go. We would always be at the shooting-lunches on moors or in fields or the farmer's parlour, eating mutton pies or Irish stew and jam puffs and Stilton cheese, with sips of cherry brandy or Grand Marnier to keep the cold out, while the head keeper brought in the list of the bag and was rewarded with half a tumbler of neat whisky. I would be at dinner according to requirement for numbers or sexes, and I would go tearing round asking brother and sisters for topics of conversation, always in a panic of drying up.

On Sunday afternoons it was the practice to take walks through the woods and fields à *deux*. I have a typical letter received of a morning:

Dearest Diana, please please come for a walk with me this afternoon—for choice a long magnificent one stretching from luncheon to tea, but if you have guest-conscience then a hole-and-corner one tucked in here or there, but anyway a WALK. P.

These walks petrified me. If we could only form a group, so that I need not have the sole responsibility and fear of being discovered to be stupid and dull. What shall I talk about? This particular fear seemed to continue down dumb vistas to my life's end. *What shall I say?* Today? At dinner? When I'm proposed to? When alone with my future husband? Why was I so inadequate in response and imagination? I've never quite lost it. The dearer the friend the greater the fear of their disillusionment and consequent loss.

Parties caused these frets, but half the time it was family life with only two or three staying with us. Then there was a lot of music and duets and puzzling out opera scores and Mr Knox playing the fiddle badly. There was tennis and letter-writing and reading aloud, and antique-buying in Nottingham and Leicester, and hunting shop and hunting neighbours, whom I am ashamed to say I despised. But we were happier at Rowsley in the summer. It was more romantic, more of a Sans Souci, and the smart visitors were so gloriously incongruous.

But the place of all others for romance and gathering rose-buds and making hay and jumping over the moon was Sutton Courtenay. This lovely sixteenth-century manor house belonged to my Uncle Harry Lindsay and Aunt Norah. There once a year I was allowed to go before I came out. The garden was famous for its imagination and fertility. Flowers literally overflowed everything and drifted off into a wilderness. The house was furnished impeccably "of the date" and lit by acetylene gas that simulated candles to perfection. We ate under a loggia from great bowls of chicken in rice and kedgeree and mushrooms and raspberries and Devonshire cream and gooseberry fool and figs—all in abundance. I would arrive carrying a letter from my mother entrusting me to Aunt Norah's great care—not too late to bed and above all not to be alone with young men. The chief object of the visit, as I knew and as Aunt Norah knew, was to drift in a boat all day long with one of the Oxford heroes through the reeds and inlets of the Thames which flowed by the garden—a dinghy full of poetry books and sweets and parasols and bathing-dresses—and better still (or worse!) in the moonlight with the best loved. So the letter was ignored by my aunt, who was younger much than my mother and did not mind anyway if I came to no good. I loved her very dearly and miss her today. She dressed mostly in tinsel and leopard-skins and baroque pearls and emeralds, and her exquisite hands could play the piano with skill and feeling. She had what was called *Gepäck*—favourite poems and pieces cut shamelessly out of books and stuck into another, and she taught me to appreciate a lot that was new, as I was apt to stick in my own mud. Sutton was quite near to Oxford (my Mecca), so these yearly visits were schemed over and anticipated with ecstasy by me and by the undergraduates I so loved. Uncle Harry had bathing-dresses for twenty of them, and four dozen tennis-balls where other players used six. Never was there such generosity, for the Lindsays had no money and for this reason Sutton did not survive. The moment came when there was not enough money to control the flowers, which rose and submerged the house.

I wanted first to be loved, and next I wanted to be clever. By clever I meant something dreadfully superficial, I fear. Knowing that I had no education and therefore no power of learning or concentration, I had to make good with tags, like bright-coloured flags that would beckon and please. I wanted to assume learning though I had it not, so I listened with attention to music, went to museums and art galleries, and learnt reams of poetry word-perfectly. Meredith was in high repute in those Oxford days, so we all knew "Love in the Valley" by heart. I managed to recite "Modern Love," which impressed the few if said in small quantities, all the odes of Keats (I stuck in "Hyperion"), hunks of Shakespeare (*Richard II*, *Romeo and Juliet* and *Hamlet* practically entire), the "Ode to Immortality," "Annabel Lee," "The Forsaken Merman," lots of Browning, *A Shropshire Lad* and Scotch ballads. It was our fashion to set other men's flowers in a great book of thick paper in monkish script. I still have mine with vellum back and Italian paper sides and art-strings to tie it. It is rather touching—so much time and effort and love of the poems are there to see—and so is the failure of the little initial keyhole pictures of a "white owl sweeping" or a "bright star." Some departures from the classic black-and-white lettering are more successful. "On a starred night Prince Lucifer uprose," for instance, is written with white ink on a black-as-hell ground, and pages of Jehovah speaking to Job from the whirlwind have black letters on leaf-green.

Meredith was particularly important to me. My mother had

christened me after Diana of the Crossways and I had once seen
the very beautiful old writer, supported by two attendants, in
my mother's morning-room. When I wrote to him for his
birthday (thank God there is no record of what I set down) he
answered in his hieroglyphic hand:

Let the younger Diana know that her good wishes come to me
like the break of the cloud throwing sun on a wintry day. And if by
chance she should happen upon Crossways, may she have an index
within to direct her whither the right one leads.

On my birthday came his *Poems I and II* with this less happy
inscription:

Lady Diana Manners: her book.

But if she my muse had been
Better verse she would have seen.

This and a photograph (immediately hung over my bed) sealed
my vows of adoration. In 1909 he died. I blush now to think
how I carried on. It seems extraordinary that my family encouraged me. They must have, for my mother lent me her
own black clothes (to the ground) with a large black hat. Thus
attired, accompanied by Podgie and carrying a treasure-armful
of purple irises, we took the train to Golders Green and I saw
to my sickening horror George Meredith carried in a small
casket by his daughter. It was lowered into the grave and I
must needs fling my flowers upon it. Broken with salt tears I
was supported back to the special train, where a little dark
gnome put his head through the window saying "All you can
du for him now is to be a gude girl." It was J. M. Barrie. I am
quite certain that I was not conscious of showing off or attract-
ing attention. I remember my emotions too vividly, but what
onlookers of this mawkish exhibition must have thought fills
me with shame to this day.

It was a maudlin phase. A letter to Patrick Shaw-Stewart is nostalgia without a past:

> Then to bed in this deserted Woodhouse, become through cold and misery a home of regrets and memories. This was Patrick's room, this Julian's, this the road we travelled in the dead of night to the earthly goal of cherry-brandy-drinking with Harry Cust and Charles Whibbles [Whibley] at Matlock Bath. There the swing without the Grenfells. "I feel chilly and grown old."

I am getting very muddled with dates, but these memories jostle around 1908 and 1909 when I was not "out" but grown up in my own eyes at least and plainish in spite of years of pain from plates to straighten my teeth. I had broken the corner off a front one playing hide-and-seek in the dark (a game forbidden) and crashing into an isolated marble pillar that held a lamp. My mother had renounced going to the Delhi Durbar "in case the children break their front teeth," she had said. It was a poor return for her sacrifice. I was by no means slim in spite of the punchball and the banting, yet I was happy and hopeful (in spite of unaccountable fears and glooms), absurdly ambitious for love and admiration, God-fearing but a little shaken in faith, which had not surged in my soul as I had hoped it would. Confirmation I had dreaded, because to talk of God to anyone but oneself was taboo. Even the word God stuck in my throat, as I feel it might have in Mr Knox's outside his pulpit. To be instructed about the unmentionable appalled me. Canon M'Cormick of St James's, Picadilly, was asked to prepare me at the age of fifteen, but I received nothing spiritual from his honest talks. I learnt the Catechism, said I believed (which I did nearly always) and he told me that God had a book with Lady Diana Manners written in it, and that my sins and my merits would be marked beneath and above my name—steps to Heaven or Hell. He was a good man but no evangelist. The Bishop of London blessed me in St Paul's Cathedral with a lot of other bewildered girls in white.

Naturally good until now, I had never lied, for nothing tempted me to lie except fear of wounding and I had nothing to fear. But now with the advent of the young men—benign serpents—came the apple. Though it was never offered or nibbled, I felt guilt at my pleasurable excitement, and a practice of deceit began—hidden letters, denial of hand-holding (my mother felt strongly on this score) and many little lies to save her disappointment in me. I felt that it was for happiness, and the only difficulties of the untruths were the crimson blushes and fears of detection. Childhood was over.

CHAPTER FIVE

The Coterie

"ONLY one year before I'll be out-and-out 'Out'."
It was a happy year, a lot of it spent writing letters to the swains. I have been re-reading and re-living these old letters written and received, all carefully tied together with sensible string in their dated order, interspersed with telegrams, postcards from abroad and even dinner-cards: "Will you take in Lady Diana?"

My own letters I find difficulty and shame in reading. It is dreadfully facetious stuff, half written in quotations from poems—"Richard is not the captain of my soul," "Yesterday, when I saw you in that little moment mercifully given." No one dies—they "outsoar the shadow of their night." Girls who yield to love have been "taken with a sigh." I don't seem able to speak of the *Odyssey* without mentioning its "surge and thunder" or of a great house except as a "stately pleasure dome." They are shockingly solicitous of admiration and "dewdrops" (compliments), and both writer and reader lose all dignity in their passionate prayers for letters and more letters and today and quickly. Those from Patrick Shaw-Stewart, whom I had found at Brancaster, tell of his life till its heroic end in 1917. They describe his years at Oxford working for his examinations—Greats, in which he got a First, and later for All Souls—his life at Baring's, his delightful pre-war holidays in English houses and in his native Scotland, his loves

and changes of love, his fidelity and his interest in my education, the whole campaign in Gallipoli and his last months in the
trenches of France. These letters, in his neat, scholarly hand,
have moved me to tears and laughter and admiration and
tenderness. They clamour shamelessly for more and more of
my silly, extravagant scribbles, which clamour too, and nearly
always abjectly. This odious little glutton writes in 1908:

Send immediately detailed dewdrops and don't tease me by saying you heard them without saying what you heard. They are only
crumbs, and I'll never get enough to make a loaf big enough to
grow vanity-fat. The older I grow [I was fourteen] the more un-
quenchable my thirst for dewdrops.

What shall I read Homer in? More grown up than Church, not
so grown up as Chapman. Butcher & Lang? You say.

A typical ending reads:

I'm sorry, darling, you must *forgive* but I fear never *forget* the
stupidity of your loving Diana.

There are P.S. injunctions never, never to show my letters to
others. I see why only too clearly. I was spinning too many
plates unskilfully and was in terror of letting one lapse. I
realise now what a strong influence this doomed group of
young men had upon me. Yet in spite of wiles I was not fickle
and loved them all truly till their death.

In the year 1910 many of us were lured into acting a tableau
play written by Mrs Alfred Lyttelton about St Ursula and her
eleven thousand virgins. I represented a thousand of them.
Cynthia Asquith, in her radiant *quattrocento* beauty with her
heavy gold hair falling to her knees, was the young saint lying
in her Carpaccio bed, visited by Mrs Patrick Campbell in
angel's wings. This pretty, foolish performance was given
several times and the young men roared applause from the

boxes of the Court Theatre and sent us prima-donna bouquets and baskets. It was my first stage experience and I was to have no other till twelve years later.

Mrs Campbell I loved to distraction. I saw no beauty in her because she was always telling us she was "older than God." She had beautiful hands that liked giving. I see them fondling her horrible little griffon Pinkie-Ponkie-Poo, and snatching necklaces from her neck to put on to mine.

It was in the February of 1911 that Letty married. Ego Charteris had been a lot to Belvoir and Arlington Street, and Letty and I went often to Stanway in Gloucestershire where his family lived. Letty, we knew, was very much in love, but love was more secret in those days. It was not talked about easily, even to one's nearest sisters and friends—not in our family, at least. So we speculated and hoped and fretted and thought wishfully. When they became engaged the whole family cried for joy. Of all men Ego was the nearest to a knight of chivalry, but there is no echo of laughter from the Round Table, while Ego's humour was a riot of fine flowers and herbs. No one had such flavour, or such humility and philosophy.

It was our first wedding—St Margaret's of course, and of course the bridesmaids were Floras from *La Primavera* in blossom-strewn dresses with rosy wreaths and veils. Veils were "the thing" for bridesmaids—no more hats. Sometimes they were blue to be like love-in-the-mist, and the wreaths could be flowers or appropriate myrtle.

Letty looked radiant. Her beams lit us all as we sped them off in a shower of rose-petals over the cobblestones of home to a honeymoon in Morocco. She wrote from Africa enraptured with Tangier, *diffars*, the Prince Menebe, rides to the Harris Villa, and the Biblical clothes.

I had lost my playmate to her love and I could not have

wished it otherwise. Marjorie and I in consequence were growing ever closer. I found it hard to remember that all my life she
had been first a fearsome stranger and then an awe-inspiring
exemplar, for now she and I were of the same age and understanding—not of the same temperament. Marjorie was the
stuff genius is made of, and suffered the weight of it. She
taught me much, including melancholia—though not, alas!
her philosophy, nor yet her arts. She had a crowd of suitors,
but her heart had been given many years before to the man she
was to marry, and in spite of the changes of fortune and the
chances and obstacles that Romance or Eros weaves, designed
like a ballet to separate the lovers and hinder and obstruct the
happy ending, she never tried to take it from him. Everyone
of our age was marrying. I never thought of my own marriage
except as of a far-off day that could not disappoint.

The stage became ever more closely woven into our daily
life. My father had brought us Maxine Elliott as a glorious present. She loved both him and his family. In her house near
London she gave us dazzling fun. Country-house tennis was
at its most vigorous. There, at Hartsbourne, was the champion
Tony Wilding taking infinite pains to improve my game—
with no success. There were Lord Curzon and Lord Rosebery, both seduced by Maxine's eyes and wit. There was the
most beautiful of all young men of his day, Lord Rocksavage.
"We see a lot of Rock. I think he's probably Apollo—anyhow
some god." He was proud and aloof and loved to dance the
one-step (something quite new) to Maxine's gramophone.
There, never-to-be-forgotten, I drank my first cocktail.
Cherry brandy was the pink basis and it had a sugared edge and
something floating, and I gulped it down behind my mother's
back, and so delightfully amusing were the taste and the daring
and the anticipation that I gulped another one and went reeling

in to dinner, all my old fears allayed, confident, in high humour,
ready for the world and whatever it gave. I remember today
the sensation as vividly as that night, countless years ago, when
I discovered an ally that I have never quarrelled with. Tipsy, I
floated round in Lord Rocksavage's arms, dancing those innocent steps that were barred at smart dances. It was during the
years when one still said to partners who asked you to waltz
"Do you reverse?" and before the Austrians had taught us to
be spinning tops.

I don't suppose Lord Rosebery knew I was tipsy nor yet
Lord Curzon. They were both very fond of me. Lord Curzon
had once given us three sisters twenty pounds apiece. I had
never been tipped more than a pound and it seemed *le gros
lot*. We all bought antiques.

He used to invite me with my mother to his very elderly
parties at Hackwood, made up of the "Souls" and Cabinet
Ministers, with their wives or the ladies they loved. They
strolled, high-heeled, with parasols on the lawns, through the
aisles of beeches, but I was a stranger in age so was not too
happy. It was there that I was rude unwittingly to Mr Balfour
when playing some guessing game after dinner. Over-keen, I
suppose, I shouted "Use your brain, Mr Balfour; use your
brain." It was one of many stories told against me, but to
make up for my remorse for pertness Lord Curzon chose me
in another game as his hypothetical companion for a journey
because I was "both gentle and vivacious."

Harry Cust was naturally my rock in this "old sea." I had
known him from earliest Hatley days. He was our "familiar,"
an evergreen olive tree, classic, fresh, tender and funny, easily
convulsed with silent laughter. Very beautiful, I thought him,
with noble hands and impeccable filbert-shaped nails. He wore
a coat such as I never saw another wear—dark blue cloth,

flaring full, short with a flat sable Eton collar. It was like Holbein's *Ambassadors*.

These Hackwood parties were composed of the "Souls," but I did not know them as such. Only later did I hear this group of intelligent, cultured men and women, who knew how to live and love and serve and savour the best, referred to as "Souls." Headlines in cheap papers called me "a Soulful daughter of a Soulful mother," and my mother would tear the page in pieces. To her the name was pejorative, but not to me. They were mostly admirable and grew to be famous. Harry Cust was a cherished "Soul" and a man I loved with all my heart. His promise was never fulfilled—too soon he wearied of ambition, too soon he died for me to realise his wonderful worth. I clung to him at Hackwood and walked through the beech-groves and capped quotations and giggled over our fellow-guests.

Our own Coterie was to be composed of children of the "Souls"—the Grenfells, Listers, Asquiths, Horners, Trees, Charterises, Tennants and Herberts.

I do not know how it came to be the Coterie—the "Corrupt Coterie," to give it its full title. As a name I am a little ashamed of it, as my mother was of the "Souls." There was among us a reverberation of the *Yellow Book* and Aubrey Beardsley, Ernest Dowson, Baudelaire and Max Beerbohm. Swinburne often got recited. Our pride was to be unafraid of words, unshocked by drink and unashamed of "decadence" and gambling—Unlike-Other-People, I'm afraid. Our peak of unpopularity was certainly 1914 and 1915. But criticism, jealousy and disapproval were all forgotten in the catastrophe.

In 1910 King Edward had died. The Belvoir bell tolled from dawn to dusk. I had seen him only at Garden Parties in a very tight frock-coat, jovial, top-hatted and cigarred. My mother loved him loyally though he said she never brushed her hair. I had been so long an undetermined débutante, contented to be neither out nor in, that I must have been asked to Buckingham Palace garden-parties before presentation. We were often taken as children to smaller parties at Marlborough House. My mother's nonpareil of beauty had been Queen Alexandra and she saw her still as radiantly beautiful. She told me that when as a shy young girl she was asked to dance, she would say "I'd rather look at the Princess of Wales, thank you." If asked to supper she said "Thank you, I'm not hungry," and "I'm not thirsty" to suggestions of lemonade or tea. I went to dances only in our own house, where one man at the piano played for great ladies in tiaras and for boys and girls to dance. It was not thought essential for plain or pretty daughters to have a coming-out dance. I emerged reluctantly at the dreariest of hunt balls near Belvoir. We drove (about twelve of us) in the Belvoir bus. The horses took an hour each way and there was no pleasure in it.

But the summer brought a Coronation and a London at its most brilliant. Not that the balls were half as elaborate as to-day's. Derby, Lansdowne, Londonderry, Bridgewater and Stafford Houses were all magnificent, gilded and marbled, and not to be tampered with. There was no imaginative bedizening, no floodlit trees, temples or ruins, no flowery merry-go-rounds and swing-boats or statues made of moss erected for a night. Marquees there were—uncompromising red-and-white-striped tents and discreet fairy lamps twinkling red, white and blue along the grimy garden paths. It didn't look in the least like fairyland, though we always said it did. Florists were ordered to bring suitable begonias and smilax to edge the stairs and sprawl over dinner and supper tables. A crude blaze of electric-light bulbs from chandeliers and sconces did nothing for the beauties and robbed the fabulous crowns and jewels of their smoulder and sparkle. I remember no candles except on dinner-tables. At supper there were quails, too fat to need stuffing, and *chaud-froids* with truffle designs on them, hot and cold soup, lobsters and strawberries, ices and hothouse peaches. It never varied. The Queen of Beauty was Lady Curzon.* When first I saw her at Devonshire House I knew it could be no one else. She wore a turquoise crown on the small golden head that flowered proudly on her long throat. Another Helen, I thought, for she had the proportions of Venus. The elderly ladies all danced with dear old prancing partners, jangling with orders and decorations and with coat-tails flying. Gambolling does not go with weary faces and unlimber limbs. Quadrilles and Lancers were better suited, though no one ever mastered their intricacies and, except at Court, they generally ended in chaos.

The young girls were raw and shy, innocent of powder and on the whole deplorably dressed, with their shapeless wispy hair held by crooked combs. They must wear gloves drawn above their elbows, and which of us could afford a new pair nightly? So the not-so-clean were worn and we often reeked of cleaning-petrol. Shoes were of pink or white satin and were smudged after the first dance by clumsy boys' boots.

We poor creatures suffered great humiliation, for between dances we joined a sort of slave or marriage market at the door, and those unfortunates with few friends or those who had been betrayed by a partner, or were victims of muddling the sequences of their dances, became cruelly conspicuous wallflowers. Those who found such shame unendurable (and I was one) could only sneak downstairs to the cloakroom, ostensibly

* Later Lady Howe.

to have their dress mended, and hope not to meet fellow-wallflowers in the same predicament. The mothers sat all round the room encouraging or glaring at their daughters' partners. They loved it, and were loath to go home.

The *Bals Blancs*, of which there were three or four a night, were very trying to me and I would welcome the dawn breaking and the red-breasted, top-hatted linkman at the door—Mr Piddlecock he was called—bidding us "Good Morning" as he packed us into the carriage.

"Taking them all home, my lady, taking them all home!" he had once said to a lady like Mrs Bennet, with five unmarried daughters, who had not given him his end-of-season tip.

As the sun rose the men in rubber boots and hats would be out hosing the streets. Pointed shoes in which one had danced for six hours hurt on the cobblestones of our courtyard, and the flights of stairs seemed long and steep before one saw the friendly bed. Counting eight on your fingers from bedtime, you jotted down appropriately "Call me at 10, [11 or 12]" on the pad that hung on your door, and gave yourself to the sleep of the exhausted.

In 1911 I was presented at Court. My mother had been given by Queen Victoria the *entrée* at the time when she was nursing her first baby. The *entrée* has the advantage that it can never be taken from you, and you do not spend three hours queueing in your carriage to the main door of the Palace, but can stalk in through a smaller but nobler entrance.

I had made my own train—three yards of cream net sprinkled generously with pink rose-petals, each attached by a diamond dewdrop. The dress was adequate and the three feathers springing out of my head looked less ridiculous when everyone was wearing them. I stood in the Arlington Street ballroom, self-conscious but pleased, while all the servants and a few old friends with nothing better to do came and had a look. I was nervous of making my double curtsey. The courtiers are very alarming and martinettish—they shoo you and pull you back and speak to you as they would to a wet dog, but once the trial is successfully over you have the fun of seeing others go through the same ordeal.

The King was to be crowned and Crown Princes were assembling for the ceremony. The great houses were swept and garnished, the smaller ones had new coats of cream paint; their window-boxes were spilling over with lobelias, geraniums and marguerites. We went to the Coronation in the best of places—Queen Alexandra's box. We looked down on my father and mother in their robes and ermine and we sucked our iron rations (meat lozenges) against starvation.

I was given a medal to commemorate the Coronation, which I wore at Grosvenor House with two swimming-medals won at the Bath Club and an eighteenth-century silver St Esprit on a pompous blue bow. It made a brave show no doubt, but why did no one stop me? The Crown Prince of Germany ("Little Willie"), who was present, immediately spotted the enormity. He was amused and took me aside and sat me down and asked me about my medals. I told him, and I told him too that lots of people thought there was going to be a war between our countries. He said that if there was he promised to spare me. He kissed my hand and picked me out another evening to walk in the garden at Stafford House. I was on my way to an artists' party dressed as Perdita, and I was proud and flattered and generally idiotic and thought I had made a conquest, but beyond a postcard of himself with "*Vergiss mein nicht*" written across the corner, nothing came of it.

The medals (which I hide today since I have three commemorating Coronations) keep shining into my memory.

This first Coronation medal I wore on my knee at a Court Ball. I was wearing a curious dress, half nightgown, half a black drapery that fell back and front from my left shoulder to meet again at the right knee. Being my own copy of a Lucille model it was insecurely stitched. When curtseying deeply in the Royal Quadrille (into which I had been commanded only because I knew the figures) the vital stitch gave. I considered it an inspired solution to use the medal as a linchpin. The courtiers were on to me like bloodhounds, but could do nothing, and I finished the quadrille with my knee decorated.

The medals won at the Bath Club, which I came across lately blackened with age, evoked the only athletic pleasure I have ever known. I would start undoing belts and buttons in Berkeley Street, the quicker to plunge into that delectable green pool where I learnt to splash, to swim and then to dive reasonably well ("seventeen feet in front of Royalty," I used to boast). After an hour's hard tuition my friends and I, wrapped in bath-towels, would stagger into the hottest room of the "Turkish," send for large strawberry ices from Gunter's next door and shock the older, fatter ladies with our giggling gossip.

Lady Constance Stewart-Richardson was the star turn at the Bath Club. She dived like a swallow, her beautiful Greek boy's body, strong as an arrow in flight, pierced the water without splash and left us marvelling. Later she took to the "halls" to compete with Isadora Duncan, and though she was severely criticised for her audacity and lack of art I still believed in her.

Maud Allan had made a sensation at the Palace Theatre. Greatly daring, she had appeared in a wisp of chiffon and bare legs with pipes and cymbals. My mother, who despised the art of ballet exemplified by Adeline Genée and very second-rate dancers, was enthusiastic about this new Grecian frieze form of movement. She sent us weekly to watch and learn, in spite of the number finishing with "Salome's Dance"—considered scandalous, for she was all but naked and had St John's head on a plate and kissed his waxen mouth (a business later forbidden on the Covent Garden stage, where a dish of gravy was substituted). My mother was untrammelled by convention.

The Russians were the next to explode on the Palace Theatre stage—Karsavina and Baldina, with a little *corps de ballet.* Again my mother forgot her prejudice against blocked toes and *tutus* and we would stand every Saturday behind the circle, not believing that the legendary Pavlova could outshine such glory. Of course she did. Pavlova was a leaf, a rainbow, a flake, an iridescent foam, her bones of music made. Secret and unsocial, even when she sprang toe-first out of baskets of roses at the most extravagant private parties, she never let us meet her in the flesh.

Looking back, I am surprised indeed by my childish vain ambitions. I bought ballet shoes, puckered up my sylphide skirts and hopefully signed on with Miss Dietz so as to swing my heavy legs on the bars and totter on my points. I went to Lydia Kyasht to be taught to glide like a Russian peasant, flicking a provocative red handkerchief. A year's work taught me to stop learning.

When the Imperial Russian Ballet arrived, Lady de Grey, with the zest and zeal of a girl, moved down to the centre stalls the better to see the whole, and would often lend us her box whence to swoon over Karsavina and Nijinski in *Pavillon d'Armide, Spectre de la Rose, Sheherazade, Tamar,* *Les Sylphides* and *Carnaval,* and as if all this was not enough the next year brought Chaliapin and the Russian Opera. Never since, I think, have we in England had our eyes so dazzled with new light. The comets whizzed across the unfamiliar sky, the stars danced. The time-revered old Italian opera in its buskins and farthingales, its tights and its cap-doffing, had wearied an audience older than me. Boxes at Covent Garden were hired for the season, but not for music. The darkness hid many sleepers. Wagner nights were more musically alert, because only enthusiasts could stand them. Now came a blast to awaken the dead, a blaze of blinding gold, the Kremlin bells clanged and crashed, and Boris was there, a humble giant on his way to be crowned.

My mother thought Chaliapin looked exactly like me. I found it difficult to trace my features, colour and shape (he was six foot four) through the most skilful dark Muscovite make-up, but later, when I knew him, and loved him desperately, I boasted about this resemblance, although there was very little beyond colouring, a good disposition and maybe a line of chin.

I was certainly an artist snob, but had I not been I would still have worshipped and put myself in his way for crumbs, and, getting the crumbs, I wanted praise, and after praise, love. My head was turned, and I behaved outrageously. I think he was pleased with me, for I was perhaps a little shield against the onset of what I then called "rapacious women." He would bow to me from the stage as he must have done to the Czar. He would bring flowers to the box when he was not singing, he encouraged me in amusing pranks, such as dressing as a peasant or a boyard's wife and singing in the chorus. Hearing him sing so near to me on the stage made the stalls pall and the box an anti-climax.

Everything Society criticised me for I now realise my mother encouraged. She was proud and pleased with my love for Chaliapin and thought I was quite right to forbid him to go to a party given in his honour to which I had failed to get invited. This insult to his host was even more outrageous of him than it was of me. No doubt he did not want to go anyway, but I thought it was for my sake. I triumphed. Maurice Baring reported the party-without-the-prince and reproved me for showing off. I felt repentant.

Maurice loved Russia, spoke its tongue, translated its poems, told me what its picnics were like and imitated the gypsies' raucous voices. He loved Chaliapin too, and through him Maurice and I became devoted to each other.

I had known Maurice always as the most amusing of myths and the most heroic. He had been to the Russo-Japanese War as a reporter, and he went to a cholera camp somewhere else, and then I met him at a very young party and he took me to supper and said, "I'll show you the game of risks," and he cut some crusts up, with a very sharp knife in his trembling hands (they always trembled) so fast and close under his blind eyes that one knew blood would be drawn, and it was. Then he set fire to his sparse hair and it would fizzle a little and go out, and he would light it again with a match till it was all singed off, but his scalp never burnt, and he laughed uproariously as I did, and we made too much noise, and were half-mad with hilarity, and it was said that I was showing off again. Next day he sent me a telegram every two or three hours. One said "*O toi, mon beau soleil*" and another "I loved you long ago in Thessaly."

I was intoxicated with pleasure and haunted as usual by knowing the moment must come when he would discover that I was not all he thought me. I could think of nothing amusing or poetic, nothing at all to write in answer that I did not discard with disgust.

This iridescent season of music, dance, pageantry and fluttering flirtations turned to the calmer joys of the country and on to London's winter wet.

The young men came to tea in the ballroom at Arlington Street. They played chess with me and we practised the *csárdás*—eight of us—for some fancy ball. I had, at eighteen, my first bona-fide proposal from a gentleman twenty years older. I cried with embarrassment and tried sophisticatedly to laugh it off. He accused me of lures and wiles and worse, but I was surely innocent. I had known him as a child and I loved him as a child loves.

It was all games and courting, and in a corner of the ball-room was Jacques-Émile Blanche, painting one of us. He was to me as familiar as the piano. His English was fluent and he had an accent we loved to imitate. We treated him with all the affection you give to a cherished dog. We had no idea he was famous. He knew more than we did about our staff, knew the maids' names and the pantry cupboard's contents, and where the paper and string and screwdriver were kept. It was perhaps he who brought into our lives Reynaldo Hahn, who would come and show Marjorie how to sing *L'Heure Exquise* or *Infidelité* and sing himself under his breath the songs he had newly written or old ones by Gounod—*Venise* and *Printemps* —all now buried and unknown.

There was the Slade School season. Letty and I both went to Gower Street by bus and sat shivering in the vast studios, absorbed in fixing the Discus Thrower on to our drawing-boards. A dear myopic man (the great Ambrose McEvoy, but I didn't realise it till later) would shyly tell me what was wrong —everything, really, but he made it sound as though the hope-less drawing was very nearly first-class.

It was warmer in the life class for the sake of the nudes, though for all the heat the poor things were very cold and livid and sagging and goose-fleshed. There the alarming figure of Professor Tonks would set me trembling as though he were Justice itself. I saw the drawing through his eyes as a silly in-sult to the human body. Having no talent and knowing it, I did not hope to improve, but the life was new and absorbing and here I learnt to love McEvoy. Lessons over, he took me to his little slum studio in Millbank. The lean-to in which he painted was not wide or high enough to hold his canvases. There was a half-finished picture of a Chilean and his wife and four children. I little knew that this unknown father was called Gandarillas and would be my friend for forty years.

McEvoy would crouch on a camp-stool, his face close to his water-colour. Above me was a cruelly unbecoming skylight and in my eyes a strong electric bulb. He was surprised that I was surprised at the unnatural elaboration of light. That and a stiff toothbrush which he took to his all-but-finished portrait account for the strange etherealness—the blue lights and the yellow, the day and the flame—that strikes one in his pictures.

It was a joy sitting to McEvoy. His conversation prattled and laughed, and friends—beautiful women and their admirers —crushed into the lean-to and talked scandal and art and love. Augustine Birrell would sit and read aloud to stop my chattering tongue. McEvoy painted me several times. Some pictures I have lost sight of. One I sought, sorrowing, for years— a water-colour of me in a big black dress and a serious top hat ("That silly Welsh hat Diana wears," Margot Asquith said). One I still have. It was christened "The Call to Orgy." He was fond of orgies and would love to come to our wilder parties. We took him to our hearts, and when he died, too young, a knife went through mine.

CHAPTER SIX

Pleasure at the Helm

IN the spring of 1912 I went with my mother for the first time
to Venice, to stay with Anthony Drexel in the Palazzo Balbi
Vallier. The Campanile had just been rebuilt and we watched
its unveiling. The bells rang and forty thousand doves were
liberated. The giant belfry dwarfed St Mark's domes and the
bronze horses, and generally the new tower looked too big and
too new. Again no one reproved me for making myself a
cynosure by wearing an Italian officer's white cloth cloak, and
on the side of my head a *bersagliere*'s hat, plumed with cocks'
feathers.

That summer Lady Cunard, a new light in our lives, took a
small *casa* in the Via dei Catecumeni. It was with her we
stayed. The fabled Louisa Casati lived in the half-built Palazzo
Vanier dei Leoni. I saw her drifting down the Grand Canal
under a parasol of peacocks' feathers, but this surprise was
nothing to the succession of glorious shocks that were to come.

At the first of her parties she received us in her roofless
palace by the light of a brazier on to which a nakedish slave for
each new arrival flung a fuel that flared up into white flame.
Another slave struck a reverberating gong announcing every
guest while she, the Casati, tall and elegant in a lampshade
skirt, seemingly growing out of a wide bowl of tuberoses,
presented each of us with a waxen flower. I remember thinking
with what grace the foreigners received the flower and how

clumsy we poor English were, saying "Doesn't it smell good!" when another said *"Quelle émotion—Madame!"*

The next party outshone the first and failed. It was planned that we should meet in the unbuilt palace dressed and masked as Longhis and Guardis and process in gondolas to the Piazza San Marco, there to disport ourselves—no one wondered how. The Casati wore the trousered Bakst-designed dress of an animal-tamer. On her shoulder was a macaw, on her arm an ape. She was followed closely by an attendant keeper leading a restive leopard, or puma it may have been. His hand was dripping with blood (doubtless paint). We were about sixty strong and had not reckoned with the normal Piazza crowd nor with the sensation we should make arriving at midnight with a menagerie and masks and a Turkish major-domo in gaberdine, pumpkin turban and stick of office to prepare a way for his procession. The Piazzetta was black with Venetians. The fine girls, dressed in their classical black-fringed shawls, made us the more garish. There were shouts and ribald screams and peals of laughter and we fought our way through a density that would have been impenetrable but for our leopard. Somehow we jostled our way across the immensity of the Piazza through the columned archway to the nearest embarking steps. For me it was no failure. I loved crowds and didn't mind being a spectacle, and I enjoyed madly the jostle and even the discomfiture of the elders, who must have heard the tumbrils behind the mob's howls, but the party must be written down a failure.

No longer a fledgling, I was allowed more liberty and choice after the first year. I was still forbidden to be alone with a man except by chance in the country. A married woman must bring me home from a ball. For walking and shopping and even driving in a taxi, a sister or a girl was enough protection. I could go to the Ritz but to no other London hotel. But generally there was more freedom. I was not forced to Ascot or to "young dances" and I had more courage in choosing my friends. I desperately wanted my mother to approve of them, but she could not.

I had earned the hard name of a "scalp-collector" and I expect the cap fitted. The more the safer. Many would save me from one. I did not want to be possessed by my heart or by another's.

Like all good mothers she planned to see me married to an Adonis reigning feudally in a palace, while I was looking for a romantic struggle with some Unknown by my side. So the tangled web of deceits grew thicker, though it barely affected my love for her. The shadow crossing her face when she saw me with an unmistakable ineligible said "What waste of time!" This annoyed and perturbed me. The eligibles she put in my way were leprous to my eyes. Today I wonder why. I should have seen it as part of the romantic struggle instead of resenting it.

Was Tommy Bouch eligible or ineligible? I do not know in what category my mother put him. I was very fond of him, so he cannot have been eligible. Before the war he was a Master of the Belvoir Hounds. He came from a hunting world in Warwickshire and with the courage of a Siegfried braved the fiery ring of taunts and ridicule and warnings of spells without a name that encircled the Castle, to become an intimate. The Belvoir Hunt thought the air too rarefied and theatrical. Perhaps they did not know that their Master was a poet—a poet whom Maurice Baring praised to the skies. He was imaginative and generous and a benedicton to those of us in trouble with scandals, debts, love or lack of a thoroughbred mount.

Then there was George Moore—George Gordon Moore, who hailed I believe from Detroit. He was certainly not eligible. I had met him at Stanway—a most unusual man of thirty-six, Red Indian in appearance with straight black hair, flattened face and atomic energy. I understood very little of what he said, but I caught his unclear accents of admiration. I "penetrated his consciousness," he said, and he courted me in his own exaggerated way although he had a wife and children. He gave me to understand that these hindrances could be liquidated and that his every living hour and his vast fortune would be dedicated to me—to me and to Sir John French. He moved in a shower of gold. He doled it out on the just and unjust and on his whims. His riches were evident but maybe an optical illusion, so his countrymen said. Harsh things they whispered—"Kicked out of the States," "Just a crook," but we all believed in him, especially the Charteris family, whose protégé and patron he was. He had no snobbery. I would have liked him a lot had it not been for his infatuation for me, which frightened me into flight.

He loaded Letty and me with presents, Letty being now a Charteris and I his idol—silver foxes for Letty and an ermine coat to the ankle for me (my mother chose it from Jay's), a monstrous little monkey called Armide with a diamond waist-belt and chain, Maupassant's works in full morocco, countless *éditions de luxe*, a cream poodle called Fido cut *en papillon* with pompoms and bracelets of fluff and a heliotrope bow, and twice weekly, wherever I was, arrived a box the size of a coffin full of Madonna lilies.

It seems odd today, and no doubt seemed odd at the time, that we were allowed to accept such presents. I never thought it strange because my mother saw no harm. She liked the children to be spoilt and enjoyed nothing better than choosing gifts from wise men.

George Moore's devotion and admiration for Sir John

French led him to buy a huge corner house in Lancaster Gate and there install the General. It was a ghastly house, which in the war was to be a shelter and playground for our diminishing Coterie. The dreary little parties he gave in 1913 developed under the stress of early war into uproarious ones behind barred doors which were called by our enemies the "Dances of Death."

A foreign eligible didn't carry the same stigma. Count Clary for instance was very eligible. He taught me the Viennese waltz and we would spin ourselves to a standstill to the strains of Cassano's band. Count Wilczeck was eligible, so was Count Hoesch, another Dream Waltzer. But the most eligible of all was Prince Felix Youssupoff. He was later to kill Rasputin, but at that time he was an innocent at Oxford and deeply in love with my sister Marjorie. A mystic, and of transcendent beauty, he sang to his guitar the Russian gypsy songs, now so hackneyed, then new to us. At the many fancy balls he wore his eighteenth-century Russian dress of gold and pearls and sables and aigrettes, with embroidered boots and jewelled scimitar. He rode in the procession with me at the revived Eglinton Tournament. This historic second-time failure took place at Earl's Court. The tickets were fabulously expensive —twenty pounds, I think—so very few were sold. The challengers were the Duke of Marlborough, Lord Ashby St Ledgers, Lord Craven, Lord Tweedmouth and others. Lady Curzon was the Queen of Beauty and I was a lady of her Court. Letty was part of the musical ride mounted on ordinary-looking horses loaned by the Household Cavalry. The Queen of Beauty's steed was little better. These well-bred animals were not dramatic enough for me, nor were the ugly Elizabethan costumes, so I designed myself a black velvet Holbein dress (quite out of period) and hired Richard II's stage horse,

Roan Barbary, with mane and tail that swept the ground. It was as broad as a circus galumpher, but never mind. Felix wore his Russian robes and mounted himself on a mettlesome snow-white Arab, foaming and flecking and pawing. Of course they were cross with us for cheating, and another score was marked up against me. I see why—now. Publicity was building me my pedestal. I never encouraged it knowingly. I think I was not aware of it. If I was, I simply didn't care.

I prayed for Marjorie to marry Felix. I bought her a *Hugo's Russian Grammar*, but her heart was set and its desire at hand. In a few months she was engaged to Charlie Anglesey and sailed away from me in a fine yacht, and I knew that, as with Letty, we could never be the same to each other again.

No time to mope—she was happy and I had friends and more friends and many that I loved whole-heartedly. There were Raymond and Katharine Asquith, and Viola, now married to my adored Alan Parsons, Felicity and Iris Tree, Phyllis Boyd, just coming into my life, and then all the young men who were making and moulding me and would so soon be lost. The favourites were Edward Horner, Patrick Shaw-Stewart, George Vernon, Denis Anson, the Grenfells, Sidney and Michael Herbert, Tommy Bouch, and Duff Cooper.

I can't remember exactly when I first knew Raymond Asquith. I remember the jubilation of two families when Katharine Horner and he were married, but it was some time later that they, living in Bedford Square, became the greatest influences on my youth.

Katharine was beautiful, serio-comical, and knew about the Rights and Wrongs that I had never thought to weigh. Though in many ways she was my opposite, she was my pattern. She explained literature and ethics in the Turkish bath over the Gunter's ices, while I sketched her a becoming dress for the next fancy ball. Duff, so newly in my life, loved her hopelessly. I loved Raymond hopelessly. Happiness was never complete if they were not there. He was ten years older than the eldest of us, yet of all of them he was the most discipled and loved. Everything he taught me by example became direction through my life. I cannot write about Raymond.

Duff had been brought to our house one dancing night by the Manners cousins. He was young—three years older than me—and a little shy and famed for every accomplishment I loved—poetry, daring, charades and romanticism. There was no sudden sympathy. He grew into my life as I into his. Never with him alone did I suffer my fears or flee from his scrutiny. From the first meeting he wrote me love-letters, sometimes three a day, in the lightest vein and gaiety. The first one, in answer to my acknowledgement of a cheque (we played a great deal of poker, too high in theory but the money rarely left the Coterie), reads:

Dear Lady Diana,
        I adore the way you spell my name. Please always spell it so. It looks like the picture of a crocodile, and is alone well worth two guineas. The ball was worth much more to me. It made an epoch in my life and will not be forgotten for days.
    We must play again and dance again, please.
                                Your DUFF COOPER—
or as you much more amusingly would write—Cooowper.

My calligraphy was always and remains even worse than my spelling, which is atrocious and so phonetic that I write bs for ms when I have a cold.

And then what of the script itself? I have always known that you wrote with your feet, but this alone is far from sufficiently explaining the look of your page. Foot is the member but what (in the name of Art and Science) is the instrument? The Koran is said to have been written by Mahomet on shoulder-bones of mutton with a mother-of-pearl pen 1500 miles long, but what do you use? A boot-jack, or coconut, or candle-end? Or just any old thing picked up for a song at the Caledonian Market?

Or again:

Your letter was divine though very unintelligible. Mr Browning might have envied your obscurity as much as Mrs Browning might have envied your brain. But what I nearly did understand rather frightened me, for it seemed that beneath all your sweet ravings you were making a frantic effort to write sense.

In 1913 Duff went to Hanover to learn German for the Foreign Office examination, and from there to France. From Germany came the letters that I learnt to rely upon:

Well, well do I remember stumbling up the stairs of Arlington Street, dazzled by a vision that waited at the top, but on that occasion I was not only dazzled but dumbed and felt in fact like stupid Dante:

> *Tanto gentile e tanto onesta pare*
> *La donna mia quand'ella altrui saluta,*
> *Ch'ogne lingua deven tremando muta,*
> *E li occhi no l'ardiscon di guardare.**

I'm late for dinner, late for the play but never too late to mend.

DUFF

In the following early spring there was a long low-fever illness in the Trees' house rented from William Nicholson at Rottingdean. I was several weeks in bed. I saw myself the girl in a decline. Down the village street at Hillside lived the

* The first stanza of the sonnet in chapter XXVI of Dante's *Vita Nuova*, translated by D. G. Rossetti as:

> My lady looks so gentle and so pure
> When yielding salutation by the way,
> That the tongue trembles and has nought to say,
> And the eyes, which fain would see, may not endure.

young men on a reading party (my mother never could be free of them) and they would wave at my pale face at the window from their horses, and it was there that Duff's poems touched my heart, and I would look for him through the window more eagerly than for the others:

Rottingdean   *24 March 1913*

A sonnet written in a quarter of an hour and a noisy room because I thought it would make good fun for an invalid. Don't as you love yourself show it to a soul, and don't rate my intellect by its merits. But get well quickly for the love of heaven, or I shall swear never to write you an elegy.

> Because your skin was whiter than the snows
> Which jealous winds of March have blown away,
> These cruel harbingers of summer say
> "We will not bear her whiteness—nothing grows
> So pale in summertide—the whitest rose
> Seems yellow in her hands." So cruel they
> Blew bitter poison to you yesterday
> While you were gathering the pale primrose.
>
> But I who never cared about the spring,
> Fonder of autumn's faded brown and red,
> Sit wondering what the summeriest day can bring
> To make me up this spring day that is dead,
> Sit wondering how the birds have heart to sing
> Now that the glory of the spring is fled.

A sonnet every few hours is my prescription for every malady. Deal kindly with it as you did the first. The poetry gambit is a bit old-fashioned in the twentieth century. But I like old methods best, and I hope you will find the sentiments very affecting and the numbers monstrous ravishing.

> I saw a ghost-white face look down on me,
> Ghost-white and spirit-beautiful—and then

PLEASURE AT THE HELM

As by enchantment I was back again
In the far fairy world of chivalry.
And such a white lost maiden I could see
Shut up by magic and by evil men,
Watching with weary eyes that wondered when
The fairy prince would come to set her free.

And that which conjured up such ecstasies
And made me dream in high romantic strain,
See visions of wild terror and wild bliss,
Of knights that fought and loved and died in vain,
Was nothing more and nothing less than this—
A lily face against the window-pane!

London   *March 1913*

Here is a very hasty sonnet while waiting for dinner. I did not want
you to blame poor God for withholding from you the daily nourish-
ment for which you prayed, especially as he is so careful of the
sparrows. But don't thank him for it—thank me. Your prose is as
welcome as my verse.

I have a message from the flowers to bear,
For as I came along they cried to me
'Oh listen to us, of thy charity,
For we would send a message unto her.
Her casement is so high we never dare
To climb and whisper to her—therefore we
Have chosen out of many only thee
To write to her and be our messenger.

Oh warn her that the Spring has come, and say
That in the land of flowers we cannot tell
Who is the Queen of Spring, whom to obey,
For while she lingers 'tis impossible.
Oh! let her not make all too long delay:
Go thou to her and say "Get well, get well." '

Later from Hanover he wrote:

A POETRY CURE

19 April 1913

I hope you are still ill. I cannot bear to think of you as quite well
and with a hat on. Also you will appreciate an unexpected letter
from me so tremendously if it finds you in bed.

> Art thou still ailing, pretty one?
> How dost thou dare be ill?
> Now that the laughing Spring's begun,
> Now that the sun
> Makes promise to fulfil
> All our wild hopes of summer fun,
> Why art thou ailing still?

"Ailing" is a bad word, isn't it? But can you think of a better?
However let's go on with it:

> Pitiful primrose, droop no more,
> Hold up thy golden head,
> For May is knocking at the door,
> And all her store
> Of garments white and red,
> Her motley mummeries of yore,
> Are waiting to be spread.

> Throw open wide the door to May,
> Let her come in to thee.
> She shall with kisses charm away
> All thine infirmity.
> So shalt thou see
> How sweet it is to play
> The livelong day
> With such a joyous playfellow as she.

I think that will do for the present, so will leave it at that.

By the way, I always meant to ask you whether you would marry
me or not? Probably not. I am mouse-poor and should be a vile
husband.

Next summer a delightful house in Venice was taken by
Maud Cunard, who had become real in my eyes—real and

unique—and who was to be loved and served by me until her life's end thirty-five years later and mourned to this day. She asked my mother and me to stay in September. Nancy, her daughter, was there and Harry Cust and Ronald Storrs, also the Prime Minister and Margot Asquith and Elizabeth their daughter.

In another palace, once Lady Laird's, lived for a month my nearest, my very dearest friends. Fired, I think, by my accounts of Venice and her people, George Vernon had taken this *palazzo* on the Grand Canal and brought with him the Raymond Asquiths, Billy Grenfell, Duff and his sister Sybil Hart-Davis, Denis Anson, Edward Horner, Irene Lawley and Felicity Tree. "*In questa casa ogni sera è festa*," a gondolier had said in answer to a newcomer's question about its "feasting presence full of light."

The Casa Cunard was more staid. Mr Asquith was interested in his daughter's friends and I was one. A lot of my passion for Venice came from him and his *Baedeker*, and the gruelling questioning of an evening on the day's learning. On his arm I would climb the stairs of the Miracoli Church and plan to be married there. (From its slippery steps Elizabeth fell into the narrowest and slimiest of canals.) Hand in hand we would gaze up at Colleoni, read from *The Stones of Venice*, peer at the Carpaccios in S. Giorgio de' Schiavoni, then quite invisible from darkness, and buy presents for Margot or white Longhi masks for the evening's masquerade.

This was a time when Conservatives did not speak amicably to Liberals. Margot Asquith had always been in our house and we in Cavendish Square to children's parties. My contemporary, Elizabeth, the youngest daughter, frightened me. Though a bit younger she was far in advance of me intellectually and in social graces. Violet Asquith and her ringlets I had been in love with at Mrs Wordsworth's dancing classes. Cyril Asquith, the Judge to be, I can see turning scarlet head over heels, but I do not remember Mr Asquith until he was Prime Minister and I was aged seventeen. I used to go rather surreptitiously to Downing Street. It flattered my snob side, but also I really loved Mr Asquith. He delighted in the young and the young's conversation, and would talk of poetry and people and weddings and jokes, and he wanted to hold one's hand and feel equal and comforted.

In Venice on his birthday we dressed him up as a Doge and hung the *sala* with Mantegna swags of fruit and green leaves and loaded him with presents, tenderness and admiration. I think he was ecstatically happy that day.

But in spite of my poor mother's misery, it was to the Casa delle Feste I was always trying to escape. There were the young, and no authority or sobriety. There was dancing and extravagance and lashings of wine, and charades and moonlit balconies and kisses, and some amateur prize-fighting with a mattress ring and seconds, and a girls' sparring match and, best of all, bets on who would swim the canal first, Duff or Denis Anson, and in their evening clothes. I can see Duff now, jacket flung to me, miraculously climbing up one of the great posts that moor the gondolas at the entrance steps—posts quite fifteen feet high and in part slimy from sea-water. There were some wires for creepers to climb along from one post to an-other, and with no other help he swarmed to the top in a trice and dived into the black canal. Denis I had no eyes for, but I heard him plop and saw them both breast-stroking to the other side. Duff won. What fun we thought it! And it was done for love of one of us, or so exploits were always said to be done in those romantic days. (I knew a man who ate a centipede to please or amuse his wanton love.) The canal exploit was much condemned next day. It was the first over the years of scandalous "goings-on" by the English in Venice.

All of us, pretty and unconventionally dressed, were naturally followed and stared at by the perambulating Venetians on the Piazza at night. Today, no longer wearing their own black shawls, they are surprised at nothing, but there was a general new look in everything in those last years before the first war —a Poiret-Bakst blazon and a budding freedom of behaviour that was breaking out at the long last end of Victorianism. We felt it and revelled in it.

One evening our knot of gaping citizens seemed smaller and less interested than usual. "What shall we do to people the Piazza?" I said thoughtlessly. It was enough for Denis Anson, with the help of a piece of soap, to throw an epileptic fit in a space at one end of San Marco's. In a moment a crowd had coagulated, plus a posse of *carabinieri*. The sad case of Denis's infirmity was explained to these alarming men of the law by Charles Lister, who was an attaché at the Embassy in Rome. The epileptic would be taken home by his friends, he said, and he offered apologies for causing a scene in a public place. The officers moved off, the crowd solicitously followed the poor Englishman, who within three minutes had sprung like a mad ape away from his keepers and flung a far worse epileptic fit in another part of the Piazza. Repetition was too much for the police, who this time frog-marched him off in the direction of the Bridge of Sighs and clapped him into a cell, from which the long-suffering Charles Lister had to extricate him next morning, using the Embassy as leverage.

All Venice was shocked by these frolics, not unnaturally, I suppose, and I came in for most of the blame, but there was no remorse in the House of Feasting and we all vowed to return yearly. The war was too near when the vow was made. In fact this was the *Carne Vale* of 1913. Only Duff and I ever did return.

It had been a very gay year. I was enjoying life more than ever before. Lit by the common day I all but forgot the prison shades:

God of Battles, Patrick, those three vampire months in London. How far from the Brahms level * I sank, to what depths of dance-love, dewdrop-slavery and crowned-head worship did I fall. Lord, it was a primrose path of dalliance. I never mean to forget my first "intoxicating year". . . . Swimming in cool river pools with Grenfell gods and another young god, Alfred Lyttelton, who dropped his years with his clothes . . . Olympic zeal in his face, and that dancing star Alphy Clary with equally starry teeth—foot and mouth perfection.

A lot of letters were written in those leisured days. They were my daily bread when exiled at Belvoir. The evidence is in my big tin boxes that hold these treasures of youth. Duff writes:

I think it would be rather fun if you were to write one letter to every ten of mine. You would then probably receive ten a day, which would begin to crowd uncomfortably a small house like Belvoir, and lay up a lifetime's occupation for some remote descendant of the young Marquess with a similar taste for antiquarian research. Perhaps he would publish *Letters from the celebrated Mr Duff Cooper to a Lady Diana Manners, 3rd daughter of the 8th Duke etc.* in 10 vols. and I hope copiously illustrated.

One can see from the following snippet how Duff's life did not help to recommend him to ambitious mothers:

A hasty moment snatched from a busy feverish day. Interviewing bankers at breakfast time, having lost £500 at the tables overnight. Oh! if only I had won as much, I would have bought you

* A private language phrase indicating the highest excellence.

something so pretty but now I shan't, in fact I doubt whether I shall put a stamp on this. It is hard to lose at cards and at love, and very expensive in gold and tears, but bankers are delicious people and help one so cleverly to consume one's capital, and mine are particularly charming. They always ask me how Lord Farquhar is, and as I have only met him once in my life I always answer that he was looking very well when I last saw him, which makes them very happy and they immediately do everything I ask. How are you looking?

And again money seems to be a difficulty. We played too high. One morning Duff sent me a little bag of golden sovereigns, the normal currency before the first war:

Didn't you say at dinner that you wanted £160 and didn't I say that you should have it? Perhaps you have forgotten, but if you said it, it is true, and it is terrible that you should ever want anything, especially anything that I can give you, but it is heavenly that you should want it at one of the rare moments when I should have it. . . .

I am weak and weaponless before you and say as Charles II said of the Prince of Denmark "I have tried you drunk and I have tried you sober, and there is nothing in you"—nothing that I don't *adore*. How right and wise you were to quit a little commoner, a little little commoner, an obscure commoner, for a well-known and notorious Duke.

This must refer to "Bendor," the magnificent Duke of Westminster, who dazzled me for a few weeks of 1913.

We had become an even closer Coterie, very irritating to others and utterly satisfying and delightful to ourselves. There was a hard core and its shifting outer rings. There was Gustav Hamel, the young pioneer, a gold-haired, intrepid Swede. He belonged to our "ring." He was a lot with us, dining at odd restaurants (a new excitement for me and allowed only if chaperoned) and motoring with great danger in his racing car at night, and dancing, and for all but me there were flights in his mothy aeroplane. My mother forbade me to fly and it was a humiliation deeply resented. Lady Dudley looped the loop. Sybil, Duff's sister, took up two piglets to prove that pigs could fly. Duff flew from place to place as a means of transport. All the girls were leaves in the wind. Then one tragic day Hamel was flying back from Hardelot in France to London. A crowd was on the airfield to welcome and cheer him, but he never returned. London was struck with horror. Newsboys screamed rumoured reports of his safety. Friends, unable to bear the suspense, quickly took ship to Hardelot in some hope of hearing good news. Dances were abandoned. Hamel was never seen again. I was hysterically upset, more really than my affection for him warranted, and Duff wrote me a poem of grief and another about Hamel's loss for *The Times*. It was the first violent death of a young man in my life, but within a few weeks there was to be another.

The Russian Ambassador, Count Benckendorff, had the happiest Embassy in London. His son Constantine and Edward Horner arranged a party on the Thames one July night. The guests were Claud Russell, Katharine and Raymond Asquith, Duff and his sister Sybil, Iris Tree, a lovely Swiss girl called Jacqueline de Portalès, myself and Denis Anson. A little ship had been moored to the Westminster Bridge steps, a supper laid, and a quartet from Thomas Beecham's orchestra was already on board when my mother unwillingly took me to the embarkation. Venetia Stanley and Maurice Baring were on the jetty havering. The evening was not perfect. Drizzle threatened. Denis arrived and was swinging in the rigging before we started. Whether some premonition urged Maurice to abandon us I do not know, but he and Venetia went home with my mother and orders from me to assure her that all was beautiful and Charles II in feeling—Water Music, Youth at the Prow, Pleasure at the Helm. We had talked of bathing-dresses but had not brought them—enough with supper, the Thames, music and ourselves. We glided away, the sun set, we feasted and the musicians played us into serenity on deck.

Who suggested bathing? I cannot tell. It may, it *may* have been me. I have so prayed it was not and now I do not know. Anyhow no one was keener or more pleased at the project than I was. Denis the intrepid, Denis the steeplejack, strong as a stag, will surely be the first in! He was. It seems odd now that none of the older ones should have cautioned. It may have been too quick and too dark, they may have been half-dreaming to the music. Before he jumped he gave me his watch and chain. We could see his head in the trail of mirrored light from the further shore. For a moment I lost sight of it and screamed my fears to the one I was with. "You always fear the worst," "Of course I can still see him," "He's a strong unsinkable swimmer." The ship's captain, knowing the cruel Thames so much better than we did, stopped the ship as fast as he could, but already we were far beyond the place where Denis had dived in. The realisation came when a member of the quartet jumped into the river as a rescuer. In another moment Constantine was also overboard. Then it was our turn to hold on with all our physical might to the other men who were throwing off their coats and trying to be rid of our restraining arms. In a few moments a little craft had come alongside and men were dragging Constantine, utterly exhausted, into their boat. The tide had the strength of a bore. Light was breaking and showing me the hideous scene. No one looked like themselves.

Water had drained from their faces and left them like painted corpses in bright shrouds.

The police had arrived and were telling of the tide and the idiocy of our action and of the certainty that both men would drown. They were taking our names too and our evidence. The sun was up. Time had no bearing on anything. The sanguine felt sure that the divers had swum to shore and that we should find Denis at his flat. We drifted up and down calling and searching. At last Youth (the music over) left the Prow and our distraught group landed on the steps of Westminster, dripping and haggard, where a few hours before we had danced aboard.

At Denis's flat the old housemaid knew nothing of his return. His bed had not been slept in. Edward and Constantine went to break the fearful news to the missing men's families. I was frightened to go home and the lovely Swiss Jacqueline offered to stay the night with me. My mother never shut her door. She must, asleep or awake, know the comings and goings in the house. Never till she died did I not look in on my way to bed, whatever the hour. This early morning's call was the worst I ever had to make.

The next few days were memorably terrible. Mad youth was blamed for the death of this fine young man. I seemed to get the brunt from the Anson family and from all elders. When at last the inquest was called, Denis's family engaged a very eminent lawyer (one wonders what to prove) and, not to be outdone, F. E. Smith, in whose chambers Edward Horner was working, volunteered to appear for us. My mother, in spite of my arguments and assurances of the futility of an appeal, called on the coroner, with the result that at the inquest I was not made a witness. It was a dreadful story. The young musician was consumptive and was due to die. The Great War was upon us and Denis would surely have been the first to be killed, but with all my resilience this was a gruesome soul-shattering end to the carefree life I knew.

I was held guiltiest as being the most conspicuous. The travesties of truth told against me stimulated me to ideas of retaliation, but now it was July, and August 1914 was very near.

CHAPTER SEVEN

Nurse Manners

WE were staying with the Trees at Robertsbridge—many too many of us for the beds. Herbert and Maud Tree were there, presiding over abundance of food and fun. I remember we disrespectfully "loaded" their cocktails, thinking to make them more lenient to our strange midsummer night's dream. There were a hammock and some deck-chairs, but not enough for all, so we settled for no rest till sunlight and danced and feasted the night through, and at dawn took cars to Battle Abbey and breakfasted at Bodiam Castle, returning with the papers which carried the news of the assassinations at Sarajevo. It meant very little to our sleepy consciousness. War had of course been talked about by the so-called alarmists of the day, with stories of *Der Tag* and the wicked Kaiser, but this poor murdered couple seemed to us unlinked with our country or ourselves, and yet Sir Herbert that Sunday morning was plunged in apprehension and gloom and prophecies of war. We fell upon the hard daisied grass and slept the sleep of happy ignorance.

So, on August 4, war was declared. We were at The Wood-house, Rowsley, playing the war game, then very much the fashion, elaborated by Winston Churchill into a pastime for strategists and involving hundreds of tin soldiers. As my brother, Bunt Goschen and our adored Ego Charteris lay on their stomachs in a stone courtyard lining up their army corps, they quarrelled more hotly over the campaigns and planning of battles than summit generals were ever to quarrel over war itself. From the day of declaration my fearful vision saw it all as it was to be, but a lot of older people thought of it as another Boer War and said, "It'll take a week or two to roll 'em up."

One of the young men returning to England on August 8 wrote to me from the train:

About affairs—I won't discuss the military situation, nor the diplomatic, nor even the financial, which is exciting beyond words: but I want to lay my position before you as a psychologist and a sometimes inspired counsellor. Shall I go up against Ramoth Gilead and prosper? Look now: I am the most unmilitary of men. I hated field-days at Eton. I hate the very thought of taking the field now: I do not particularly dislike the Germans; my chief European preoccupation is the ultimate hegemony of the Russians, which it seems to me we are fighting to achieve: and I know full well that though I may be a bad banker I should be a hundred times a worse soldier. Again, I frankly recoil from the thought of wounds and death.

These things being so, ought I to go? When I say to myself that I am doing more useful work in the city, do I mean that I am earning a better salary, and that I should be ruining my chances if I went, as well as imperilling my most precious life? Honestly I don't know. Meanwhile I seem to myself to have temporarily solved the problem by proposing to enrol myself in the London Volunteer Defence Force (for business men to drill in their leisure moments), after a month or two of which I shall:

(a) be moderately efficient.
(b) have thoroughly introspected my position.
(c) have some chance of seeing whether this is a war crying for every able-bodied young man, or simply a war for the suitable with others in reserve.

One might also perhaps attend to one's French and German, and have an eye to a possible vacancy in the interpreterships. But God knows—and I beg of you to communicate anything you have been able to glean of His purposes.

I feel myself excused from entering upon your peace-letter to E., it not having been written to me. I saw very unexpectedly your mother last night. She was very sweet and alarmist. Are you always at Rowsley now? Or where else?

Three weeks later he was in France. This letter I put in to show that realisation of what the war meant seeped in very slowly. (In 1939 we knew it would be worse than it was, hence the wringing of hands six years before the bells.)

August 1914

The atmosphere here is appalling. The crisis has brought out all that is best in British womanhood. K. still keeps her head but C. and her Ladyship have sunk all their political differences and are facing the enemy as one man. They have cornered all the petrol, sold all Charles Kinsky's hunters, knocked off two courses at dinner and turned my child's pony-cart into an ambulance. How I wish you were at the War Office—Diana instead of Kitchener. We should all sleep easy in our beds, or I for one should make a bee-line for the colours. . . .

Certainly in London the fog of war, as they call it, had got into everybody's lungs and the air was thick with the feeling that England expects everyone to make a fuss, and that if you did make a fuss—even quite a small fuss, for at a time like this no fuss is too small—you would be personally thanked by the Prince of Wales. I saw at once there were two things to be done:

(1) to make some small unobtrusive fuss of my own.
(2) to interfere as much as possible with the people who were making more serious fusses.

So I put my name down for a thing called the London Volunteer Defence Force organised by Lovat and Desborough, having the following among other advantages:

(a) It is not yet in existence.
(b) The War Office may stop it ever coming into existence.
(c) P. belongs to it.
(d) No member of it can be called upon to perform even the simplest act of duty for several months.

(e) No member of it can possibly be killed till Goodwood 1915 at earliest.

Then I went to the most amusing place called the National Service League offices, where a vast swarm of well-meaning and inefficient patriots are employed for fourteen hours a day in first classifying and then rejecting the applications of a still vaster swarm of still more well-meaning and inefficient patriots for posts which they are obviously incapable of filling—Baptist Ministers who volunteer as *vivandières* and so forth. I spent a very pleasant afternoon trying to put these people into classes. There were four classes, but the qualifications for each class were so peculiar that none of the 2000 applicants whom I examined were eligible for any one of the four. Next week the committee are going to alter the classification, and it is hoped that someone may scrape into one of the classes. It will be a proud day for England when this happens.

As to hopes and fears. . . . There is in the Regular Army John Manners:* "Let determined things to destiny hold unbewailed their way,"† but if the Yeomanry begin fighting our hearts will be horribly wrung. And why do I say "if"? It's a certainty, I fear. If that wretched old K. of Chaos had only been able to carry out his scheme for a Second Army! But it was always hopeless and now he has definitely climbed down and taken shelter behind Jack Tennant;‡ and two Divisions of Territorials are to go abroad first. However if the war is really going to last three years (as K. says) we shall all be under the sod, and as well sooner as later. Poor old Edward went off to the North Somersets last week with Cicely's two best hunters and a body-servant and Mrs. B. But all these conveniences have now been confiscated for the use of the Regiment, and old E. sleeps on bare boards, rises at 5 a.m. and guards bridges in Surrey. It makes one's heart bleed.

We all dispersed—my brother to the Derbyshire Terri-

* My cousin, killed at Mons.
† *Antony and Cleopatra*, act iii, scene 6.
‡ The Rt Hon. Harold John Tennant, M.P., then Under-Secretary of State for War.

torials, Ego to the Gloucestershire Yeomanry. I was left to comfort my weeping mother who was losing her only son, to toss around some late Midland hay, and to think of schemes to stop the war.

I have found my Peace Letter, written to Edward Horner on 7 August 1914:

Edward darling, I think it's up to the Coterie to stop this war. What a justification! My scheme is simple enough to be carried out by you at once. It consists of getting a neutral country, either America or Spain or Italy or any other you can think of, to ask each fighting country to pledge their word—on condition *each one's* word is given—to cease hostilities, or rather suspend them totally until a treaty or conference is made. That they should then meet, agreed not to dissolve until a decision of Peace is come to, and not a collection of worm-eaten Ambassadors to do this but the Edward Greys of each country. It seems to me an admirable suggestion. For God's sake see to it, backed by Patrick and the P.M. How splendid it would be. "Who stopped the war?" "Oh, haven't you heard, Edward and Diana, members of that Corrupt Coterie." You mightn't believe it, but this is written more seriously than I've ever written. My fears are your own war lust. Perhaps Maurice [Baring] would be a better man to put it to a neutral country's Head—that's all that's wanted. Then a few hours with the cable. *Do* see to it. God, if I were only Judith or Jael or Salammbô or Corday or Monna Vanna—or at worst the crazy Kaiser's mistress.

Love

DIANA

It might have been signed by Daisy Ashford. As the plan didn't mature I began scheming to get to the war as a nurse. Women were taking Red Cross hospitals and dressing-stations to France, and they were taking their daughters and their daughters' friends. I wrote to the Duchess of Sutherland and Lady Dudley and the Duchess of Westminster and others. Maxine Elliott had a plan for a barge on the canals of Flanders, packed with clothes for refugees. I got nothing but discouragement and tears from my mother and a pi-jaw from Lady Dudley, whom my mother summoned to reason with me. She explained in words suitable to my innocent ears that wounded soldiers, so long starved of women, inflamed with wine and battle, ravish and leave half-dead the young nurses who wish only to tend them. I thought her ridiculous and my mother ridiculous too, and could not believe Rosemary Leveson-Gower, my cousin Angie Manners and other girls I knew, already in France, to be victims of rape.

Regretfully I abandoned the Front in favour of nursing at Guy's Hospital (Aunt Kitty's refuge many years before). This took a stiff fight, but as an alternative to rape at the Front the civil hospital was relieving to my poor, poor mother, who knew, as I did, that my emancipation was at hand. Still she did write to the Matron, while putting up every obstacle. She begged and warned and apprehended, and ordered the hideous print for my uniform, while I went to the kitchen and saw a hare's insides taken out to prepare me for operations. I think few nurses were killed in the war—Nurse Cavell of course, but not by chance. Sights were terrible, suffering ghastly, but I would rather my daughter had been nursing the wounded in France than in the wards of a London hospital. It must have been Guy's that was responsible for my silly hypochondria, now outgrown: threatened leprosy, lockjaw, T.B., cancer, foetid bronchitis and dementia were for many years a great handicap in my life.

Two reactions—one from England:

Are you really contemplating Guy's Hospital? I can't help thinking it is not a thing like the Slade School to be lightly undertaken as a mere essay in parent-dodging. The contract is lengthy, the drudgery unbearable, and the uniform disfiguring. I don't believe even your genius could make the headwear tolerable, and I doubt if you would be more accessible in the Borough than at Belvoir. A hospital has all the material discomforts of a nunnery without the spiritual glamour of chastity. Quite the contrary indeed. But anyhow I feel pretty sure that their Graces won't let you go and that the Matron won't let you stay. How glad I am that you did not whip off to the Front with Lady Dudley. R.

And from France:

I'm *thrilled* to hear of your resolution; it will be simply bloody but I think it's well worth while and I'm sure you are right. Also I'm sure you will be able to do it without an excessive amount of nausea. I approve it all the more heartily as I am now out of the country and have nothing to lose by your seclusion—"internment" is the word, I believe. Now you will be well out of the reach of those Yeomanry boys with their generous leave and their wild ways. Be chilly to the medical students, won't you? P.

So the die was cast. I had won, but with the winning came anticlimax and cooled enthusiasm. My mother drove me down sorrowing and silent to Guy's Hospital. I had not been there before, but she had.

It was a grey cold day. I felt ashamed of having triumphed, but not in the least apprehensive. I do not think my mother was at all proud of me; she just hated the sordid, unvirginal aspect of it all and the loss of authority and protection. Guy's looked very Dickensian that afternoon beneath its dark drizzle. A few shivering nurses in cotton dresses were being blown about the wide courtyard and open arcaded passages. We rang the bell at a side entrance. The door was opened by an old housekeeper in black with a hospital cap. She was as dry and grey as cinders. She led us to an upper bedroom giving on to the courtyard. Here I unpacked my modest little trunk—some underclothes, some books, concealed cosmetics, clock, pencils and paper, and a pampering hot-water-bottle. Every movement was watched by the old house-Gestapo. Then they dressed me. My mother writhed. I felt myself more a nun leaving the world than a V.A.D. probationer. There was no long glass, but I later saw what was making my mother so appalled, for indeed I did look horrible. The dress was just off the floor and gathered at the back only. The print was of a minute and colourless mauve-and-white pin-stripe. The apron was cut to deform the figure. The stiff collar, cuffs and belt gleaming with starch gave cleanth and trimness. The absurd cap attached to the tip-top of the head by an unreliable pin protected one's hair neither from lice nor from contagious germs. There were the universal black stockings and flat black shoes. I was led away from my mother who left disconsolate. I could not feel myself naughty, only perhaps heartless.

They took me to a women's surgical ward called Charity. There I was passed on to Sister Charity, a very comely, shy young Sister in well-fitted becoming blue, with a cap held on by fresh white strings and a pleated bow. No smiles. A training hospital in 1914 was as inhuman as the army. No speaking to superiors before being spoken to. All these rules had to be learnt by trial and error, as I found out when next day I said "Good morning" to Matron. One could be schoolgirlish with the probationers though not with the Head Nurse (still unqualified), whose cap was tied on and was therefore unofficially referred to as "Strings."

That evening I hung around not knowing what to do with myself—shy of the patients, no one naturally paying any attention to me. I had had no preparatory first-aid training, nor was this asked for. I had never been into a hospital ward before and knew no more about nursing than Nanny's plasters and doses. I was given a very unattractive little boy of two or three as my own patient. He was recovering from an appendicitis. I clung to him and tried to ingratiate myself. There was a pretty girl of twelve who had had her tubercular leg amputated (I saw her eighteen years later still in bed at her home, lined and dry, smiling and patient). Jessie she was called. I felt I could love her. Then there was Mrs 12, who was mental. I had never talked to anyone mental. It was hard to believe that one could not personally find the clue or break through the mazes diagnosed as impenetrable.

It was a fine old L-shaped ward with deep embrasured windows on both sides. It held between twenty and thirty beds with a few children's cots scattered around. It had an atmosphere of brightness and even happiness—a big fire in the grate, the convalescents sitting round it, the pretty Sister and a pleasant bustle. I left it after Sister had said prayers at eight o'clock, had some supper and went to my austere little room. There was a bath and hot water for the bottle. I had my orders for the next day and altogether felt satisfied with the beginnings, and ready for hardships. The first came at 10.15 p.m., when without appeal the only (centre ceiling) light went out. No reading, but tiredness took its place and I was awoken sharply at six a.m. by the same light blazing into my sleepy eyes.

How hard it is to get up when there is an hour to do it in! "Another few minutes—I can do it in ten." "I can do it in five—in two." And then the hideous scurry—new difficulties with collar-studs and caps, no washing, of course, the room left in chaos, the inadequate black-flannel cape thrown over shivering shoulders, the scramble with a dozen others down the Georgian wooden stairs and out into the court. A biting wind blew us into the beautiful old chapel, where for a quarter of an hour we prayed to be given strength and patience with the patients and for the safety of an ever-lengthening list of Guy's nurses abroad with the Forces.

From chapel we filed over to a modern building where our very nasty breakfast was waiting for us—tea limitless, off-white "standard" bread, marge (in those days uneatable), tinned eggs (then a novelty and considered poisonous), good sausages or stalish fish. My trouble was wanting not to eat as I was both vain and rather fat, yet knowing that a high-graded Sister on a little rostrum was eagle-eyeing each nurse who was late, who was ill-dressed or who appeared fastidious. Often in later days I would be called with several other miscreants after the meal and reproved severely. Did I not know that nurses were different from other people? Their lives were dedicated to the sick, maybe dying, and they must keep up their strength by sensible diet in order not to be found wanting.

By seven-fifty breakfast was over. The roll was called—no cheating possible (often tried and always exposed). Before the zero-hour of the ward there were ten precious minutes in which one doubled back to one's room, brushed one's teeth, made the bed (no dusting or sweeping), collected mail, did up the buttons one had left undone and tore back to the cheerful ward. My first job was to clean the glass trolley. The fear and dislike of asking where things are impede one's speed the first day. "Clean it with meth, nurse." Where's the meth kept? one wondered. Meanwhile beds were screened off and the miserable unresisting patients blanket-bathed in turn. Convalescents dragged themselves off to a washroom. I was told to give the horrid little boy a bath and dress him cleanly. This meant a spate of agonising questions. What bath? Where are the clean clothes? What soap? I had no idea how to wash a child (half-invalid) of two. I seemed to have done nothing practical in all my twenty years. The child yelled as though I'd put it on the rack. The clean clothes were a frightful problem as there appeared to be none. Later I learnt to wait for the clean linen when it was delivered from the laundry, and if I had a child patient to grab the best of a few poor articles and hide them for future use. We all did this, so there was naturally nothing in the common cupboard.

At ten o'clock a cup of tea was snatched by half the nurses in the little kitchen attached to the ward. There the ward-maid operated. She was never off her knees except to put the kettle on—she was called Polly—and to heat up the excellent food the patients were given—good meat, chicken, creamy rice-pudding, fresh fruit compôtes. Soon after this break the doctors would arrive, followed by a knot of students. Matron had already passed through the ward, met and escorted by Sister, silent and inscrutable. She spoke neither to the patients nor to the nurses. She was formidable. To be sent for by Matron (if a probationer) meant tears before, during and after the interview.

I was called behind the screens by Sister to watch a dressing on a woman who had had a kidney removed. She had a biggish hole in her side, and as Sister squeezed and pressed her stomach and flanks a stream of green pus oozed slowly into a kidney-dish. I felt sick and weak. Dreading operations, I had never expected some dressings to be worse, but they are to me much more terrible—the patient's own consciousness and shame and pain, the smell and the realism and all the horrors the theatre overcomes by its unearthliness.

Very soon it was 11.15, at which unexpected hour one shift of nurses went to dinner. The second shift went at twelve and returned at one, and took over the ward with an interval for tea till eight p.m., while the first shift was out from two till six and remained on duty till nine. Dinner was very nasty, but one could wolf it and regain one's room, put one's aching feet up on the bed and read the papers and one's letters. Feet hurt more when one got up. Back in the ward by twelve to serve dinners. This was done ceremoniously by Sister, extra-aproned like a chef, sharpening her carvers on a stone and dispensing to her understrappers plates of different robustness and lightness—"Mrs 10 and little B's (cot)," "That's not enough for 22, add some more sprouts."

At one o'clock bed-making, general tidying up, preparing for operations and visitors. And at two, my first day out and away, in a bonnet not unlike the Salvation Army but less becoming, and a long tubular narrow cape to the ankles—no arm-movement possible. We looked like caterpillars. Later I would dress in plain clothes for outings, but on my first day there was no question of not showing myself to be a nurse *par excellence*. I got back to Arlington Street by bus before they had finished their 1.45 luncheon. Eagerly awaiting me (I was by then the Pride of the Family) they bombarded me with questions and I gave, probably, an exaggeratedly dramatic account of hospital life with no details omitted or extenuated. I rested and was petted and tucked into a fine tea. The hospital provided tea, but I think no nurse whose off-afternoon it was took advantage of the Indian stew and rock-bottom cakes.

In the ward at six, more washing, four-hourly fomentations, tonics and bed-pans, temperatures, pulses, respiration-charts, convalescents, prayers and hand-over to the "night people." There was a traditional dislike and distrust of the "night people." The most popular nurse, when her turn came for night duty, became one of these heartless, negligent, half-asleep murderesses who let No. 15 "go," i.e. die. Deaths are rarer in hospitals than laymen imagine, especially in a surgical ward. Accident and medical wards have more. But death in Charity came in a blue moon. I do not know if it is true that the small hours take the biggest toll of mortals, but the dying certainly did tend to flicker out at dawn, and it was always the fault of the night people, particularly in the eyes of that poor creature's day nurse. For we each had our own patients. I don't think that is so today, so all the pride in one another is lost.

We handed our pampered victims over to the nurses who would take our places on off-afternoons with a mass of instructions and injunctions not to forget their idiosyncrasies—"Boil the eggs her mother brought her for three and a half minutes," "She'll drop off about three—don't wake her." So of course we thought had we been there at night she would never have died.

The third day held good and bad. In the morning the blood-curdling message "You're wanted in Matron's office" froze my bones. I had already graduated to doing simple dressings and fomentations. I had two or three patients of my own besides the horrid little boy. Jessie I had, and the mental Mrs. 12, and I was feeling safer and successful. Here was a whack to send me spinning off the ladder's first rung. Unroll the sleeves —what did I do with the cuffs? "Nurse, your apron's not very clean. You'd better change it before going to Matron," from Sister, her face inscrutable. "What have I done? Will she dismiss me? Give me something for courage?"—all these remarks were not voiced. The nurses saw me off, sympathetic and comforting. "It isn't as bad as all that." "Isn't it though?" So with a whiter apron and a whiter face I knocked on the lion's bars. She was an old lady, I think (I could hardly look), all in black with white-frilled cap. She ignored me for some minutes while she finished writing a report—an old trick. And then it came out.

I had been home the day before. I had told my story. I had given all the details possible to my relations and friends. Did

I not realise what a sacred thing a hospital was? How vowed we should all be to discretion and respect? In our hands were the sick and dying. The responsibility of their death was often with us. Outside its walls it should not be talked about and certainly not ridiculed. By this time I was in tears, unable to deny or defend myself.

"That will be all, nurse."

I left having said no word. I have thought since that perhaps, as I came from a society house, she felt safe in assuming my crime. She may even have felt her way. "You went home yesterday, did you not, nurse?" "They asked about your work?" My nods, for I could not speak, confirmed her suspicions, but I did not think of this, so thought "Who can have spied? The footman? A friend? An eavesdropper belonging to the hospital?"

So I got back to the chorus of "How was it?" and to make up for all the suffering Sister said: "I've arranged for Nurse Manners to take Nurse Shepherd's patient to the theatre this afternoon."

Another moment I had feared was upon me. "You'll have to see operations!" my obstructors used to say, and old Dr Hood, in my family's pay, would pull out stories of the Guy's of fifty years earlier—his Guy's, when the doctors kept their old coats for operations. These coats lived in the theatre and were so stiff with old blood that they stood up like armour. The students were always fainting, he told me. Neither student nor nurse ever saw their first op. without passing out.

There was not very long in which to worry. The poor victim had a cancer of the chin. Of all dreadful operations it is the worst to watch. A face must always be more affecting. Stomachs and limbs are less concentratedly human. On the table an abdomen is so shrouded and strange, and, except for the little square amid the sheets, iodined to a brilliant orange where the scalpel is to cut so whitely, then so redly, you can see nothing. The doctors and nurses in their caps and masks are a secret society incognito, and the intestines themselves are as familiar as what we know in pork-butchers' shops. But a woman's face—who can imagine worse than to see most of a chin cut off?

So she was put on a trolley. Two orderlies whisked her away and I trotted importantly alongside, carrying a tray of I forget what—something that always went to the theatre with the patient. She was wheeled into the little anaesthetic room and I held her hand. In those days anaesthetics were very unpleasant and alarming, not to say suffocating. They got her "off" protesting, and unconscious she was wheeled into the hot glaring theatre. The doctors were being dressed by theatre nurses and sisters—masks adjusted, sterilising-drums opened, rubber gloves soaped and drawn on, sluicings of water and antiseptics, unsterile taps and wastes turned on and off by unsterile feet, a lot of talking about outside things—racing, theatre plans, hospital appointments. This I had been warned of as something callous and disillusioning, but it seemed to me most natural and necessary. The conversation turns to the patient when the operation is in full swing. If there are students watching it develops into a mask-mumbled lecture delivered as talk is delivered when one is very tense and absorbed in any concentrated handicraft. I did not look very close or very long. I thought small doses would teach me not to faint, and I never came near to it—not with unconscious patients.

I enjoyed the months at Guy's. V.A.D.s (it was the first month of their infancy and there were but two of us) were very well received. We dressed the same as the staff and were

treated in exactly the same way. I was allowed to do everything the upper nurses were allowed, except dispensing, but in
a few weeks I was giving injections, intravenous and saline,
preparing for operations, cutting abscesses and once even saying prayers in Sister's absence. In some respects I had an easier
time than the first- and second-year probationers and more
variety of work, as my rank changed with whatever nurse was
off duty. There was no sweating at classes with examinations
looming ahead. I could go to the lectures, but I was not
eligible to enter for the examination. The first year took a lot
of probationers off the list. The life was excessively hard if you
were not very strong. Their feet and mine suffered intolerably.
We were not allowed to sit down during working hours, so
that it meant (meals excluded) eight solid hours on one's feet,
and a ninth hour walking the hospital.

One could steal a minute or two in the kitchen, where there
was a chair, also a cupboard of left-overs, cold creamy rice-
pudding, cold chicken perhaps. Finding was eating. I was
never a real martyr to my unseasoned feet, but some of them
came to felt slippers, much disapproved of, and some to a day
in bed. Often in the afternoons we would stand bandage-
winding and rubbing plaster of Paris into open canvas ban-
dages, padding splints, etc. The table was just wrong for all
heights and one's back ached as well as one's feet. There was a
perennial pleasure in leaving the ward for any form of mission.
With a huge basket on my arm divided into squares for bottles,
I might be sent to the dispensary. Oh, the "Sistering" that
went on:

"Please, Sister, Sister says can Sister Eyes let her have the
lotion? Sister spoke to Sister this morning, but Sister hasn't
received it, Sister. Thank you, Sister!" It was great fun. I
would linger and draw out my missions—"Sorry, Sister I

couldn't get Sister's attention"—all the schoolboy wheezes. One could drag a mission out to twenty minutes. Later in the spring it was lovely to cross the court and the so-called gardens and hope to see Henry Lamb, now a reputed painter with white hair, then a gold-thatched student. With luck one might see Sir Arbuthnot Lane himself arriving to operate. That would make a day, for I was in love with that unusual man. Operations became a frequent and uncloying treat, with no squeamishness left and ward-monotony relieved.

To be discovered going out with a student could mean dismissal in your third and last year. Punishments were severe. Twice late for closing-time at ten p.m. would forfeit your long-desired week-end, and less serious misdemeanours would stop your rare theatre-leave. To me all this discipline spelt liberty. I had never been allowed to go out alone on foot. My every movement at all times of the day must be known at home. Now, suddenly, my non-working hours up to ten p.m. were my very own.

At eight o'clock in the evening I would fly out of the ward, across the court into my room, noting as I ran the taxi waiting outside the great iron gates. Five minutes would see me painted and powdered and dressed (as I hoped) to kill, and into the arms of friends or friend. It had all the excitement of an escapade and was as short-lived as a sunset. The Borough is a long way from the fleshpots. The nearest restaurant was called De Keyser's. A quarter of an hour to get there, a quarter of an hour to get back—two crowded hours of glorious life and no more for forty-eight hours. The other days were limited to one hour's evening leave, and I never discovered whether one was allowed to leave the premises, but I did not ask and was never caught, and in an hour could make London Bridge or a romantic drive with a favourite. A note would read:

I will surely be at the iron gate. I will order food and drink to attend us at De Keyser's. Fat sausages wallowing in crushed potatoes, cheeses, fruits and great quantities of champagne.

And another:

Send me, O send me, a message to say that some 9 to 10 or 8 to 10 I may come to carry away my golden nun from her dark cloister to take her to have a drink at the Cheshire Cheese.

The big party evenings were thrown at the Cheshire Cheese. This was a bit further away, but the atmosphere was alluring. There was a little cubicle on the left of the entrance. It would hold about eight of us, all rollickingly young, I perhaps the gayest, the sailor ashore, the hours so short. I would have to leave the candlelight and merriment and like Cinderella tear back to my brooms, shouting "Hurry, hurry" to the taximan. Twice I missed the fearful hour by a minute or two. I saw the closed gates and almost gave myself up to despair, but both times I was able to plead with the porter to overlook so slight a breach. He relented and did not report me.

Officers' Mess, Crystal Palace   *November 1914*

Do try and make a night of it one night next week. I'm sure you can if you exert yourself—surely either the Matron or the Sister is in love with you. We left our cards on you last night. Did you get them? To testify to our grief at your not dining. Don't do more work than you can help; you looked frightfully tired yesterday. P.

They didn't understand. Of course I never got the cards.

Some nights, leaving the cloister gate, I would cast a fearful look to the shadows in case Mr Taubman should be there. Mr Taubman was a lunatic fan. Everyone, with however little publicity, collects them. He had written to me for several years from Hampstead, frail fluttering pages, traced over with the most exquisite calligraphy, weaving memories of a love that never was. Often the letters were illustrated with a tree, a street-corner—the pictures did not fit the text—and with them were sent presents of punched bus-tickets, old corks, gnawed pencils, sealing-wax-ends, once a silver ring. A friend called Hugh Godley knew this artist and knew him as perfectly sound-minded. Since my retreat to Guy's he had said he would be waiting for me, and it frightened me unduly, but I never saw his shadow.

I got on very well and was popular with my fellow-nurses and I think with the patients. Nurses took it in turn to bring a cake for two o'clock teas and there were "dormy feasts" in Matron's house with hot blackberry tisane, delicatessen, sweets, cigarettes, suppressed songs and laughter, the larks that I had missed by never being a schoolgirl.

I was moved after a few months from my dear Charity Ward down to Ashley-Cooper Men's Accident Ward—very different —a high, gaunt, sunless ward, busier and sadder much. Here were the old paralytics, spinal cases that in a minute years ago had lost their powers utterly. They lay there, three or four of them, resigned I think, on water-beds, their heels and elbows and buttocks on air-rings, nothing to be done save to protect them from sores they would not have felt. They talked to one another chiefly about food, for food they could still taste, and I wondered why we never gratified their longings for tripe and winkles and many other curious delicacies of their upbringing. There was a funny D.T.s man I was rather fond of. He was given prescribed doses of spirits, but not enough to still the fears he had of his feet, which he took for two white bogeys sitting at the bottom of his bed. It was a depressing ward with too much to do to do it well. Men were brought in to die in a few hours, and never was there an empty bed. Old lags, so the belief went, would slit the surface of their throats at the hospital doors so as to be brought into warmth and idleness, especially in cold weather, and they were said too to be well up to all the tricks, even to infecting themselves deliberately when they were on the mend. I was moved again to a medical ward, but it's all the same story till I left after six months.

CHAPTER EIGHT

Frustration and Folly

I CAN'T remember why my mother grew a determination to
move me from Guy's to a hospital in France. It could not
have been my persuasion. I was standing up to the wards very
well, and what mattered to me more than anything else was to
spend every free hour with the beloved friends in London.

George Moore, who since the war had become a neutral of
the greatest importance, London host of the Commander-in-
Chief and a man of power and privilege, played a big part in
this scheme, which looks as though I was not reluctant to
further it. He found us a château at Hardelot, contributed a
few thousand pounds to equip it and put us in the charge of a
competent American organiser. I left Guy's to prepare for our
imminent embarkation. Mr Selfridge gave me £2000. Two or
three rich Americans, friends of George Moore's, subscribed
generously. I had to do the begging and loathed doing it. The
equipment was bought, a Matron engaged and doctors be-
spoke. We visited the château, approved and ordered altera-
tions, came home and suddenly, after a six-month struggle to
survive, the whole scheme collapsed.

I cannot remember how or exactly why, but there was something sinister, I know. It was the Red Cross who at the last
minute refused to sanction the unit. Lady Angela Forbes had
had some trouble with her hospital in Boulogne. Was it our

backing by the suspect George Moore? Was it my name that was beginning to be overloaded with publicity? Impossible to remember the alleged reasons, but collapse it did. The château became a centre for military training, and two years later Patrick Shaw-Stewart wrote:

I might tell you of our last eight days up the line, in which I went through several gas-alarms and built myself a wire bed—really comfortable—in a front-row trench. I might tell you of a subsequent hellish five days beginning Intensive Training, and how I was suddenly despatched to the Army School on a Company Commanders' Course, but I must hurry on to break to you the remarkable fact that the Army School is where? In that notable château where Her Grace and you tried so courageously and so lucklessly to establish a hospital.

Isn't it extraordinary? I remember it all rather vaguely and I had no idea how far the preparations had gone, and then on going in, the first room I saw was labelled "Marquess of Granby Ward." Beside it was "Violet Ward," upstairs "Marjorie Ward" and opposite "Diana Ward"! You would think that Destiny might have had the sense of fitness to put me in the last-named, but no—I am assigned a bed in a neat hut under the château wall.

The *comble* came when, on hearing blankets and sheets—nice ones—were to be had up at the top, I toiled up past "Diana Ward" (somehow they looked so much like surnames I wondered for a moment if you had married Bobbie Ward or—worse—Arnold Ward) to the "Duke's Room" where a Lance-Corporal stood guard over a heap of superb blankets and sheets. I asked for some and he said: "Sorry, sir, these are the property of the Duchess of Rutland and she cannot allow them to go outside the château." The temptation was almost overpowering to say I was sure she would be *delighted* to give *me* one, producing the blue Peace Charm round my neck as evidence, but I kind of felt that something similar must have been said before to that Lance-Corporal, so I meekly toddled off to draw an army blanket from the Quartermaster several kilometres away. Incidentally some humorist has inserted an N before the T in "Violet Ward."

Frustrated and disappointed, my mother spiritedly decided to turn Arlington Street into an officers' hospital. My father was passive; I was keen. We still had a good bit of capital, and the Red Cross, guilty and thankful to have triumphed, encouraged and contributed to the new scheme.

The golden drawing-room—a real room-of-all-work—became a ward for ten patients. The ballroom held another twelve. The centre-skylit salon was the dining and club room. The walls were hung with glazed linen, the floors covered in linoleum. My mother's bedroom was equipped as an operating theatre, divided by glass from sterilising-machines and administrative desks. Sister White and two trained nurses, Manley and Malony, were engaged. (Manley was to continue to live in my house till she married one of her Rutland Hospital patients several years after my own marriage, and Malony remained with my father till his death in 1925.) There were to be several V.A.D.s. I was one of them.

While the battle for Hardelot was being fought and preparations for the Rutland Hospital being made, there was a pause in nursing. I think I was pleased. It meant more leisure, less independence but more time for the friends, and, when the hospital opened, less—in fact no—discipline and a becoming red uniform with a big organdie Red Cross headpiece.

A few days were snatched early in March by Edwin Montagu Venetia, Duff, Patrick and me for a fishing spree to a primitive inn on the River Beauly. It was Scatters's scheme. Scatters's real name was Sir Matthew Wilson. He was a dashing soldier-baronet from Yorkshire via India, and had married an elder sister of the beautiful Laura Lister, by now Lady Lovat. I had thought as a child that he was funnier than any of the clowns, and he could still keep the table of all ages in a roar. In the North of Scotland we were desperately cold and ridiculously happy. Only one bedroom had a fireplace, and this was given to me, as I had pleaded sickness to get permission for some convalescence. Solemnly every evening the hotel's only hip-bath was set out on its flannel mat before my fire, and for it we queued, carrying our hot-water cans. When Duff's turn came he was an unconscionable time behind the locked door, enjoying by a candle's light in the fire's flicker my diary, unlocked by the key that locked his own. Five years later the chance came for me to spend a happy hour getting my own back.

Back in London, the new hospital seemed soft and de-moralising after spartan Guy's, with Scatters arriving from Rumpelmeyer's laden with chestnut-cream cakes and sherry for our elevenses, with plenty of snug bolt-holes for escaping moods, with usable telephones and hourly contact with the friends, who came a long way before duty, the good of my character, or anything else on earth. They were all scattered by 1915 into various regiments, some abroad, but all of them either training in England or on leave from France gravitating to London. Our dearest pampered George Vernon was training in the Yeomanry; the Grenfells, the Sitwells, Michael and Sidney Herbert, Tommy Bouch and the many others all, all dispersed. Raymond Asquith was training with the Grenadiers at Richmond. Maurice Baring had joined Trenchard, then creating the Royal Flying Corps. Brother John was with General Stuart-Wortley in France. The girls had various war-work in hospitals and canteens. Venetia Stanley had been from the beginning of the war at the London Hospital, Marjorie a new mother lonely at home. Duff was at the Foreign Office—he and Alan Parsons the only two for whom, as Civil Servants, I had no fears. Alan was a victim of an atrocious form of asthma and could never be accepted for the forces, and Duff, whose position was not easy with all his friends gone for soldiers, showed me for the first time his extraordinary strength and serenity of character. He envied his friends and envying them had no false shame at sticking to his office. His closest friend, my cousin John Manners, was killed in the retreat from Mons. This death, the first in the war to hurt us, was of all the losses the one that affected Duff most. John was a glorious young man, a soldier by profession. Raymond Asquith wrote when he died:

I find it terribly easy to be soppy about John. You see he whipped the Greeks into a top hat at their own game—beauty, temperance, vigour and reserve—and all their tags, the only ones I know, fit him like a glove and drop into their sockets with a sob of joy.

Patrick Shaw-Stewart, after a short training in England, was on his way to Gallipoli;

Hood Bat. R.N.D. Med. Ex. Force   *25 April 1915*

Rupert Brooke died two days ago, which has cast a considerable gloom, not the least part over me who had succumbed to the usual magic. He was not leading a charge (we haven't led any yet) but got the pneumococcus in his lip which killed him in two days. We buried him the same night in an olive grove on a noted Greek island of incredible beauty and appositeness. I commanded the firing party, in so much terror for the correctness of my ceremonial drill that I was inaccessible to sorrow or grandeur. It's very like Byron, really.

Venetia Stanley in 1915, free of the London Hospital, was on the brink of marrying Edwin Montagu, then in Asquith's Government. Edwin was a new Coterie member who being "very old" (not forty) and very eminent we called "Mr Montagu." We had a struggle to change to Edwin (a difficult name) but he felt the "Mr" put him out of our category. Duff wrote of him:

He was a man whose ugliness was obliterated by his charm. He had a huge, ungainly body, a deep soft voice and dark eyes that sparkled with humour and kindliness. . . . He was very nervous and absurdly pessimistic. Whenever he talked about the future he would interject: "But I, of course, shall be dead by then," and he did die at the age of forty-five.

In his face shone a benevolence that made me think he must be under some spell and that a magic word, the fall of a sparrow, would allow him to cast his cruel disguise and turn into a shining paragon.

In this summer of 1915 he would say "My fires give no heat." That was his attitude to all things, but they blazed brightly enough for us. At his house we saw not unadulterated Coterie, but the Prime Minister and Margot, Winston and Clemmie, Augustine Birrell and most of the Government, politicians, new bloods of the town, and Edwin's brother in the Naval Brigade, "Cardie" Montagu. But of all these Edwin liked us best.

Edwin, for years in love with Venetia, had won his hard fight for her hand and was to marry her in July. A week or so before the wedding Katharine and Raymond, Edwin and Venetia went for a Sunday to Brighton. I overcame the usual home obstructions and, claiming the need of sea air, joined them together with Duff. Anxieties and apprehensions were allayed temporarily by the pleasure of escape, the sea, the invigorating bathing and conversation. Edwin was at his most cheerful and appreciative, his noble eyes softer than usual with love for Venetia.

After a dazzling dinner Duff and I sought the moonlit beach and tipsily staggering down a fragile wooden stairway that led to the shingle, fell like Jack and Jill down the rickety flight. My ankle I thought to be twisted, but it hurt too much for twist or wrench or tendon. I was carried back to the hotel and the doctor who was summoned thought my leg might be broken. Consternation! I did not remember how many fibs I had told at home. I had certainly not admitted that Duff was of the party, and how the goodness could I have broken a leg on a sober Sunday evening? And what passing witness might there not be who would betray me?

They drove me up to London the next day in writhing pain. Hospital experience made my new lies plausible. It was a Pott's fracture, I diagnosed, liable to happen to anyone getting clumsily out of a car in a hurry. The others had seen it happen. It seemed incredible to them that so normal a twist could break a bone, but Pott's fractures were like that. The X-ray confirmed my diagnosis, and ice-bags and Sir Arbuthnot Lane, my surgical hero, were sent for.

One of Sir Arbuthnot's specialities was bone-plating, and my delight was great when he decided to operate on me. So I went to a nursing home in Manchester Street and a four-inch piece of silver was screwed across the break.

There, nursed and entertained by adorably witty Irish nurses for several weeks, I held my court—and what a fantastic court it was and what a lot going on at it! Venetia's trousseau was brought to show and with it as a present two vines trained on to trellises. Some pinioned budgerigars arrived to perch on the grapes. Shopmen brought wares for approval, and plenty of balloons floated at different levels, some buoyant against the ceiling, others multi-coloured floating imperceptibly down as their gas seeped out. Banks of flowers, bells, bows, crystal pistols, masks and witch-balls, fortune-tellers—strangers even came to have a look at the nonsense of the town and, in a narrow hospital bed in the middle of the room, the greatest nonsense of all. Soon out of pain but tied by the leg to a "cradle," ringletted in emulation of Mary Pickford, the "World's Sweetheart," pillowed and counter-paned with a hundred muslin frills to look like Aubrey Beardsley's *Rape of the Lock*, I lay there for five weeks.

The war at that moment was not overwhelmingly terrible for us, though Julian Grenfell had been killed earlier in the year. Ego was still comparatively safe in Egypt, and Letty with him. Billy Grenfell, one I dearly loved, was still alive, so were the Herbert brothers and Tommy Bouch, though all in France. Patrick, Charles Lister and George Vernon were in Gallipoli.

It seems today so extraordinary, even inhuman, to have been able to divorce one's spirit from the funereal reality, but all survivors of that most wasteful of wars will tell the same story. A resilience was bred to sustain the battered people. Any pause gave us a momentary *allegro* supported by the resolve to keep the living buoyant.

Mr Asquith came to delight me and swell me with pride before the nursing staff. Venetia and Edwin came straight from their marriage ceremony, Venetia in aigretted beauty and Edwin in unaccustomed smart and painful clothes, with tight new boots.

Often into the sickroom's frivolity came the two Sitwells in their unsuitable uniform. Curiously ignorant of such conventional things as the army, I did not know before the war what a Guardee was. I remember asking Lady Cunard, who told me I would find out when I sat next to one that night at her dinner. My Guardee opened the conversation by asking me if I thought much of Stravinsky. It was Osbert. He brought to my sickbed his very young brother Sacheverell, and also Ego's youngest brother Ivo, an enchanting child-soldier predestined too soon to die.

They took me in a wheel-chair all over the British Museum. The nursing home gave up their rules and schedules. Meals at all times, dinners on my bed, a girl in the stocks and jolly nurses made a fine rendezvous for soldiers and other girls:

Shall we come up to you now, or are you snowed under by the usual blizzard of nurses? What for food? A cold bird? A cold fish? A cold peach? Or the cold fruitless moon? Just jot down anything that occurs to you.

Maurice Baring sent me a daily trifling or sentimental keepsake. He was splendid too for Gunter's ices. Mr Birrell came always for reading aloud, Alan and Duff after office hours, the girls at all hours, and even the friends of friends to see the silly sight.

On August 12 we had grouse for our greed and at ten p.m. Sir Arbuthnot Lane, visiting another patient *in extremis*, looked in to say goodnight and found eight of us round my bed, picking birds' bones and drinking champagne. He looked pleased enough and joined us in the ices and the hilarity. He was a rare man.

In a few weeks I was up, my leg two inches shorter than the other and viced into a shining Hessian boot, one of a pair. Defying crutches, I limped around in freedom. My mother ran, as well as the Rutland Hospital, a convalescent home at Belvoir which kept her part of the time in the country. I had limped to Welbeck Street to have dinner with Alan Parsons on the night of the first Zeppelin raid. In a trice we were on the roof of his house to watch the fun and being hauled off it by an old char who thought us foolish. So I hobbled off with Alan to Downing Street for latest news, and on to Olga Lynn's to hear other people's tall stories about the raid. The tallest was of "the Zepp being so low that I saw their horrid German faces in the searchlight." That "they passed right over where we were" every one of us said and believed. Then more champagne, Olga to sing Debussy's *Enfants de France*, Basil Hallam to dance with, and heights, and the fearful depths.

CHAPTER NINE

Dances of Death

LOOKING back on these nightmare years of tragic hysteria, it is frightening to live them again in memory. People stung by the tarantula doubtless forget the mania forced upon them. The young were dancing a tarantella frenziedly to combat any pause that would let death conquer their morale. If one of them fell with pain, he was tenderly lifted and treated, but strangling tears must not stop the salutary delirium. It was even encouraged.

I read a letter from Patrick written in 1915:

Naval Brigade

O it's fun to be a sailor and to be going to fight the Turk. No mud, no cold, very little danger and infinite glory of avenging the Paleologi and entering Byzantium.

I am not 1000 miles from the plains of Troy, where I expect to meet the enemy, and before meeting him I feel impelled, on the exceedingly off chance of his registering a score on my cautious retiring person, to tell you just as far as three lines will carry me what I thought of you this winter. I thought, one may say, everything.

You know several of us have been thought ill of in connection with this war. Evan once told me in no measured terms that R. and I had. In the same way eminent women have described our parties as the "dances of death" and others have cast doubts on your professional career. Still others have cast doubts on (a) my (b) N's (c) E's sobriety on various historic occasions. In fact those of us who survive this war will without doubt undergo yet a little more opprobrium than we are already used to. This makes it the more essential to keep our mutual admiration. What I say is that I have never seen you one half so glorious as in these times. You were (and by God's grace are) surer of yourself, more central, more indispensable, fairer, wittier, more seductive, than I have ever known you before, and I have known you wellish since 1907 and it is saying a good deal. If one circumstance or another has prevented my making this as clear to you as I could have wished (the most permanent and irritating circumstance is the number and assiduity of your first-line lovers) that makes it all the more imperative that I should now make it clear beyond the shadow of a doubt.

Darling Diana, just in case I should be killed I do want to impress it on you that you have practically the burden of this generation on your shoulders. Be fruitful and multiply and replenish the earth and SALT it, and encourage the good and cause the undesirable to *writhe*, and never say that you forgive little moral obliquities only because their perpetrator comes straight from the trenches.

Wine helped and there was wine in plenty—it was said too much. George Moore's dances of death flowed with the stuff. They became more frequent as leave became regular from the training centres and the trenches of France and the Middle East. The parties were left to the Coterie to assemble. Parents were excluded. We dined at any time. The long waits for the last-comers were enlivened by exciting, unusual drinks such as vodka or absinthe. The menu was composed of far-fetched American delicacies—avocados, terrapin and soft-shell crabs. The table was purple with orchids. I always sat next the host, and the dancing, sometimes to two bands, negro and white (and once to the first Hawaiian), so that there might be no pause, started immediately after dinner. There were not more than fifty people. We kept whirling to the music till the orchids were swept away in favour of wild flowers, for breakfast eggs and bacon which appeared with the morning light. The noise of carts rumbling to Covent Garden called a revelling group, singing catches, to board them.

I should have liked to have danced all night with Basil Hallam, being a little in love with him—Basil Hallam, the original of "Gilbert the Filbert, the Knut with a K." The Coterie loved him dearly. Harsh things were said about his dancing in London at the Palace Music Hall, instead of marching to war. He had an infirmity which he did not choose to use as an excuse, so he joined the captive balloons and was killed in France.

George Moore used to dismiss the band when I left the party. "When you leave, the place is a morgue," which meant my staying too late and unwillingly. I wanted to leave at a reasonable hour, drive twice round Regent's Park with a swain and be dropped home at an hour compatible with hospital duties next morning. I wonder if the young go round Regent's Park as often as we did? I suppose not—they go to coffee bars and dark night-clubs. But then that "little house on wheels," as we called our taxi, represented the only complete immunity from surveillance that I knew.

Coming home in daylight, I must by law call in on my mother to report my lies about the guests and my partners, but of George Moore my mother could not disapprove. He had become, through French's position as Commander-in-Chief, a man of omnipotence. My mother's obsessing hope being to get my brother to G.H.Q., she thought that only I could coax this boon out of Moore. The parties were the delight of my friends but I, who could not like him because of his passion for me, found the position acutely painful. To get my brother to G.H.Q. would answer my mother's anguished prayer and my own. "To me the war's the General, England's you" was Moore's theme, so it should not be too difficult.

He would do all I asked and he had extraordinary power—power great enough to arrange transport for Sir John and

Lady Horner, their daughter, Sir Arbuthnot Lane, a special nursing sister, my mother and me, when we heard that Edward Horner was gravely wounded in France. We all travelled across the Channel, blown up in Gieves waistcoats against drowning by submarine attack, and landed at Boulogne. There waited a G.H.Q. car to take the family, surgeon and nurse at full speed to the front-line hospital. Edward was desperately ill, had an operation to remove a kidney and was brought back to Boulogne in the dead of night on a stretcher bound for England.

The scene is marked in memory's eye like a familiar picture —outside the station, pencils of searchlights and a procession of stretchers that seemed never-ending to me, looking at each sick face for the one I sought. And then there it was—very, very ill and looking ecstatic. The bearers broke the procession and laid the stretcher down, and round we crowded, crying with relief, to see our precious Edward alive and due to recover.

"O darling, this is heaven," he said.

Against the march of the sick and the wounded returning home, tramped, in the dark, the men from England bound for the trenches. I wondered if they looked with envy or dread at those on stretchers.

It was, I suppose, natural that this privilege—worse, favouritism—was considered outrageous by the many. One cannot but sympathise with their deprecation, but which of those many would not have grasped at the same chance? I could not mind therefore my portion of the blame.

Naval Brigade

So swings the military pendulum, and now I hear of a party at George Moore's on Friday, and I suppose it's about 9 to 1 on getting there. But (like a good sailor) I pray and prey on the feelings of my Company Commander who also has loved.

The Commander-in-Chief himself would look in on the revels at Lancaster Gate. He would not stay long. My mother and I used to lunch there when he was home from G.H.Q.— small parties of importance, politically demure and low-voiced. Moore's twinkling little black eyes would catch mine, both of us hoping my mother took this to be the normal tone of the house.

So Brother John went to G.H.Q. There was great rejoicing and blessings upon Moore's head. He needed them, because although he was the most loyal and selfless worker in the Allied cause, the fact that America was still a neutral and he in the innermost councils of England gave the papers a chance to libel him. There was a case in court in which the Commander-in-Chief himself was made a witness. I was there but I cannot remember anything except Moore's winning it.

In the autumn of 1915 we had to suffer more losses, hard indeed to weather. George Vernon, that dependent boy we had so cherished and petted as one does the youngest and weakest of the family, got dysentery at Suvla in Gallipoli and died, too slowly, in a hospital in Malta. I wrote to Patrick:

Poor darling little George, always spoilt and pampered, with more frailties than any of us. No one knows what it cost him to be brave. He told me he would be woken in the night by a frozen sweat of fear and dread of being afraid. Yet Henry Bentinck, his Colonel, writes that his courage was proverbial. His fears then were unfounded; he was not more afraid than the bravest. It bears no thinking of, his dying in Malta, conscious of death and wondering if we even knew, and then, if knowing, we loved him? And, if loving him, we were not by now half-callous to loss?

Billy Grenfell, the titan cherub who outshone his brother Julian in scholarship and athletics, was killed in France. Charles Lister, after many woundings, died in Egypt.

146

Days were very heavy, heavy with one's own heart and the hearts of others. The Rutland Hospital expanded, taking in another twelve officers. More girls and young widows I knew came to work as V.A.D.s. For me it was not whole-time work. I had plenty of leisure to be with Duff quietly.

Now with the Hospital running full tilt my mousy intriguing little Italian maid left me. Her name was Adelina and she would pass me letters, however unimportant, between a pair of gloves. In her place arrived Kate Wade, a little older than me, more courageous and balanced and much taller. She was to become my friend and the cornerstone of my home. She was to maid and support me and my husband and my son through many vicissitudes and adventures for forty years "not out."

Having only my bedroom in our hospital-home, I spent most of my free time in Duff's flat, or in the houses of our well-wishers—the Parsonses, the Montagus and Katharine Asquith. There was no longer a Tree house. Sir Herbert Tree had died, Iris was married at eighteen in America, and Felicity too had a family. Duff and I used to cry together in his flat at 88 St James's Street—cry secretly, and then brace ourselves to the sad revelry.

A haven was the Montagus' house. We had given Edwin all our affection, ragging him for his gloom and forcing him sometimes to be carefree. We seem by letters to have been there several times a week. Hospital goodnights said, I would tear out of the house (with luck ahead of the warning howl of the maroon) and run down St James's Street to Duff. There we would split a half-bottle of champagne and then stroll past the birds and the swards of St James's Park to 24 Queen Anne's Gate ("The Green Griffon," Mr Birrell called it), to the stimulating company and all that was left of the loveliest and the best.

Last night at Edwin's I survived a double-barrel spike from Margot: (1) "What a pity that Diana, so decorative, should let her brain *rot*." (2) to Duff, "I'm fond of Diana. I know you are. She's pretty and amuses Henry, but she reminds me of what I most dislike—German-Greek."

But it was an amusing evening. Venetia had brought two of the old flower-sellers' baskets from Piccadilly Circus, packed high with spring flowers, for the drawing-room. Mr Asquith at his happiest asked a riddle: "What is it God never sees, kings rarely see and we always see?" Raymond improved on the real answer, "An equal," by guessing: "A joke."

The Parsonses we would also frequent, but those delightful literary evenings are too well described in *Old Men Forget* for me to re-tell them here.

Now people returning from Egypt told of Letty's confidence in Ego's safety. He had been missing since April. She had reasons of rumour to hope that he was a prisoner, but the rumours were to prove false. She returned in May, cruelly anxious but wearing a brave face, stalwart in her hopes. Soon we were to hear the glorious official news that he really was a prisoner in Turkey. Radiant with relief and thankfulness, she sent innumerable parcels of food and clothes, books and daily letters. Our own joy was out of bounds. We couldn't care for anyone else's safety, least of all Kitchener's.

I remember, a few days after the torment of anxiety had been stayed, going to St Paul's Cathedral and standing godmother, beside Duff the godfather, to Raymond's little son. The Dean was officiating and Margot held the child at the font. She wanted to whisper to Dean Inge that Kitchener had been drowned, but he was too deaf to hear. After two attempts she broke into the service and bawled the story into his ear. It was dramatic, and I found myself hurrying directly after the ceremony to some big charity function at the Caledonian Market, praying that I should be first with the news. I was not. It had preceded me and already when I arrived the inevitable false rumour "Kitchener safe and sound!" was being shouted out by a man on stilts while the crowd sang spontaneously, though not with one voice, "Now thank we all our God."

There was a memorial service for Kitchener in the great Cathedral. Kneeling beside me, Letty whispered "To think we might be at Ego's requiem." And all the while Ego was dead. He had been killed in a flash near the Sinai desert.

Patrick, evacuated from Gallipoli, had joined the French in Salonica. He had been awarded the Croix de Guerre and wrote happily enough from all theatres of war. But the fatal tug to join his last few friends in France soon dragged him back to the Naval Brigade, now commanded by Arthur Asquith (the Prime Minister's son) in France. Patrick had been "a calm thought" to me, but his last leave was weighted with the dread of war and blackened by the deaths of his dearest friends.

Edward had recovered enough alas! to be sent to Egypt and from there back to his regiment, only to die in France in 1917. I was to see him but once again. I felt my spirit too low to recover. Only a few months before we had had to bear the worst of all our losses. Raymond himself was killed. By his death everything changed, except the war that ground its blind murderous treadmill round and round without retreat or advance, with no sign of the beginning of the end. The letters say repeatedly: "Write and tell me what hope you hear of the war ending."

I wrote to Patrick in 1917:

Driving home from the ball with Duff, feeling a tragic jester, I gave way to a flood of tears such as I have never had without acute cause. I have so often promised myself that I have no illusions so that there could be no sad disillusions. Now I am broken to find youth failing me. The young today are far, far from our young ones —blameless from Eton predestined to an accepted routine. No Oxford, no soul-racking career-decisions to light and colour them. They have not the seriousness we carried before the war, nor the conscious hilarious desperation the war developed in us at the beginning when we never let the candles expire. They have only their pathos, and some veterans of twenty-one their maimed limbs to qualify them.

It's half mood I suppose and half my surrender of Duff who left the F.O. today. I must stop writing, my tears are incontinent. Be careful and lucky, darling Patrick. I feel a straw will finish my back now—let alone a fair pillar of my house breaking on it.

Duff had become the most precious treasure in my keeping. The day when he would march away was bound to come, and bound to destine him to death. We had been spending every moment snatched from my hospital and his Foreign Office work with each other and for each other. To be together being all-important, it is surprising that we did not think or talk about marriage. It must have been instinctive or superstitious or a sensible resolve to give it no consideration till the war's end.

My poor mother, saddened as she was by the death of Harry Cust and no doubt distressed by my unhappiness and secrecy, stayed much at Belvoir. We had no longer a sitting-room in London. Our relationship was almost at its worst. But I must quickly say (because I cannot bear it to be thought otherwise for a page's minute) that these jarrings were never more than a temporary eclipsing of my great love for her. I was impossible. My nerve had gone. Dread had taken possession. I kept her more than ever in the dark. My lies bandaged her eyes. At least I thought they did, so how could I expect her to understand? She perhaps knew and felt and guessed a lot—

knew perhaps of the drinking, and the Moore orgies, and the nights wound up at the Cavendish Hotel, with Mrs Lewis leading her Comus crew around and around and into a room where a man was dying (not *in extremis*) "to take his mind off," or to fetch from the cellar Lord Somebody's champagne, and to stay making fools of ourselves, dodging the police who were sleuthing for lawbreakers, till morning light—a dangerous, dissipated, desperate life for her daughter to be shaken into. She had been deeply sympathetic about Raymond's death and the others too, for their mothers' sake more than for mine, but her three worst fears for my future were constantly preoccupying her—Edward, Patrick and Duff—and the worst of these was Duff. I suppose she really thought only the highest was good enough.

So to Patrick I wrote:

The Duke of Connaught said the other day in the strictest confidence (so respect it) that I was the only possible wife that could keep the Prince of Wales his throne! I'm getting every day and night more fit for the Palace—soberer, staider, less yearning for orgy.

When I think of the 1915 debauchery I smile. One used to wake in the morning with only the longing to be (till death-released) an anchorite, to feed on fresh bread, hear babbling streams and contemplate flowers. So was one's soul pure in a piebald temple. But now that I am purged with carbolic and have been given a lot of heavy and awkward crosses to drag with me to the feast, the temple's tenant craves for riot and artificial paradises.

Duff and I would go on Sunday picnics to what woods there were near London. I remember once on a day of days preparing all morning a meal to be worthy of the lake and pines near Cobham. There were eggs in jelly and chickens' breasts, rationed butter, fresh bread, strawberries and cream from

Belvoir and a big bottle of hock cup to be cooled in the lake-water. With this treasure in a cardboard box, I came tripping down St James's Street, over-excited, when the bottom of the box fell out and on the callous pavement lay all the broken meats, unpickupable! I ran to 88 and arrived in a flood of tears. But Duff could comfort me—it was one of his qualities. When the same swords stabbed us, I would run to his arms thinking, I remember well, "Who will comfort me when Duff is killed? Who will comfort me for *his* loss? Who will keep me sane?" This fear was ever with me.

In the spring his release from the Foreign Office was probable—almost certain—and one warm night in a Sussex garden, within the house the guardians of my sentiments Viola and Alan Parsons, he told me he was liberated and had joined the Grenadiers. A subaltern in the Guards had then as short an expectation of life as a fighter pilot was to have in the Battle of Britain. I knew that for a little time he would be sent to a cadets' training college. I would see him less and less, until he went to France. Then, with fair luck, once or twice on leave, then never, never, never . . .

We all dread seeing him in the King's uniform. He shares the horror but thinks he'll only look supremely ridiculous in his hat.

He had a very big head.

At Chelsea Barracks there was more leisure than at the Foreign Office. Our Matron was glad to be putty in my hands. The summer was a generous one. With the help of protective friends and houses and the peace of 88, where we rested and read aloud and felt safe, we saw each other daily. We had long had the habit of lunching at a rather dreary little restaurant in Jermyn Street called Bellomo's at 12.45. "*C'è amici?*" I would ask. And Duff, after careful scrutiny, would answer:

"*Nessuno*." No one I knew had ever heard of Bellomo's. It served us well, and after a happy meal I would dash back to Arlington Street for a second lunch at 1.45.

The beautiful days were overshadowed by coming events. In July he left me for the Cadet School at Bushey, which was to be four months' hard. His first letter was a cry of pain:

I have been here for three hours, but I will not tell you about it for fear of making you cry. One is not allowed to go to London except with special leave, which I'm told is hard to get. I shall not see you for a long time. . . . My uniform is as shameful as a convict's. I sleep in a room with seven others—no sheets. All this however I mind not at all compared with separation from you. Just when I am bearing up and facing the discomfort, the thought returns that three summer months with you are being lost.

I shall try hard to get to Eton on Saturday. The cricket match is just the sort of excuse these mugs prefer. By the way, you mustn't say you are going to Eaton when you mean Eton. People will think you don't know the difference between strawberry leaves and strawberry messes. . . . I shall really have to abandon vanity—I consider it the supreme and final sacrifice to Armageddon—and meet you in my convict's garb.

But in the next letter he had got to London, dined at his club with an imperial pint of champagne and *Alice Through the Looking-Glass* to read, and his "untroubled mind" had come back:

bringing courage, joy and hope so that I was happier than I have been since I left you. I'm ashamed of my former misery. It was because everything was so different from what I expected. Now I shall enjoy it.

Bushey

I like you for not avoiding the theme of death, and I think to talk of it is a form of insurance. I am not frightened of it, you know, just as I wasn't frightened of coming here. I'm too curious and too avid of novelty to fear the unknown.

Things improved. We were enterprising and contrived meetings imaginatively. There was a Golf Club in the Bushey grounds and, any night I could get away, Venetia and other friends would take me there. Duff was always the spoilt darling. There were country houses within the ten-mile radius where we could meet for thirty-six hours, and there was one long week-end spent with the Horners at Mells. Edward was home on leave. It was to be his last real one, shooting in the September sun with Duff, Michael Herbert, Tommy Bouch and Katharine Asquith. Her heart was broken and mine desperately ill with love's fear.

Duff wrote that his return to Bushey was shattering, and I could not help him as I was pledged to go with my parents to Ireland, where my sister Marjorie and her husband were on some mission. "Now at my lowest ebb at dawn departing I think of you," I wired, and I wrote:

Dublin

A wearier journey I never remember taking, perhaps a little modified in horror by my lovely new clothes and an oily sea, but interminable and the prospect of arrival offering no relief. And yet once there, a line of Wicklow mountains, a charred house out of which some rebels had been burnt, rows and squares of gentlemen's houses of the best epoch, and a slap-up bouquet from the Viceroy [Ivor Wimborne] encouraged me a lot. I went straight up to dinner at the Viceregal Lodge in grandest *tenue* and alone. Perfect, I thought—don't believe a word said against it. Forty to dinner—Convention men, Labour ones and Peers—red ties, diamond studs and stars. The Laverys, McEvoy, Léonie Leslie, "A. E."—in fact a court as we would choose one. Her Excellency clotted and weighed down with jewels. Ivor flashy, but very graceful—flashy from being unlike *the* King, but not unlike *a* King. The table and its pleasures a treat—all gold and wine and choicest fruit. One Conventioner said he had never tasted a peach before (I didn't believe him). The footmen too, such beauties, battling with their silver cords, blinded by powder.

"Gentlemen, the King" was good. The curtsey in the wide-vistaed door a positive danger, as the lady-in-waiting had warned us before that Her Excellency favoured the Spanish curtsey, and very beautiful it was as she did it, with the stamp of her heels and flourish of her fan. The rest of us made bobs. After dinner, talking to the Conventioners, some of them a bit unintelligible, and smoking gift cigars. One said of Lord Oranmore, who looks as prosperous as he is: "Sure he's as stout as the Lamb of God." To-morrow a dash to see the Augustus John picture of Iris [Tree] so as not to feel too removed from the Coterie. . . .

P.S. I have just heard that Basil Blackwood is dead. It came through to his mother from the Crown Princess of Sweden. You will have seen too that Uncle Bobby is killed. The long habit of death disinclines us to any demonstration.

And later:

I am going to the Viceregal for my last three days. The life there amuses me. You get your orders—the rest is free. I take a jaunting-car from the town to Phoenix Park—to shock I'm afraid—also because it's great fun. I went over to a place called Powerscourt. I was much impressed by the beauty. An ancestor who discovered Italy with the rest of them in the eighteenth century stocked his garden with great marble Nikes and fauns and tender Ganymedes and Tritons blowing fountains a hundred feet high against the higher mountains. I was struck too by the pathos of Lady Powerscourt, a frail pale woman who lives in strictest poverty in the gaunt house stark alone. About thirty-five, an enthusiast of life as I might be, she is facing with only faint misgivings this coming impossible winter with two servants and no petrol. I know I shall think of her just as I get into my stride one happy fire-warmed evening, perhaps with you at 88—damn.

London   *3 October 1917*

Thank God to be back even in these discordant nights. I dined with Ivor last night in the cellar of Wimborne House, after an hour in the Arlington Street basement, with some of the wounded, and screaming kitchenmaids—most trying. Later at Wimborne House arrived Jenny [Lady Randolph] Churchill and Maud Cunard, both a little tipsy, dancing and talking wildly. They had been walking and had got scared and had stopped for a drink. Maud had a set purpose to get to the opera, because it being raid-night the public required example. She really, I expect, wanted to die with Thomas Beecham if Covent Garden was to be hit. So we let her out at ten. I hope she was all right. The streets are opaque black with only the dear brave *mauvais sujets* about, thieving and vicing, and now this morning I have spent an hour and a half in the Reville & Rossiter dug-out, so maybe it's an ill wind which might blow me good when I claim that Bushey is a safer dining place than London.

I've ordered myself chemises embroidered in hand-grenades and a nightgown with fauns.

My brother John had married Kathleen, the youngest and most beautiful of the Tennant sisters. She was pure and lovely as an anemone, and we gathered her to our house with delight and good reason. John was to survive the war and live happily with his bride for many years. That summer she was living with her baby at the old Rowsley house, which I revisited.

The Woodhouse, Rowsley

It was here that I have seen twelve hot summers fade into cold winters—here been injected almost to suicide with Marjorie's melancholy. Here was born and here died that regrettable friendship with R. One would think with such records the place would hold no ghost of sentiment, and yet the forty days of heat and bathing and Grenfells and Ego and Edward, Bunt and Patrick blot out all the horrors. The place is crowded with objects of my own that I loved before I became anti-possessive, and though I have no great desire to retrieve them it enrages me to see them put to mean uses. I had a low dark room which I equipped through the years with necromancer's and alchemist's properties—curious bottles coloured and crusted with iridescent sediments from elixiral experiments, that now are scoured and used for tooth-water. Delicate gold scales, hung for allegory over my mirror, now have to determine whether fish weigh more or less than a mean lb. A painted ivory ship is only produced should the baby whine. George Meredith's palsied head becomes a nursery picture. It made me sad. I am thankful you were never here to make it more poignant. At dinner I gave them a slight description of your Bushey day (faintly blushing) and Mother said "Do him a lot of good to rough it a bit," upon which John and Uncle Charlie flew at her—no need for me to utter. Blessed be their hearts that wish you well.

Arlington Street   *9 October 1917*

This is bad news—it is muttered that you stand a chance of "not passing" and in consequence remaining more months at Bushey. It hurt me terribly when it came to my ears. I love your record to be brilliant. . . . I shall find complete consolation, if you do fail, in remembering that the further from London the further from the war . . . but it has worried me terribly all day. I told my fool informer that I had just heard from somebody in authority to the exact opposite. It was the same story with Edward's course at Cambridge. God! can I never put down my whitewashing implements for a minute? I had to walk from Marble Arch home in absolutely flooding rain at seven tonight, thinking how terrible everything was, and that really if I fell down I would not get up again.

Bushey   *12 October 1917*

How silly you are to believe that I could fail. Be assured that such rumours are due to the nicety with which I calculate the very minimum of trouble one need take in order to achieve some tiresome business. I think the grenades on your chemises the most romantic thing in my life and they strike a note of poetry and high chivalry worthy of the sixteenth or perhaps the fourteenth century.

Arlington Street   *18 October 1917*

Jack Pixley has been killed. It upsets me a lot. My endurance is weakening. Osbert told me as he often does—a great ill-omened bird—in the middle of the opera, and I have come home and cried and been beastly to Mother on the subject of my lovers, which O shame! comforted me. I must try and be better. At what? . . . Your future is always with me, a jagged companion. I may no longer draw a cheque—so not a rag to put on or any luxuries. . . . Don't fuss about passing.

Arlington Street   *20 October 1917*

I am so sad about poor "Lucky Pixley" and for the first time in my life a little remorseful that I wasn't nicer and didn't come up from Chirk two days earlier though he begged me to. If only one happened to know Death's plans.

I couldn't write yesterday as it was "Our Day." I worked hard and scraped £700 together. The lottery was drawn by the un-interested hand of F. E. Smith and was won, I regret to say, by Teddie Gerard.* Last night just as I was starting for Edwin and Alan's farewell (they leave tomorrow for India) and Maud Cunard was in the hall to fetch me, the raid warning was given. Till 9.30 I argued with Her Grace. I had no case save that the guns had not begun—a poor one for they didn't begin even when Piccadilly Circus was demolished and a knot of the proletariat killed, not even when the *élite*, represented by General Lowther, had his hat blown off. I got away in the end and found myself between Alan and Edwin, the latter divine, in the mood of the doomed, speaking bravely enough of his thankfulness for two Heaven-given years with his wife, of his reliance on me to look after her widowhood, and of several significant omens that signalled his approaching death. His fear has been quelled by complete resignation. Alan was little better—ashy-white with an unshakeable belief that he would be left to die at Aden. . . . After dinner I talked to Winston a great deal about you.

Bushey

I have been sitting under a wall reading all the letters you have written me since I came here. I found them entrancing and I feel they would bear the test of the typewriter better than mine. Some day I will type them with my own hands lovingly and you shall read them again and mount in your self-esteem.

* Miss Teddie Gerard, most popular music-hall artist of the day.

They are in my hands today, only the self-esteem has not mounted.

So Duff passed his examination and came back to London and soldiered at Chelsea Barracks, and six firelit winter months were before us, two of them to bring unbearable sadness. Edward was killed in November while defending a village near Cambrai. It was overwhelmingly dreadful. His mother and his sister had had enough to bear. Katharine broke it to me. Together we told Lady Horner. My mother was sympathetic. She, like everyone else, had found Edward irresistible. He had a lot of real melancholy woven into his *joie de vivre*. He could not bear to be humdrum. He thought life could do more than it can, and it had not given him much except a loving family and friends. Duff, though battered by the blow, was invincible in spirit, while I felt like pulling the clothes over my coward's head.

To make the sadness more poignant and the situation more macabre, Patrick Shaw-Stewart was on his way to London from Salonika for what was to be his last leave. He had not heard of Edward's death. Venetia told him on the telephone. The festivities arranged for him were muffled, however much we tried to make them glitter. His leave was, alas, unspontaneous and sad. The thought of return weighed heavily upon him. Those of us who were left felt we must inevitably be crushed on a stupid pitiless wheel.

Duff wrote in his diary: "So ends 1917 which has been, I think, the least happy year that I have lived." As he wrote, he did not know that Patrick had been killed in France the day before. A bullet in his head brought him instantaneous death—and an end to his brave heart and his mind teeming with methodical designs for a life of fine aims, fortune, fulfilment. His memory will last as long as we who knew him live to remember, and perhaps a little longer, for his classic mood and courage live in a poem scribbled on a leaf of *A Shropshire Lad* that was always with him:

I saw a man this morning
  Who did not wish to die:
I asked, and cannot answer,
  If otherwise wish I.

Fair broke the day this morning
  Against the Dardanelles;
The breeze blew soft, the morn's cheeks
  Were cold as cold sea-shells.

But other shells are waiting
  Across the Ægean sea,
Shrapnel and high explosive,
  Shells and hells for me.

O hell of ships and cities,
  Hell of men like me,
Fatal second Helen,
  Why must I follow thee?

Achilles came to Troyland
  And I to Chersonese:
He turned from wrath to battle,
  And I from three days' peace.

Was it so hard, Achilles,
  So very hard to die?
Thou knowest and I know not—
  So much the happier I.

I will go back this morning
  From Imbros over the sea;
Stand in the trench, Achilles,
  Flame-capped, and shout for me.

DUFF GOES TO WAR

As the weeks galloped along towards the spring offensive, the more listless and crippled my inner self became. The hospital routine did not avail, nor did new friends. Alan, my sentinel, was in the far Indies and sadly missed. There was only Duff now for consolation—Duff my most loved and most feared for.

The dreaded day of his departure fell in April. His mother, the most selfless of women, whose love for Duff was her whole life, would not be there to see him go but rather chose to say goodbye in the hall of some hotel and to walk away without looking back. She knew of our deep attachment and gave it all the blessings she had to give. Duff, more resilient, was excited at his prospects. He wrote in *Old Men Forget*:

So I enjoyed those warm April days in London. My duties grew lighter and finally ceased altogether. I had more time to spend with my friends. . . . The last night was the best of all.

It was my very worst. We dined with a friend, Harold Baker. Venetia was there and Duff's sister Sybil, Michael Herbert and Hugo Rumbold. But let Duff tell of it:

The atmosphere was a little strained at first, but under the influence of wine it all went well enough, I thought. We sat long at the table. Mother telephoned to say good-bye. We walked over to Venetia's, where we had a final bottle. I found that I had left my coat behind. Sybil volunteered to go and get it in a taxi. She returned with the wrong one. Diana and I then went for it and this made me late, so that our last drive together was marred by my worrying about the time. She dropped me at Chelsea. It was very dark on the square. The draft was already formed up. The Adjutant was there and only laughed at my being late. The officer in charge of the draft had arrived, but was in no state to march to Waterloo, and so had gone away again and was coming on by taxi. Teddie [the Adjutant] thought that I should probably be in the same state but I explained to him that I wasn't. As I was senior to the two other officers, I took charge and marched off the men, leading them, with the drums in front. The band played nearly all the way from Chelsea to Waterloo and I felt proud, romantic and exalted. There were a lot of people at the station, the Baroness [d'Erlanger], Hugo, Ivo, Gerard Brassey, Sybil, Venetia and Diana. Diana had changed her clothes or wrapped something round, I didn't notice which, but she appeared to be all in black, and her face so white, so white. We had some time to wait at the station though it seemed too short, and she and I found a dark deserted waiting-room where we exchanged our last embraces. . . . At last we left. The band struck up again as the train moved out of the station.

I went home and wrote to him:

Arlington Street   *2 a.m.*

I think of all my extravagant dreams and demands that you have fulfilled. I adored your glorious spirits. Your salute to the Colonel deserves a page of praise. I am terrified that I clung and clamoured too much—a bright trite mask might have helped you more. It seemed unnecessary with you—you needed no courage. . . . So pleased I was that M. was too drunk to lead a dog to the water, so that you marched the men to Waterloo. Pray God I have word of you soon. Good-night.

In France Duff wrote in his diary: "I wrote to Diana and tried to say how much I love her, but failed, failed." So little did he fail that re-reading those dear letters from France, I see it was in this battle-time that marriage became the true goal of our days. I thought, if death will only spare him we will live our lives together.

Arlington Street   *Midnight*

At all moments I ask myself what you are doing, always hoping you are warm and asleep and dreading most your loneliness. If only the others were with you—it's all easy then. If only I were with you like Serbian and Russian couples we see illustrated. Never think of me lonely. They are all so good—Venetia etc.—and do their best. Letty terribly concerned if I cry at night.

CHAPTER TEN

The Glory and the Dream

To continue the same life of the Rutland Hospital and move among ghosts and desolation was unfaceable, and I determined to return for a month to the austerity of Guy's. I knew it would hurt my mother deeply, but I would perhaps have hurt her more with tears and sulks and love-sickness at home. My sad sister Letty was living and nursing at the Rutland Hospital.

Arlington Street *   *April 30*

It all went off far worse than I feared. When Her Grace came in I started bravely enough with "Now darling, about Guy's," then God! hands up, shrieks, gasps for restoratives, so I withdrew into my own pleasant sheets' warmth and sent Letty to calm her, and they wrangled, poor souls, till three a.m. . . . I long to know how much she connects this intolerance, this great remonstrance, with love or sorrow for you. Now this morning the continuance of scenes and ravings makes me waver, and again if I waver now I shall always waver, so I must try not to. My determination I find greatly strengthened by your absence. It's understandable—so much was tolerable while dallying and philandering secretly with you, so much that I was content to pay in forfeit and sops. But now it seems any single straw will break me.

Arlington Street   *11 p.m.*

I've had it out with Mother. She was pathetic—tamed—and bleated of the loneliness of her life. She thinks Guy's is a penance. For what? Too much life? Too much love, or too much suffering?

* All my letters in this chapter are headed simply with an address, and Duff's with *B.E.F.* They were all written in 1918.

163

So my mother was almost reconciled, and I must have had a lull and licked my wound at Belvoir, for it is from there that I write on 4 May 1918:

John and his wife are too happy. I think all the time how happier we should be. I saw them this morning running about picking flowers and cherry-blossom boughs, and they brought me millions of cowslips, laughing, and asked me to make cowslip-balls for their baby. After lunch I had to take Father to see the pheasant's nest and found the eggs deserted, which "put him out" again, so leaving him I ran rather exultantly to a far garden I knew of, and there I found so many thousands and profusions of red and white camellias that you would have been by me in the first flash, if summoning by wish or will was possible. All round were high blood-red maple trees and I climbed one because it was a very easy kind of tree and I hadn't done such a thing for fifteen years. It was so hot and bird-haunted, and so much the day we have waited for, I remember, that I gave up and sobbed on a little stone. There was no one to ask me why I wept, so soon I stopped, but knowing that this year at least my spring is in you, and that alone I might as well be without eyes or ears—better in fact.

My nerve is wavering terribly about Guy's—not my determination. I shall loathe so much, not the hours, discomfort and life, but the dirt, suffering, smells and squalors. I had forgotten foot-day and hair-day.

Guy's Hospital   *May 8*

Am I not naughty about dates? You said "to please me," still I can't keep it in mind. It's antipathetic, but these days I have to write it on twenty-two charts daily, so I will be good. I arrived this morning and was sent to a women's surgical ward—not bad, you know, cleanish and a few lovely children, glowing consumptives who shame one very much when the soul bleats or revolts. I lunched at the unusual hour of 11.15 off a portion or parcel of a dreadful past fish. It could not have been worse fish, not even if it had harboured a Jew like Jonah in its stomach for months, so I shall fine down I hope, though tonight I made good with a melon that dear old Venetia sent me the first day, bless her, and mugs of cocoa and toast and butter and cold rice puddings at a "feast" in the kitchen with my co-wardworkers. One has to *hide* everything. I spent fifteen minutes looking for a suitable cache for the remnants of a melon, a bottle of methylated for sore backs, a cloth and an ounce of margarine, but whenever I thought to have found a niche a nurse would whisper "I shouldn't leave them there, nurse; the night people know that place."

Guy's   *May 9*

So little time to write. 7.30 a.m. to 8 p.m. and with the exception of $\frac{1}{2}$ for lunch and $\frac{3}{4}$ for tea, during which I hang my legs in cold water just to calm them, one is not off one's feet. I don't remember it being so torturing last time, do you? Perhaps novelty and patriotism stiffened my sinews. It was one of our spring days, but one must lead the leisured life to appreciate weather. I'm glad to say once busy it matters little except to one's general spirits. The poor don't notice it at all. Another thing about the poor that surprises me is that when friends, or chiefly relatives, come to see them sick, they as often as not sit in a complete silence for an hour and a half, rather self-consciously too, occasionally broken by "Feelin' very poorly, dear?" or some such rhetorical remark. But what *amazes* me about them is their lack of question or curiosity about themselves. They all are afraid of cancer. They have all got it. They have the words "Diagnosis: carcinoma" written over their beds, big. They say as a rule "What is glands? Not cancers, are they?" I say "O no, dear, not cancer," and there they leave it. There is a lovely woman of thirty-five not unlike me, with a glimmering skin and breasts like the Milo's, but if you touch them it's like touching stone, so they were both removed today, and yet she doesn't ask what's wrong.

Claud was at the iron gates at 8 for me and gave me an enormous dinner and half a bottle of Burgundy. A note from Venetia to the effect that Edwin and Alan probably arrive Sat. or Sun. I'm so dead and stale and unignited without you, Duff darling. They won't love me as much as they did, I'm really afraid, and how broken they will be to find the Dove flown.

Guy's   *May 10*

O the pain of the bones of my legs and feet, they send shivers down my back and a dull sickness as I walk the wards. My hands too would frighten tame bulls, and my neck is like the man they couldn't hang though they tried to six times—from the collar's sharp grip.

Do you remember (I think he struck your fancy) the idiot in *Boris* who wore a saucepan on his white hair and moaned gibberish? I have just such another one, a woman, in my care—a real delight, very old and playing like a child in terrible earnest. Sometimes for three minutes she swims out of her craziness and groans for her "poor, poor brain—it's that that's gone, I know it has," she says, "because I can't smile and I can't cry and I'm dreadful afraid to do some harm to those pretty children." She's called Mrs 2. The other patients shun her and every day I walk her down to the Light Department. It's as sensational as the camel coming out of *Chu Chin Chow*. People stop and watch. Only she's not easy—it's more like driving a pig. And when I get her there I leave her on an iron slab, between four old men, syphilitic I guess. They are half-naked and more bled than bladders of shining lard. Their four noses have apparently sucked all the blood from their bodies and scalps (which are the whitest part of them and hairless as china), for these glow like flame in a wax surround. Over them sit four pretty girls directing a blazing light upon them by way of cure. It's enough to unhinge shaky minds.

When I returned to my room tonight, tired enough not to think any more of this work beyond bearing, I could scarcely open the door for red and white roses, sent by Ivor—five hundred I should say. It's a joke. It *did* give me pleasure.

Guy's   *May 12*

I drove home at 9.30 alone (you could not have let me do that— O God to have you), a little fuddled in an open taxi. The search-lights were playing magically and I found myself addressing a very complicated and exacting prayer to the Power of Lives aloud, to the effect that you might not be killed, or might be restored very quick to my very arms, that nothing should touch your face or arms, at least not both arms, but I didn't mind your leg or rib, and so on for ten minutes before I caught myself up.

Guy's   *May 13*

Today, in consequence no doubt of my night out, I dozed off after the bell had rung and woke again to my panic when the watch indicated the hour Home Sister takes her estrade seat above the breakfasters. To come in behind her is punishable. I clapped my uniform over my nakedness, took no look in the glass, and ran 300 yards to the hall holding and tugging at my ungartered stockings. Providence had made my watch two minutes fast, so I thought myself safe as I sank into my chair exactly beneath Sister's empty chair. But my table of twenty started sniggering, I hoped at my flaming hurry and pantings, then when twenty mouths had whispered it to me I found I was collarless—always ridiculous, you know. Think of yourself stalking into Ava's with a bare neck and a stud like a star. I was distraught as my great flashing nape was the first thing Sister's eyes must rise on, after Grace. But a grubby choking collar was handed me through three hundred hands beneath the table from Nurse Philip Sidney sitting in an inconspicuous place, and I swept into port very weary. No. 2 can no longer remember when she has washed and starts loading herself with soaps and brushes as soon as I have got her back to bed. She will speak no word more, and because her arms are swollen I have tied her two hands up to a rod above her head, till she looks like a crazy *Kamerad*. Can the poor mad thing be sleeping? She can't, I know.

Guy's   *May 14*

No. 2 is dying, I think. Her arms are like thighs and her legs are strapped to her bed, which has been removed to a black corner of the ward where she can give no trouble. I have had a sickener today with the treatment of the poor, beginning with the hiding of No. 2, and going on all afternoon with a poor young woman being operated on for appendicitis. She was anaesthetised and then Fripp could not be found. He was discovered, after half an hour of the patient's unconsciousness, having tea, but even then etiquette prevented his being hurried. In his own time he came and the operation was performed under his supervision by a beginner, while Fripp shouted, "No, no, not like that." "That's the mistake you all make." "There! now you have hashed it; you'll never get an incision of that sort to heal, my boy," and then she comes round two hours later and Sister says "Feeling much better, old lady?" The poor must give themselves since they have no money. Money is fine. I think so specially tonight, because Ivor W. picked me up and took me to dinner at Oddenino's. He paid the taxi £1 on a 4/- clock because "You're in it," he said. He gave me a £4 uneatable dinner, with two nice bottles of claret (I thought of you). He bribed the porter £1 to give us a taxi he had secured for another, and bribed the taxi £3 to go to Guy's when he was set on picking up a theatre customer at ten, so I guess his evening out cost him near a tenner.

B.E.F.   *May 7*

I dined here last night and shall tonight. The food is better than 1918 Ritz but the champagne, of which they have only one brand, is very inferior. Censoring the men's letters is sometimes amusing but usually monotonous, and their love-letters are so shamefully like one's own in thought though not so prettily expressed. One man wrote today: "A lot of ships were needed to bring the British Army to France. Only two will be wanted to take it back, one for the men and the other for the identity discs." I thought it so "good." There is a rumour that we may be going to where Katharine is. I don't think for a moment it's true.

B.E.F.   *May 12*

Yesterday afternoon I went for a walk with young d'Erlanger. He described to me his parents' palace in Tunis, which sounded all that we have ever dreamed—terraces going down to the sea and orangeries on the beach. Thinking of you I muttered that it sounded a suitable spot for a honeymoon. He (aged nineteen) said he intended never to marry, that he was like Alfred de Musset and that all he cared for in love was "*la conquête et la rupture.*" I said—modestly —that I had never made a *conquête* and was not, I thanked God, ruptured.

I then abstracted my thoughts and built Somerset Houses in the air for you and me. I thought how happy we should be and how, because we have never been too sentimental, marriage could brush no bloom from our romance. If we survive the war, which is a serious obstacle, it seems absurd that any smaller ones should stand in our way. Tell me what you think of this if ever you think of it at all.

B.E.F.   *May 15*

While I was writing the above one of my brother officers walked by with another officer. I hailed them. I am sitting outside under an awning. They confessed that they had a rendezvous but sat down to have a drink until their friends arrived. Presently up turned a little poll with a wonderful command of the English language and with the promise of her sister and if necessary another friend waiting at home for entertainment. I excused myself saying that I must write my letter and as she led off the two victims she said to me quite prettily "If you are writing to your sweetheart, say that a French girl wanted you very much but that you were faithful." Why is it that the word "sweetheart" offends me there? I can only bear it in the vocative.

B.E.F.   *May 16*

After I left you yesterday I went almost with you to the churches we wanted to see. At the first, St Patrice, there was such a crowd witnessing First Communions that I could hardly get in. So I went to St Ouen, where also a service was going on, but there there was plenty of room and the church is most beautiful inside. I felt I could become a bore about churches. One of the little girls, I suppose the best—*la rosière*—made a long oration. She said it beautifully, enunciating every word distinctly and laying no stress on any, as though the whole had no meaning. There is a charm in the sexless voices of the young, not because one likes sexlessness but because one does like birds, in spite of oneself and although they get up too early. Then I strolled back to the Cathedral because I wanted to see some tombs there which I hadn't been able to see in the morning. There was a large one of two Cardinals which I had hoped would be

THE GLORY AND THE DREAM

more like the Bishop's, and there was a very lovely one of the husband of Diane de Poitiers—good late Renaissance—alabaster divided as it were into two stories (I mean *étages*, not *histoires*). Above the gentleman appears on horseback and in armour, very fine with smiling female figures at his head and feet representing Victory, Glory etc. Beneath him is seen a small, almost naked man, one cloth twisted round the lower part of his body, his head thrown back as though in death agony and his face *mesquin* and ugly. At his head kneels Diane quietly praying, at his feet a Virgin with a happy laughing child. I remember that he was a very ugly man and small as he here appears. Diane ordered the tomb. How well those people lived and with what pomp and fantasy they died. All this and more I thought of saying to you while I was looking at the tomb, and then I rejoined my friends, and then we dined.

B.E.F. *May 29*

I must try to carry on your education even at this distance. In the first place you mustn't put at the top of your letter "12 p.m." because it signifies nothing. 12 can't be p. or a. because it's m. itself. You must say "noon" or "midnight." In the second place you mustn't ever say "ignorami" when you mean more than one ignoramus. It would bore you if I explained why but take my word for it.

As we marched out of the station very gloomily we passed a party of W.A.A.C.s, at the sight of whom our men with one accord bleated "Quack, quack, quack" until they had passed. Apparently it is the usual thing. I think it is so funny.

B.E.F. *May 30*

I am much warmer and much happier now, for many reasons. Soon after I had finished writing the enclosed little wail, the sun came out and the larks started singing. The larks are wonderful here. Everywhere else in France they are shot by the *français sportifs*, but here since neither the English or the Germans can ever hit anything they are perfectly safe, with the result that the front line has become a regular bird-refuge, and as one has anyhow always to be awake at dawn, which as you know is their favourite hour for kicking up a row, one doesn't mind the little ——

Guy's   *May 15*

By this time maybe you are with your battalion, and though you calm me it's all I can bear, but I must wear blinkers and see it as nearer your return. This morning they said to me "Would you like to have a half-day, nurse, it's less than your due?" It was illustrative of your being far from me that I answered "No, thank you, Sister, I think there is a lot I must get through this evening in the ward." She snubbed me in replying "At Guy's, nurse, no one is indispensable. Matron says it of herself." So it was forced upon me and I could see nothing but disappointment at the waste of free hours without you to breathe the quiet warm air with me. Dropped in at 24 for an hour and a half to dinner with Beaverbrook, Venetia, Diana Wyndham and Nellie; the last two did not once speak. V. was dressed like an elephant in "howdahs" and sham Eastern spoils. Beaverbrook talked of the *Daily Express* and of how much of his interest he gave to it. Every night, he said, he rang up and told them to insert and omit so and so, and put the fact that Lady D. Manners has a new giant mastiff with a diamond collar on the front page, not the inside one. Edwin recalled an anecdote of Lloyd George at the outbreak of war, sitting in Edwin's Duchy office, feet on table, while the question of mobilisation, or ultimatum, or what? was in the air, and delivering himself of the following "I am not *against* the war *actually*, but I am certain that I could not possibly take an active part in the conducting of it. I shall, I think, resign, though continuing to support the Government. Anyway before I make my decision I must go and consult my old uncle in Wales. We shall play an ignoble part, for in six weeks we shall have starved the women and children in Germany, and not have lost a single man."

In the middle of all this I got my Guy's panic and ran wildly from the house, leapt into a taxi in Victoria Street and crossed Westminster Bridge. It looked so wonderful in the pale dead crepuscule light, and that half-finished building that we love brought my desire for you back till I stretched my arms out to it. It looked tonight so like our generation—great straight aspiring pillars cut off at the same time before they bore the weight they were built for—too lovely an edifice to be half-built, but so beautiful in its abrupt cessation. There are two high finished columns. They looked like you and me. This is written against time.

I do not remember how Max Beaverbrook became so woven into this period. It was during Duff's time in France that the Montagus and I saw almost daily this strange attractive gnome with an odour of genius about him. He was an impact and a great excitement to me, with his humour, his accent, his James the First language, his fantastic stories of his Canadian past, his poetry and his power to excoriate or heal. We went a lot to his house at Leatherhead, to his rooms and offices in London, and my letters to Duff are full of admiring references. Although Duff and he were never to be happy in their relationship, I am to this late day devoted to him, and though there is much to lament I have valuable memories of good deeds done for Duff, if only for my sake.

Guy's   *May 16*

Today was a dog day, unparalleled in beauty but of terrific devitalising heat, heat that melted etiquette and discipline. We all shirked work, and sat down in front of each other and were crusty with the patients. No. 2 regained a little lucidity when I was attending to her tonight and kept on repeating "It's not right, dear, I know it's not right. You shouldn't do it. It's not right for you to do it." For a long time she couldn't explain what was wrong, then at last "You're too clean to touch me, nurse. I know it's not right you should have to, and don't do it. I know I'm not fit for you to touch, too foul, too foul." It was horrible and all said very blankly and quietly, but it seemed to me very, very sensible. Mrs 22, opposite, says she doesn't like to see her so quiet "cos it's the quiet ones what always *springs*." It was torturingly hot. I thought I must give up in the theatre. The smell of blood seemed too strong, and I had to mop Fripp's brow for an hour, but half an hour in a freezing bath in the tea interval restored me, and at eight I was prepared to face dinner with the Montagus, but I find I dress slowly and without the happy happy hecticness of three years ago.

Guy's   *May 20*

Scarcely had I finished my letter to you at eleven and scarcely fallen asleep, when loud went the maroon, so I darted into my uniform, thinking there was certain to be some drill or law to follow. "Nurses of A. Section to take cover in T. Basement" as it might be, but only a Sister appeared to tell me I could do just what I liked—remain in bed in the papier-mâché house, or go over to the more concrete Nurses' Home, or stroll in subways, or find shelter with red-dressed fallen women in the laundry. This made it all very difficult, as I only wanted to do the usual, and I couldn't make out what that was, as everybody was either truthfully unconcerned or in the passage swanking about the lure of their beds and direct hits and yet dressing hectically and edging away out of any finding. Darling, you know I am a little frightened. If you can remember, you only just kept me right when I had measles in the big raid, but without you near me my heart did leap and flee.

Guy's   *May 20*

It is a thing that the stoutest campaigners of the school that walk on parapet-tops with eye-glasses flashing, and pick up shells wearing pumps the while, cannot endure—to wait three mortal hours in *total* darkness among strangers all alarmed, while the London Bridge gun shook our marrows and a procession of victims dead and mangled passed in the darkness. How much less can a feeble campaigner like myself endure, who when in health am used to greet a raid with a glass and laugh the bombs to inaudibility.

I wish I might stay here until your return, writing every night and a life ordered, but Mother badgers me at all hours and ticks the days off on an almanac.

Guy's   *May 21*

Last night a new patient came in unexpectedly. The nurse rushed to me shouting "What do you think we've got in?" I guessed a Hun, a hermaphrodite or a dog-faced woman. "No," they whispered breathlessly, "an *actress*," and a poor furtive little widow actress she was, with a blue ribbon in her modest nightdress instead of an unbleached calico wardgown. She threw off a blanket in the middle of the night (the one *next* her, as the heat is abnormal and the ward has eight calorifiers) and the night people declared she had done this as the House Surgeon came in so as to "catch him."

Guy's   *May 24*

I have one advantage over your sister Steffie in that I do not have to retire for an hour daily to think on you, but manage to do it day and night with no effort and in all companies. So if this simple method is to keep you safe you are strongly accoutred.

There is a woman here, who because her husband failed in the carpentering business has lost her memory to the extent of not being able to remember whether she has had her dinner, or been washed or anything. It worries her terribly, especially the terror of doing something twice. Such a condition would not suit me now, but it might have had its advantages if we had forgotten we had been to Victoria Road, or had dinner, and fun for Keats if he'd forgotten his impressions of Chapman and was able to come over queer every morning.

Guy's   *June 2*

Today I took a florid buxom young girl's nightdress off, preparatory to washing her, and there on her firm white arm I saw tattooed a large scroll encircled with red and white rose-wreaths. On the scroll was inscribed in copybook calligraphy the simple name "Bill Baldwin." Was it not charming? the confidence of unalterableness, the pain endured, the chaff of her future husband—a Maupassant might be written, I thought, on the succeeding lovers' irritation at the eternal advertisement. Do you remember the tattoo shop as we left the Old Vic and my desire for a voluntary wound "here on the thigh"? If fickle Fortune sends you back to me I think I must have a little laurel wreath or "a dove alighting" or something adaptable to other explanations and even other conditions, of course, but some commemoration of great joy I would like.

B.E.F.   *May 25. Sunday*

We argued about Asquith and Lloyd George. One of my brother-officers maintained that Asquith was "all in with the Huns" and he believed that Mrs Asquith was a "female b——" that being as near as his limited vocabulary allowed him to get to Sapphist. He sounds dreadful but is really sweet—of the Denny type, with red hair and a large nose and a slow smile. He is Acting Captain. My other brother-officer said that Lloyd George was not what he called a clever man.

I have been out riding all today—from seven a.m. to three and it was rather lovely. Such perfect weather. Quite close to the line, just dangerous enough to make one feel brave and think of gentlemen in England now in church.

B.E.F.   *May 31*

It is, as you say, very odd that our friends should be blind to our love, or blind to yours at any rate. Surely they don't doubt mine. That we should have so long and successfully deceived them thrills with pride and pleasure all the gentleman in me and slightly irritates all the cad. For the cad would be flattered—the imperious desire speaks out—he would have men mark you eyeing me, and would have them groan to be the god of such a grand sunflower. But it is very well that he should not be humoured.

Guy's   *June 3*

Today, my last day, I am rather glad to find myself so popular with nurses and patients. They bring me bunches of very tired flowers when they have their half-holiday and rush home to Peckham, and the young girl-patients wink at me to wash them and lie to get me. It *is* nice. 2 has gone to the infirmary, but 12, who has lain lost in her own dirt since I have been here, literally crawling and weighing fifteen stone and spitting unintermittently, has suddenly developed a disease, incurable, called foetid bronchitis, which makes it quite impossible for anyone to tend her unless we burn an incense cone by her bed or wear a mask. Every few hours she puts on a gasmask-snout filled with the strongest possible disinfectant and breathes it for an hour. This she thinks is a treatment but it's only for the staff's sake. All the fluid in her lungs, all she spits, has gone bad inside her. Could anything be worse?

Belvoir   *June 7*

I spent the afternoon preparing food for a picnic which John begged. It was such a lovely tea in Frog Hollow. The garden is exactly like a transformation scene at Drury Lane, azaleas and syringa and asphyxiating smells. There were *petits pains* filled with chicken and lettuce and mayonnaise, and feathery jam tarts, and cucumber. I thought I would make a meal just like it for ourselves, and somehow we should be in that garden together, for no breeze can reach it and the flowers meet across the paths, and you would kiss me as we walked, and I should not be afraid and always looking back.

B.E.F.   *June 7*

I am writing this in my tent after tea. My tent is the colour of spilt claret, a beauty which I owe to theories of camouflage, although it is the colour of nothing in nature except a copper beech half-finished or a ploughed field of very red soil. In my tent there is a little grave wherein stands my bed, so that I lie no higher than the ground. So I am supposed to be immune from bombs, and so should anyone say to me after dinner "Will you walk out of the air?" I could reply, "Into my grave."* Do you always follow my quotations, or misquotations? At night one candle makes a tent quite light and I feel very romantic in mine. I think of Saul in his and David playing to him, and of Achilles when he wouldn't come out, and of Richard's night before Bosworth, and Brutus and Cassius both in one tent and I'm not surprised they quarrelled.

There is a new moon and a new star. May they shine kindly on us and make us happy.

Rutland Hospital   *June 10*

Two letters tonight—I feel gayer. When I arrived at seven I swung round to Venetia, who told me about the new star that was coming to destroy us in two years. I turned quite white and sick with horror for ten minutes, speculating on the certain death and the dread of the price and scarcity of poisons which we would be fighting for, then I saw it all as so perfect from another aspect. The war would stop, for who would fight in hell for no gain since annihilation was certain, and you would come back and we would be so happy in those two years, with not much more dread than in these normal days. It sounds a story not worth the telling, but I

* *Hamlet*, act ii, scene 2.

enjoyed the change that thoughts of you are able to create in me, for really my fear was genuine and ghastly until you came into my mind.

Rutland Hospital   *June 20*

Great success and fun at Max Beaverbrook's last night. He lives at the Hyde Park and we had an amazing meal in a sitting-room—Edwin, Nellie, Mr Means the Canadian representative at the Conference, host and self. Edwin really stimulated with argument and Beaverbrook terribly attractive. Lloyd George's name was brought up as knowing some small point which he could not remember. He rang the bell for a confidential servant and ordered him to find out where Mr Lloyd George was dining and ask him to come round. After an hour's work on the servant's part, he appeared again, pale and exhausted, and said: "Mr Lloyd George is on his way, my lord."

It is as cold and wet as charity. It hurts me less than the warm sun, but it acts upon one too very sadly. I'm to have a tooth out this morning and I funk the gas terribly, or will it waft me to Hardelot and the woods and the little good restaurant called *Catelan* or some such nearby? Perhaps it will take me to a lovely grass-grown moat filled with irises and lilacs (now no doubt a practice trench) and put your hand in mine, and sink all fears, till I shall funk the waking.

P.S. Beaverbrook referred to my father as "a man of considerable stupidity."

Ely   *July 1*

I haven't been able to write because we had not got a stick of paper between us at that very very unformed Breccles.* We took a picnic yesterday to a distant fen or mere, so beautiful and so hot. I see at last the charm of Norfolk. It's so demoralised. The fields are half-tilled only, so that poppies and wild blue torches fight with the corn and some acres are given up to them. It is thinly populated because Norfolkians can't or won't propagate, so that the birds have it their own way and reign unmolested, except by love, and in gratitude even the high-building species in this country nest on the ground, presumably out of consideration for the inhabitants.

I tried to master some characteristics and appearances of birds.

* The Montagus' house in Norfolk.

The lapwing, plover, snipe, redshank and duck I think are stamped on my eye-mind, but they don't excite me. Butterflies in the British Isles only number about forty kinds, according to Edwin, so we will master them in a year of leisure. Jim Vincent, the Hickling keeper, was there on leave, asking after you. He's a fine man. I listened to him reminiscing for an hour. He could not tell a story that was not discreditable to poor Edwin. "That day, sir, you was so exhausted. I'll never forget your lying there panting and pleading for a trap," "That day you took fright at that little pony, sir?" The Montagus will be happy there, I think, and so pray God will we.

B.E.F. *July 4*

Three letters came from you this morning, so you do love me after all. Lovely letters from Breccles which made me laugh and one from Alan which made me cry. I laughed at "That day you took fright at that little pony, sir?" and I cried at his description of your sweetness, your beauty and your love for me. He expresses fear of my not fully realising the last. Perhaps I don't. One can hardly sometimes realise the greatest fabulous wealth, and I feel about your love as about a miraculous fortune which has come to me, which makes me proud and happy all day long, and over which I ponder and gloat more avariciously than ever the maddest miser over his heap of gold. And it is true that I never knew how great it was until I came abroad. Imagine then the miser's joy when, counting his shekels for the thousandth time, he finds that there are twice as many as he thought before. Alan goes on very charmingly to urge our marriage and makes me think of Shakespeare and Mr W. H. He will not admit impediments. And certainly it does seem wicked that so great and unimaginable a joy should be hindered by the miserable shortage of crumpled Bradburys.* Tell me truly what you think about this and about the irreducible minimum. I think I asked you once before and you didn't answer.

I thought of sending you Alan's letter but I can't spare it, so I will quote a little. "Diana is too lovely at present . . . and, Duffy, she does love you so much. Perhaps you don't realise it and will be glad to have me tell you, but it really is true and you should be very

* Treasury notes.

proud of it. She thinks of you all day, watches the post eagerly for your letters and loves to talk of what you are doing and what you have done and will do with her" (I cried). . . . "I wish you would marry her, Duffy. She would take you at once if it were practicable. And can't it be made practicable? I don't suggest that you should do what I did, which is to marry on £400 worth of debts, though I would like to point out that even a crushing burden like that is not a fatal obstacle to a happy marriage. But I wish it could be made possible. . . . Your marriage couldn't fail" and more in needless but pretty praise of your qualities and assurances, which God knows are unnecessary to me, of how perfect a wife you would make. "She is not only the most beautiful woman in the world but also the best, the most generous, the most warm-hearted, the most gentle, the most loyal. Is all this to change or wither after marriage? Surely it can only blossom the more, etc." Damn him, he appears to think that I am hanging back. He can't think that really, but is only carried away by his own verbosity. You surely, darling, have never doubted how madly proud and wildly happy I should always have been and always shall be to marry you under any conceivable conditions, how little I should mind poverty, how gladly I should renounce all my extravagances and vices, break my champagne glasses, throw away my cigars, tear up my cards, sell all my books—the first editions first, study the habits of busses and the intricacies of tubes to obtain that inconceivable honour. You don't believe this. You shake your lovely head, your pale eyes look reproaches for past transgressions and too recent ones, but, O my best, you can surely see how different it would all be then. Believe, believe me how gladly I would scorn delights and live laborious days, and indeed what would it matter then how the days were spent? But what would Her Grace say and His Grace too?

So I propose to you again. It is just five years since I did so first, by letter from Hanover in fun. Do you remember? I can still remember your non-committal answer. I wonder what it will be this time. Whatever it is, my life, it cannot make me love you more.

It was sweet of Alan to write, wasn't it? Perhaps he showed you the letter, in which case I shall look silly. You were writing to me near him at the time. He described you stretched under an apple-tree.

B.E.F. *July 5*

I am not going up to the line at present and am secretly rather disappointed. However I am leaving here and a change is always nice. No letter from you this morning, so I had to read the paper. How good Wilson's speech is, though he is wrong about the Barons of Runnymede acting not for a class but for a people. I love his phrases: "I can fancy that the air of this place (Washington's tomb) carries the accents of such principles with a peculiar kindness," and "forces . . . which have at their heart an inspiration and a purpose which are deathless and of the very stuff of triumph." "Stuff" is good. I have just looked through the new *Tatler* hoping for a picture of you where I don't usually hope for it. But now I am starved for your features. Send me a little picture to carry with me. This is a day of hustle bustle.

Bath Club *July 5*

A woman strolled in today and asked for me. She was from the *Daily Express* and much upset as to how to work the appeal for this hospital. She had had Editor's orders and was almost desperate to get the thousand pounds. I have a great fear that one morning, without even opening my *Express*, my eye may be caught by some sentimental article about the Manners' sacrifices and my merry, or sad, blue eyes. I dared not tell her to submit it, as a gift horse must not be looked at.

P.S. Ella Wheeler Wilcox met a beggar, she says, and gave him a thought. Ronnie Knox in an essay praises her generosity for what she could so ill afford.

Rutland Hospital *July 8*

Such a wonderful letter this morning about our marrying. It was my cure, my wings. I feel it may be so. I know I cannot be as happy without you, but these dread days indicate less than ever a means.

In a sense the world shapes to hide our possible squalor; no one shall have motors since we cannot. There shall be fewer servants all round, and food is not to be bought, but wine shall flow which our guests' other hosts lock up, and so they'll love us best, and never pity our poverty.

Rutland Hospital   *July 9*

I send you another picture today, for the sake of the romance in it. She was a spy. Her prettiness you can believe. Her hair is of an acid peroxide colour and her skin frail. She told her beads while Orpen painted her the day before she was shot, crying terribly. The story is told, but not believed, that she asked to be allowed to dress properly for her execution, so her maid was allowed to go to the cell taking with her an unequalled sable and chinchilla coat, and a little pair of white satin mules. She asked for no bandage, no cords round her wrists and begged for short warning. When it came she let the furs slip from her naked body and lie like a vanquished animal round her feet. Like that they shot her. No doubt she had a little hope and faith in her beauty earning her a reprieve.

Rutland Hospital   *July 10*

I was so childishly thrilled today by the Queen of the Belgians. I went to the Albert Hall and found it congested with crowds expectant-eyed on the Royal Box, and she was sent in to face the multitude unsupported for a couple of minutes. So very small she looked and dressed in gleaming white from head to toe, and they cheered as I have not heard cheering before.

I have been dining at the Café Royal with Lutyens, Barbie, Ivo (up from Tadworth for the night), Birrell and McEvoy—a strange little party, not unsuccessful. We retired to "The Green Griffon" and had general information. One story of Birrell's I remember, but I think it may be a chestnut. Lord Young to Alfred Austin: "Well, Mr Austin, are you writing still?" "Keeping the wolf from the door, Lord Young." "Do you show the wolf your poems, Mr Austin?" Birrell said too he had heard King Edward do as good as "Scribble, scribble, Mr Gibbon" when he turned to Lord Rayleigh at a Palace party and said "Well, Lord Rayleigh, discovering something, I suppose?" and then turning to Birrell "You know, he's always at it."

I still make castles half the night and they house us so regally. I have had such a million sorrows, you must have been kept to restore me.

Rutland Hospital   *July 12*

I have felt so ill all day. I slept all the afternoon while Mother drew me, and then woke and went out and bought *What Maisie Knew* because James is such a conspicuous gap in my reading, but I couldn't manage a single page without dropping off, so I tried learning the *Midsummer*. Is it from "Ill met by moonlight, proud Titania" and am I to learn both parts or only the fairy queen's while you have all the dolphin fun, and when am I to stop? And am I to learn Helena and Hermia too? Do explain. I'd rather have done *Romeo and Juliet* but perhaps you haven't got it.

The Wharf, Sutton Courtenay   *July 13*

I have touched the apex of wild despair. The party is Cynthia, Mary, Beb, Hugo, Sidney Russell-Cook, Eliza, two McKennas, Asquith, and from ten to twelve after a parched dinner Mary and I and Hugo and Beb sat in a fireless room in the Mill House. At dinner Beb had relieved the monotony a trifle by turning to the German-born Mrs Joshua and saying with intent about a battle: "We won it. No, you did. No, I think we did."

Wade I loved this morning because she volunteered some reminiscences of last year's Wharf and reeled off the guests, all with the purpose, I think, of saying when she reached your name "How is Mr Cooper, milady, has he been much in the front line?" I said "Yes, he has" curtly with 10,000 beams raying towards her from my heart.

P.S. I cannot be happy without I marry you, as these Americans say.

P.P.S. I am dull and tired and always sad. The offensive starts again and I don't know where you are.

Rutland Hospital   *July 18*

Beaverbrook took me to see a private view of a German-produced film, unreleasable because of its origin, but of such gross commonness and vulgarity that I think it should make fine propregander. Nothing I have seen or heard has bred more hate in me of the enemy —old men's lips and fat women caught bending. Max also produced from his pocket a wireless they had just intercepted from Germany making tremendous propergander of His Grace's prayer for rain. "Lord Rutland gives us to understand," it runs, "that the harvest in England is even wor se than our highest hopes. . . . All crops are dried up, etc.," and many enlargements.

My father had written to *The Times* about rain. At least that is how the news posters read. "Duke prays for rain"— "Duke's prayer answered." The poor man had only suggested on the correspondence page that prayers should be offered in all churches.

B.E.F.   *July 7*

I have just finished *The Brothers Karamazov* and I don't think I need ever read another Dostoievski, need I? He is the great writer I like least. He heads my heresies. I am now enjoying *Eminent Victorians*. I love your markings. I don't think he is good on Manning but my criticism is rather too complicated to explain. You can't write well about a man unless you have some sympathy or affection for him, and he obviously has none either for Manning or for Newman. It is very easy and obvious to mock at people who worry about religion and especially about small points of doctrine. What is interesting is that the Victorians, Manning, Newman, Gladstone, Acton—all cleverer men than Strachey—really were worried to death about these things. Strachey seems to me to make no effort to understand them or to represent what they felt and what was their point of view, but simply to show how very funny their religious worries appear seen from a detached and irreligious stand-point, and he rather suggests that in so far as they had religious worries at all they were either mad or insincere. He doesn't write like an historian but like a pamphleteer. You don't feel reading him as you do when reading Gibbon that he is looking down from the heights of knowledge and wisdom upon "the crimes, follies, and misfortunes of mankind" and that he cannot occasionally refrain from sneering at th em. You feel rather that he is out to sneer, that he is like an agile quick-witted guttersnipe watching a Jubilee proces-sion. He c an laugh at the judge's wig, the bishop's gaiters and the general's medals, can make a good joke at their expense and if neces-sary throw a lump of mud and run away. I apologise for this long tirade, the less justified as I have only read the first of his *Victorians* and am now enjoying Florence Nightingale, which is certainly not so open to the above criticism. I didn't mean to write so much on the subject.

P.S. I've just taken a deep "drop off" reading this letter. God knows what you will do. Don't write too legibly or intelligibly as I have no occupation so pleasant as pondering for hours over your hieroglyphics, and for hours more trying to interpret your dark sayings. A clearly written, simply expressed letter is too like the lightning.

B.E.F.   *July 8*

No mail today from England, which made everyone cry but none so much as me. *Nulli flebilior quam mihi.** I have just written to Alan on the subject of his letter to me. I have told him that God knows I never needed prompting and that the decision rests only with you. And I have pointed out all the arguments against—your arguments and the world's, for I have none—the arguments of the star against the moth, of King Cophetua's best friends against the beggar maid, of all which I am probably more sensible than you. So don't think, darling, that I wish to force your hand, and you may if you like and find it easier ignore the matter in your letters altogether. I only feel that in a collapsing world it would be a great bid for happiness, which the Fates don't seem likely to bestow on us unless we fight for it. As for the pecuniary aspect, while the war goes on it hardly matters. Everyone lives from hand to mouth and from lunch to dinner. Afterwards there will surely be work to be done, or shall we say jobs to be got, in the securing of which our combined talents could not fail us. People have started on less and lived happily ever afterwards. But there, don't let me bother you. Your answer will probably be the traditional one of the Old Gang† and I can't quarrel with it.

I have nearly finished the *Victorians* and though I have enjoyed it enormously my criticism of yesterday I still hold to. He tries to be detached and dispassionate but he doesn't succeed. You can feel

---

* An adaptation of Horace, *Odes*, i, 24, line 10.
† "Wait and See."

reading the book that he is pleased that Miss Nightingale grew fat and that her brain softened, and he is delighted that Gordon drank. I must say that he makes me like both better than I did before, partly out of opposition. Dr Arnold of course is a bit too much.

B.E.F.   *July 10*

How can I support these bitter months of separation? I am sorry to rant and wail like this. It takes me seldom, but sometimes the monotony of the present and the uncertain prospect of our re-union are appalling. When I think of leave and England I think really only of you, though I seem to echo Mr Moore in saying so. If it were not for you I should be tranquil and content to waste here a year or two. But years of our youth and love I cannot spare, nor months nor days nor hours. Do you remember Hotspur when the Prince kills him "Oh, Harry, thou hast robbed me of my youth"? So the war is robbing us of ours.

Now that I have complained I feel better. "Hope is a lover's staff." I must "walk hence with that."* Perhaps all will be well sooner than we dare dream, and meanwhile on "the bitter journey to the bourne so sweet"† I dedicate myself to you day and night, doing always—don't interrupt—what I think you would wish. O love, what architects we are of air-castles.

B.E.F.   *July 12*

I was delighted with His Grace's letter urging *The Times* to ask the Bishops to tell the Clergy to pray to God for rain.

B.E.F.   *July 14*

I can't bear the story about Orpen's spy. It quite worried me until I dismissed it from my mind, as the lady did the story of the Gospels, with the comfortable reflection that it all happened long ago and let's hope it isn't true.

B.E.F.   *July 17*

How silly of Alan not to show you my letter. I wonder why. It was written for your eyes, as all I write must be, and all I do. You

* *Two Gentlemen of Verona*, act iii, scene 1.
† Coventry Patmore: *A Farewell*.

say I must not love you less. Oh, my darling, fear anything but that. Surely I have more grounds of fear than you have, for you still live among wine and roses and love, surrounded by the ardent youth of England, and the still more ardent middle-age and eld, while I see nothing but dusty veterans lumbering about in sweat and lice. But even if I were on Calypso's isle with Helen to wait at table and the Sirens coming in to sing after dinner, I can imagine no enchantments or enchantresses which could lure me from my fidelity.

B.E.F.   *July 23*

A very pretty letter from you today in which you spell propaganda "propregander" and "propergander" (I prefer the second) and in which you calculate that £8 a week works out at *over* £200 a year. You angel.

B.E.F.   *July 26*

It is so pleasant here—more like one's old-fashioned ideas of war —standing on the top of a hill and seeing the battlefields all around you. We can see miles of the country held by the enemy which looks much closer from here than it does from the front line. And ten miles away we can see—and lovely it looks through glasses— the ruins of the cathedral which once graced the hiding-place of a rash old man.*

These new poets—all that I have read—seem to me especially bad about the war. They can't see anything in it but lice and dirty feet and putrid corpses and syphilis. God knows that nobody living loathes the war more than I do, or realises more fully the waste and folly and universal unrelieved unnecessary harm it does. But there is romance in it. Nothing so big can be without it. And there is beauty too. I have seen plenty from our parting at Waterloo until today. And those poets ought to see it and reproduce it instead of going on whining and jibing. And the ones that don't whine say it is all so glorious because we're fighting for liberty and the world set free, and to hell with the Hohenzollerns, and the Yanks are com-

* Arras. See *Hamlet*, act iii, scene 4.

ing. This attitude of course is even more tiresome than the other. I think Rupert Brooke might have continued to do it all right. He started well.

B.E.F.   *July 28*

This morning I have been undergoing instruction in patrolling, which means learning how to crawl, which most of us can do before we walk and I found I hadn't forgotten. But it was bad crawling weather this morning and I didn't enjoy it.

I send you a dreadful photograph taken just before the last battle. I look like a startled hare that has suddenly seen a joke.

There was no letter today. All the posts are very much upset by this tiresome advance. The last letter was addressed 3rd Battalion Gren. Gds., 88 St James's Street.

We have a new doctor whose name is Coffin. Would you believe it? I couldn't at first but it's true and it delights me. It's so Dickens.

Goodbye, when are you going to marry me?

B.E.F.   *August 9*

This must be a short letter as it is written in my sleep-time and I am tired. All last night I was crawling and I am to do the same tonight. I like it as long as the ground is dry, though the thistles rather spoil it. It's just like stalking.

B.E.F.   *August 11*

These last two nights I have spent crouching and crawling. As I lay flat on the dun wet ground I pictured your party at dinner—Birrell fingering his port-glass benignly meditating a roar, Edwin, stomach thrust forward with sunken chin and listening eyes, Scatters holding the table and the attention of all with infectious smile and slightly frog-like expression of lust, Venetia fingering her hair, speaking seldom and with quick assurance while watching with anxiety the servants, the food and the wine, Mary slightly flushed and windblown, speaking with that appearance of diffidence which conceals self-confidence and self-content, you leaning forward and from side to side like the conductor of an orchestra, calling at will for the right sound from each instrument, yourself bright and animated and beautiful as the Mother of Love. That, you see, is what I am thinking of when I ought to be thinking of the enemy and of a thousand other things. We have a password when we go out on patrol, and last night I nearly gave them "Diana" but I was too shy to. Would you like to think of fierce men crawling about No Man's Land in the darkness and whispering your name to one another when they meet?

This afternoon in lovely sunlight and heat I went for a little crawl by myself and had rather fun. I found an arm sticking out of the earth. I don't know what impulse made me take off the glove. The arm had been there a long time and there was little left except bones. The hand was beautiful—thin and delicate like the hand of a woman and the nails had grown long and even like a mandarin's nails. How much the flesh may once have hidden the beauty of the framework you couldn't tell, but it must always have been a small hand and I think the owner must have been proud of it because gloves are not usually worn at the war. It gave me no feeling of disgust or uneasiness but rather content to find that beauty can still hang about the bones, surviving the corruption of the flesh, and staying with the body until the bitter end of complete annihilation. The hand was raised and the fingers curved in rather an affected gesture. I wish I could have kept the glove. My brother-officers were amazed at my lack of squeamishness in removing the glove from a corpse, and yet they would think nothing of treading on a beetle. How different we are.

When I came in from my crawl I found a hard case to deal with. Some stretcher-bearers carrying down dead and wounded this morning had during their absence been despoiled of their few belongings by their brave companions. It is apparently understood that when a man is killed or wounded his comrades instantly pounce on his belongings, but to take those of the stretcher-bearers too was considered a bit hot.

And Oh! I hadn't finished the story of my crawl. I finished by getting back into our own trenches at a sentry-post without being detected by the sentry, which shows how clever I am and how bad is the British Army.

TO NORFOLK IN THE RAIN

Breccles, Norfolk   *August 2*

I had to leave London today unconsoled by my daily delight and I must face erratic posts in this primitive county. I travelled down by train in floods of rain with Scatters and Birrell, starting with a firm resolve of reading and silence. It hit poor Scats cruel hard, for he can't read although he had armed himself with a new-bought half-calf copy of the *Oxford Book* which I thought incomparably funny. Birrell read a life of Tom Moore and I had a little quiet cry over Eddie [Marsh]'s new edition of Rupert Brooke's poems with memoir attached (I'll send it tomorrow). Harling Road, the station for Breccles, has no cover and a platform a mile long, so in sheets of rain we descended a drop of some five feet from compartment to ground. Imagine the horror of seeing Birrell take a crowner on his back, heels and umbrella waving in air, a Victorian comic cut, but inexpressibly painful. Then I dropped Scatters's 50/- *Oxford Book* into a puddle and before we got off in our shoddy open Ford our wretchedness was crowned by the sight of 300 happy happy prisoners packing into closed Rolls lorries. The house is if possible more impossible than last time, more moths, fewer lamps, more creakings, worse belfry-smells. I heard Birrell muttering "This is a house for the young" as his head cracked on a beam, showering him with wormwood dust, but it has the advantage of transfiguring Edwin, and tonight with Mary Herbert and me flanking him, good wine and lessened raid-funk, he was a man of hope and light, till Birrell (the ox, the fool) roared at him "Why do they want to label your scheme 'Home Rule for India'? It's done now, but the phrase stinks of failure." He never smiled again. We discussed "bores" at dinner and whether anybody could steer quite clear of the epithet. I thought Hugo safe but was shouted down. Rib* was not passed. Birrell himself I think is free of any taint, but I didn't say so, then Edwin made my blood run fast and glowingly, for he cited you alone as never having bored him. Now we are all in our beds, and I have got the George Moore book that is only privately printed because of its obscenity, but it looks as dull and monotonous as a drain-inspector's treatise.† I have been thinking that journalism, with Max's backing, might be a lucrative and honourable livelihood.

* Lord Ribblesdale.   † *A Storyteller's Holiday* (1918).

Could you not write an article or so about the beauty others have missed at the war?

Breccles   *August 4*

I have never borne three days letterless. Curse the ramshackle set-up and this barbaric county. The party goes well enough. Birrell is subjected now to a weak giggling state whenever Scatters opens his mouth, like you rather, and to exclaiming repeatedly "What a fancy it is!" Scatters has no respect for his age, but pulls spoons out of his pocket before servants and calls him "darling" or "old sweet." To lunch arrived Lutyens, and Chapman from a neighbouring house. At 2.45 I suggested to Birrell a project of church two miles away at three. He jumped at it and in the twinkling of an eye Mary and he and I were tramping across country as zealous as converts. What I ask myself did Chapman think? How did he explain this piety, not seeing his own presence at the board was as good as a church bell? No reading today—chess instead and Scatters the champion beating Venetia repeatedly. A pretty spectacle was at midnight. Edwin having gone to bed, the rest of us strolled into the garden for half an hour's exercise, somersaults, standing on heads, dancing, flying machine, etc. while Birrell stood stone-still in centre holding a little candle amazed, for all the world like "This lanthorn doth the horned moon present, myself the man i' the moon."*

B.E.F.   *August 4*

There was no letter from you today but I was feeling for some unknown reason so light-hearted and happy that even that misfortune did not depress me. I had a long sleep last night with troubled little dreams of you, interrupted and awakened by the sound of guns—our own guns—continually going off.

I have been enjoying the Aga's book.† He must be a very clever man if he wrote it.

It is a pleasant sunny day—the anniversary of the war. Where were you on August 4th 1914? I think you were at Rowsley. I dined that night with Patrick, Anne Kerr, Adele Essex and her

* *A Midsummer-night's Dream*, act v, scene 1.
† *India in Transition* by the Aga Khan (1918).

lamented husband at the Ritz. After dinner we went back to Bourdon House and I left them to play a rubber while I went to the Foreign Office to hear the latest news. I came back and told them we were at war with Germany. I think we played another rubber and then George Essex went wisely to bed. Adele, Anne, Patrick and I drove round London in an open taxi to hear the fools cheering. Ringing their bells before wringing their hands, if ever bells weren't rung and hands were. They sat back to the driver because of their hair and Patrick and I lolled like Pashas opposite.

Did you read Lord Lansdowne's letter in *The Times* two days ago? I thought it excellent and sensible and written in the grand manner. There have been replies to it which mean nothing. I feel so very strongly sometimes about politics. I'm afraid you never do. And I don't find myself in agreement with anybody. I used usually to agree with Patrick. But now the *Morning Post*'s silly reactionary jingoism irritates only a little less than O.'s silly contemptible pacifism. Lord Lansdowne is the man for me. Do you know him? I like his appearance but I have never spoken to him. He had an ancestor at the end of the eighteenth century whom everybody hated and who was always right.

I suppose the country must be ruled by Northcliffe, Bottomley and (with all due respect) Beaverbrook. This letter ought to have been written to Katharine in the shape of an anti-democracy essay. I apologise for inflicting it on you, but you said the other day—God bless your eyes—that you liked me to write without restraint and let whatever was simmering in my heart boil over and pour on to the paper. Unluckily this afternoon it was politics. It shan't occur again.

B.E.F.   *August 5*

We go up again tonight. The first four days we shall spend in the unpleasant place which is full of flies and rats and smells of corpses. The prospect is not very cheerful as it is pouring with rain and, which is sadder still, Wine Red is going to leave us in three days to command another Company. However, with my full flask in one pocket, my little writing-case with your pictures in another, my *Shakespeare's Comedies* in a third and my cigars in a fourth, I feel armed to meet a sea of sorrows.

You did very well to send *Boufflers*.* I remember your showing it to me once when you were ill and I have always been meaning to read it. I have hardly laid it down all day. It has amused me almost too much, because it hasn't let me go to sleep, as I meant to do, with the prospect of none before me tonight. There are so many points in which they are like you and me. She makes him promise not to gamble, he breaks his promise, their friends do not realise their love which they conceal, they are separated, she writes him a diary of her life. At a gay party she takes advantage of the darkness to cry, and she usually writes to him at night. I have only read half of it at present.

Poor Chevalier and poor Madame de Sobran. They are on my heart today. They weren't very happy, but they had far greater opportunities than we have. He goes to the war too, but what a pleasant, easy little war. And their supper parties sound more fun than ours. He says in one of his letters to her: "I am like a miser parted from his treasure," which is just what I said to you not long ago. They quarrel a lot. We used to quarrel once, but never shall again.

B.E.F.   *August 7*

I have finished *Boufflers* today. What an exquisite end to the story. I was so glad. Their marriage didn't lessen the romance of their love. It isn't a very good book but I am very grateful for it. There is too much irrelevant history of the Revolution but I can never have too much of that.

B.E.F.   *August 8*

Did my letter cross yours in which we both suggest journalism as my future? Odd if it did. I would write the article that you suggest but I doubt whether the *Daily Express* would care for it.

Breccles   *August 5*

It's a funny situation—Birrell and three young women in the house—and rather wearing too, though mostly for Venetia who

* *The Chevalier De Boufflers: a Romance of the French Revolution* by Nesta H. Webster (1916).

192

unselfishly took him a seven-mile walk while Mary and I slept. To-night he told a story that amused me rather of Stephen, a poet (J. K.?), saying that because Heaven lies about us in our infancy, there was no reason why we should lie about Heaven in our old age. It was capped by Venetia quoting Harry Cust's phrase that Heaven lies about us in our infancy and Evan lies about us when we grow up. You probably know them both, but I did not. I submit with diffidence.

Breccles   *August 8*

They brought me news tonight of a British offensive. I turned sick and could see no beauty in the twilight glow or the country's peace, which I had relished all the day. No papers ever wing through the wastes of desolation that surround this lovely house, and in my fever and ravings of last night your danger, generally so cruelly present, was lost in the plans of future joys. I have had to bring a lot of strength and heroism forward to keep curbed a breakdown of tears and shudders and conspicuous coward-dice.

It was a jolly ten-mile drive to market this morning in a dog-cart through poppy-fields with a big gamp and a sack for the stock. Re-turning we looked like "flitters"—the trap overladen with fry-ing-pans, pudding basins, a commode, gridirons, various tins, a terrier and two of the rosiest, tenderest, sweetest grunting pigs. We chose them out of thirty and took an hour to do it, with an old Colin Clout tipping us winks about points to fasten on to. "Furst count the tits" was his happy wrinkle, seizing a grunter by the back legs and counting off in pairs. Nothing under twelve should satisfy. That is something learnt. Our two pigs are regular beasts of Ephesus.

A letter was waiting for me, or rather Wade was, because now she likes to hand me yours. It's for her a moment of intimacy in her day and I believe like mine her happiest, bless her.

Breccles   *August 11*

Alas! I didn't send you *Boufflers*. In a hundred years shall *we* be read? I fear not, but all's one.

Breccles   *August 16*

I did not hear of you from Tuesday at Ashby (which I counted as Monday in London) till Friday, and against all reasoning I thought you dead and my joy dead with you. I woke, as I foretold you I would, at first dawn, and by nine I was crying. The smoke-grimed vault of Paddington at eleven seemed, as William met me with one fluttering letter, suddenly a pleasaunce, shining with peace and light. A sad letter but very beautiful, my darling. What a strange impulse to unglove the dead hand. You could only have done it alone, and I wonder how you told them you had done it, or why you told them, or perhaps you never did. It makes a great impression on me. I have thought of it all day.

Rutland Hospital   *August 20*

It's all true what is said about love—the ennobling power of it. Tonight as I drove home alone my thoughts were of my nightly happy duty—this duty, the first I have ever found to be a fine pleasure and an unselfish one too in its search for expression and words to give you satisfaction. This evening I feared a little to have nothing to tell save the twice-told, 1000th-told tale of devotion. The fear was a proof of zeal to please you. All my home life has been a wish to please authorities (supported by a benefit to be derived from the success of it) and only through deception was it achieved. How serene, in contrast, is the belief that the nearer my utterance is to truth, the more joy will it breed. When before has one framed truth or striven for a more convincing way of declaring it?

At three I ticked off poor poor C. and took a train (standing in outrageous heat) to Wallington, forty minutes away. He met me at the station, greyer and older and cruelly stained in outlook by solitary confinement. I was shocked at his state, and in answer to my questions he admitted that the internment was indefinite. Incredible. He offered me a graveyard or a public park as a resting and talking place. I grasped at the churchyard, so we sat there for an hour on a mouldering heap with great beauty of surroundings. We strolled into the church and I was struck by many symbols denoting taste and ill-advised sentiment of whoever is in command there.

There were several inscriptions to the fallen, briefly and most beautifully constructed and chiselled into the wall itself, as I have seen only at Mells, and also I noticed that in the middle of the choirstall was a wreath perpetually renewed, and on the seat a cassock and now crumpled surplice in memory of a soldier choirboy. I wondered how long with luck it would stay there, and the sad day when it must be removed, if any who knew him still lived, and it flashed into my mind too how excruciatingly funny if in ten years, when the old men must fight and the young choirboys in the fullness of time are called up, and when all the choir have paid the debt to patriotism, how dramatic, how funny, to see a real choir invisible, invisible to all but their empty garments. O dangerous precedent!

Rutland Hospital   *August 22*

   The days I have dreaded almost most are upon us. Your letter of the 9th came on the 22nd, together with one of so much love and tenderness written on the 20th that it frightened me more than any warning. I have not known what to do with my easeless self, telephoning unceasingly to Osbert for news, which he never had, and lunching with him. Bed all the afternoon in despair, and up at seven to go and meet K. Every means of locomotion is on strike, so for ten minutes I wrestled with a man in the pub to take me to Victoria. At last he consented on condition of high payment and instant dismissal. Suddenly half-way down St James's he stopped and asked me if I was the young lady who went rowing with the officer on the Serpentine some months ago and gave him some sweets for his children. Then I started crying and he said he'd wait up for either of us all night, and I poured out my misery of fear to him, relieved to find anyone to whom I could. K. never came, though I waited for two trainfuls of uproariously happy people. It was a cruel disappointment, for she might have heard some news. I feel so certain that the Guards are in, though Osbert clings to the chance that the Third Army is all we have heard to suggest it, but *I* have your love letter. I went down to Mulberry Walk for an hour and found Alan engrossed in his typed anthology of London, dedicated elaborately to Viola, Diana and Duff (another rain of tears).

Wilton Park, Beaconsfield   *August 25*

When I put out my light last night after writing, all command of thought vanished, a surging mind vanquished my hope of sleep, and a realisation that I had neglected any formation of plans, for eventualities. I thought of you desperately, maybe mortally ill in France, and how my coming to you should be accomplished. I had to settle everything then—my first step, who I should make my appeal to? A. J. Balfour? Cowans?* Beaverbrook? A threat of *suicide* if they opposed, and how it should convincingly be phrased; my luggage and what it should include—V.A.D.s clothes, officers' khaki, in case. Whose? Frankie de Tuyll's in London and my size. Money—easily asked of Max—£50. My letter to Mother—all the wording of a frank and total confession, not to be sent till I was entrained. I know (and still know) they cannot keep me from you. Then finally my finding you. It all possessed me too much. A turbulence, not to be quieted by sitting at the open window, or smoking, or will-power, racked me. Seven struck before I slept, and today I have felt a trial to my companions though a little calmed by a morning and evening anonymous enquiry to the War Office.

Perhaps this may be all a prophecy. I calculate you went in on the 21st and that by now bad news would have sought me out, but how vague are one's conjectures. It's all imponderable. My darling, I write these silly papers about myself, when I should be encouraging you and praising you and convincing you of my courage and belief and hope in you. No one but you among the fighting millions is thought of so continuously or adored more.

B.E.F.   *1 a.m., August 23*

Had no moment to write. Am safe, well and happy. Have no moment now. Telephone to Mother to say all is well. I have been wonderfully lucky for two days, and three letters from you ten minutes ago crowned my luck. I adore you. *Don't worry.* Probably shan't be able to write tomorrow. The Germans are charming and always surrender.

* General Sir John Cowans, then Quartermaster-General.

DUFF COVERED WITH GLORY

I have so much to say, so much to tell you, so much to thank you for, so many lovely letters to answer and their beauty to comment on, that I feel like St John when he completed his Gospel in despair of ever writing all he had to say.

I am going to shirk telling you of the first day of the battle by sending you the rough copy of the official report I had to send in.* Please don't show this to anyone except in great and *safe* confidence. I fear it may not convey much to you. There was, you know, from the start at 5 a.m. until about 10.30 a thick mist. One couldn't see a yard. Captain Fryer is Wine Red.

The second day we remained where we were in boiling sun under heavy shellfire suffering from thirst. I have been thirsty all my life but never quite so thirsty as that. We thought to be relieved that night and lived on the hope. But as night came on we learned, first that we were not to be relieved, and then that we were to make another attack at 4 a.m. My platoon of thirty was then reduced to ten, and at the last minute as we were forming up for the attack I discovered that my serjeant was blind-drunk—a dreadful moment. And it was followed by the most glorious of my life. A full moon, a star to guide us, a long line of cheering men, an artillery barrage as beautiful as any fireworks creeping on before us, a feeling of wild and savage joy. It is a picture that will hang in my gallery for ever and will come next in value to three or four dozen in which you figure. The whole battalion won their objective under the scheduled time. I was the first of my Company in the German trench. I boast like a Gascon but it was what the old poets said war was, and what the new poets say it isn't.

And then, darling, but this is a secret—I am covered with glory. When first I realised this, the Commanding Officer speaking to me in terms that made my head swim, my one thought was that the Chevalier de Boufflers had thought by obtaining military glory to render himself in the world's eye worthier of Madame de Sobran. And I wondered how a medal would weigh in Her Grace's scales—lighter than a leaf, I feared—certainly lighter than a strawberry leaf.

* This has disappeared. Duff also wrote a diary account of the battle.

197

Personally I am as proud as a peacock, though I have an affectation of modesty that is very deceptive.

Darling, I haven't begun to write to you to tell you what I want to say, to thank you for letters and books and lovely pictures, but I want this letter to go tonight and I rather want now to go and listen to the band and gossip about the battle, so I will go on tomorrow.

B.E.F. August 26

Half my ease at coming out of the battle was spoilt and still is spoilt by the thought that you are probably still worrying. I do hope you may have been able to get some news before you get my letter, which I fear is not with you as I write. And I am sure that the last one I wrote you before the battle must have alarmed you as it was written a little on the farewell note. I meant it to be a paean not a *vale* but the wrong note crept in. Forgive me.

B.E.F. August 27

The incident of the taxi-driver is so beautiful that it must have lightened that dark day. Bless his kind grateful heart and remembering eyes. That was the day you cried waiting for me at the flat. Cast your secrets upon the Serpentine and you shall find them after many days.

Now I am waiting for a horse to carry me to Details. So if the battalion does go in again, which is possible, I shan't go with them. I confess very reluctantly to the faintest tinge of regret should this occur. I have come to be a little—only a very little—sentimental about my platoon, and don't quite like to think of the ten survivors going back to the battle without me. As we were coming out on Saturday evening, marching peacefully and very slowly over these quiet uplands where men didn't dare show themselves three days before, lit by a perfect sunset, the tired men crooning popular songs as they went, the Commanding Officer and the Brigadier rode by. And I heard the Commanding Officer say: "That's Duff." The Brigadier came up and praised me till I blushed and sweated. He said that the whole Brigade had done marvellously but that my platoon had simply shone. I wished so then that you could share my content that moment, for my happiness was marred by knowing that you were probably miserable.

Don't, darling, repeat to anyone all the boastful stories which my vanity makes me tell you. It is not my vanity only but my desire to make you share all my joy.

B.E.F.   *August 28*

Another cry of anxiety written on the 23rd. Poor pretty bird, I am glad you thought I should not fail. I have just read the Commanding Officer's report of the battle. It is mainly unintelligible but ends up:

Outstanding features of the Attack.

(1) The splendid leading of No. 10 Platoon by Lieut. Duff Cooper.

(2) Cooperation of No. 10 Platoon and No. 1 Coy. [Wine Red's] in taking strongly held enemy position without the assistance of artillery barrage and tanks and in broad daylight.

(3) The importance of a second water-bottle.

I alas only had one.

B.E.F.   *August 29*

Here comes the post. Is there one from you? I wait.

Oh, the excitement of the slow distribution—a cross-eyed man clumsily fingering the thin envelopes, gazing doubtfully at the officers, who go on reading, writing, playing patience, hiding their anxiety. One letter for me and that from you, darling. Oh faithful heart.

B.E.F.   *August 30*

My poor little Bushey friend, Gerard Brassey, has been killed. I am very sorry. He did so hate being a soldier and wanted so much to have fun and had so little.

This has been a bad day, for the post didn't come till 5.30 and all the afternoon was spent in waiting. I had a letter from Mother enclosing your telegram to her. Very odd about the War Office—I can hardly believe it. She, bless her heart, has had no anxiety at all. As I never told her I was going to the battle she hadn't presumed that I was. So with her my policy worked admirably. But I won't do it again with you, darling. We have got to get up early to-morrow to do a sham battle. It is really too silly to ask us to do it within a week of a real one.

Rutland Hospital   *August 27*

The light of everything is changed with a letter from you this morning. I am mad with relief and pleasure. I did not write yester-day because K. arrived at last, and I lay talking with her till 5.30 this morning. Today comes, too, horrible news of Lance Page's death —the entire tragedy to my poor old Podgie. The imagination fails to encompass but in the huge selfishness of my happiness I cannot think of it.

Will write tonight. Your scribble of safety, I must tell you, is in the style of a demented man. Is it "shock"?

Rutland Hospital   *August 30*

If you had told me of a heart grey and shaking with dread of pain, or of stabbing men that they might not ask for help, I would love you no less, nor am I in any way astonished—well, yes, I am a little surprised in Fortune's attitude, knowing her hostility to me. You have blamed me for having so little belief in the capacity of those I love, and yet I was as sure of you in this respect as I might be of the sun's shining, so all my jubilance has gone to join yours and I soar above tragedy today in thinking of your delight and sud-den tyranny over people's opinion of you. I see you as a tried Mars and would rejoice in Vulcan's net.

I cannot cease to read your letters and account. I know the direc-tion of the Shropshires' steps and the Tanks' civility and the general early tone of derelicts. I had, strangely enough, had such a vivid picture of a railway-backgrounded action. Did I write to you to that effect? I love the C.O. for pointing you out as "Duff." I love to think of your men's pride in you as you reached the guns. I love to think that even strangers will admire you as I do, and I dread to think of your disappointment if it all gets forgotten, as many such things have, without ribbons for your love's hair to proclaim your bravery.

Tell me truly any succeeding and belated appreciations and commendations. Write like a peacock of Gascony. It delights me. I told K. and Venetia and A. under seal of secrecy. Why should it not be known if you are not quoted as informer? Tell me when I may brag.

Viceregal Lodge, Dublin   *August 31*

I cannot put your success out of my head, I'm glad to say. All day wrapped round with travelling *contretemps*, I felt willing and civil and ready to irradiate my happiness to others. So you see, my dearest, what a crown you are to me and how my credit must rise and fall with your fortunes.

A dreary journey with Mother and Kakoo and no Wade, for she is holidaying, and I miss her most terribly, apart from her help technically. I love her pleasure in handing your letters and her silent loving company. There is a wicked change in this house from last year—no comforts, no royal flair, no lace sheets, worse no fires or stationery in the bedrooms. The same curtsey at the door though, and tonight an enjoyable dinner next Harry Chaplin, who, after getting me to read him the menu aloud, a merely sensual wish since he was out for two helpings of every dish though they'd been tripe and blubbers, embarked on eye-witnessed descriptions of the American Civil War. On my other side was a man name of Barrie who had been on duty at the Viceregal the night of the Phoenix Park murders, so you will see from this I was well out of the nursery.

Viceregal Lodge   *September 1*

Talking after dinner to the new Under Secretary's wife, a dowdy-looking middle-class soul, who had she been English must have been Mrs Page or Mrs Lloyd George, but being Irish and with a brogue like Maire O'Neill answered my description of the Phoenix Park fornications with "And isn't it a fine thing to ignore the public?"

Viceregal Lodge   *September 3*

I have had a true grievance. I got a letter tonight dated 30th and my last reached London Thursday and was of the 26th, so either the mails have gone crazy or it is true that you have been bewildered and puffed by pride out of touch with me, and very soon your deeds will be forgotten, and more than probably never recognised, and you'll regret the forfeit of a fraction of my love. My blessed, I forgive you, and really today I feel so sad about Brassey, who loved you so. Poor little thing, with a life spent in preparation alone.

Viceregal Lodge   *September 6*

Your mother wrote this morning enclosing a letter from Streatfeild.* It's all very great and fine for us all. Strange that such an eventuality never occurred to me before. I set no value on the hope so didn't hope, and yet now it seems this is what's made me happiest since you left. Such luck (forgive me, darling) is so seldom touchable by us that our whole strength of hope is negatively directed, and "not death" is all our prayer.

Perhaps I put your triumph too much on luck. I really in my heart think it is all your due, but in a strange kind of defence for the others I find myself declaring for chance. In valour weren't they all Herculeses? But they had little to flaunt.

Viceregal Lodge   *September 7*

To my other neighbour I couldn't help drawing a little diagram on the clean cloth of your heroism, without names and asking what it might fetch. He said a V.C. simply and quietly, but then admitted that so much depended on how important it was on the battle effects, and more on how it was represented by the C.O. It was perhaps silly, but such fun for me. If only dear General French were still C. in C. there'd be no question, for he pronounces lastly on each deed, and with me and Ghastly Moore to show him truth, your fame should have excelled. As it is, the Guard is a modest Guard, and so you'll hear no more about it. An M.C. isn't dusty though.

B.E.F.   *September 18*

The Tale of Chloe† is even more beautiful than I remembered. Perhaps I get its beauty intensified by seeing you as the Duchess all the time and Katharine as Chloe. I put it first of his works and of

---

* Colonel Sir Henry Streatfeild was the Colonel commanding the Grenadier Guards 1914–19.
† By George Meredith.

all short stories. The artistry of it is so admirable. The atmosphere begins with the lightest of light comedy, the sinister note is first struck when Chloe plays with her silken cord and gives answers full of what the Greeks called tragic irony (or perhaps what we call it when the Greeks use it, which they always do). After the most beautiful bedroom scene in the sixth chapter you begin to know it won't end happily. The light fades and finally goes out with the sun on Camwell kissing Chloe. The stage is set for tragedy and the audience ready. Perhaps the realism of the Duchess fingering the corpse which falls on her is a little too horrid—perhaps it isn't. You must read it again and tell me, and one day we will read it together. Goodbye, little Duchess of Dewlap.

B.E.F.   *September 21*

Your letters have taken to coming in pairs again, bless them. There were two today. I have written to thank Venetia for that melon. Aren't I good? I write continually to Katharine but she doesn't answer. She must have taken a dislike to me.

More officers are coming out to us, which is good. I really ought to get to Paris soon. If you were married to me you could meet me there. Why aren't you, pray? Oh, I am weary of the war—weary of the society of soldiers, the colour of khaki, the jargon of militarism, the dullness of safety, the discomfort of danger, the barren wasted country and the autumn weather.

> Tired with all these, from these would I be gone,
> Save that, to die, I leave my love alone.*

Belvoir Castle   *September 15*

I haven't thrown off my dejection yet and am so unpopular in consequence except with Father, bless him. He has a *Schwärm* for me at the present and still regards me, as he has since I went to Guy's in 1914, and through all the successive debaucheries, lethargies and "ambuscades" of the last four years, as a patriotic self-obliterating martyr, overworked and unfortunate. (Incidentally he is quite right.) We all are, thanks to this vile age.

* Shakespeare: Sonnet lxvi.

Belvoir Castle   *September 17*

It's lucky this bit of life is nearly over. The monotony is very
wearing. The only truly agreeable time is from tea to dinner (that
space you abhor so much) when I settle in John's room in the tower.
There with a nice book and a fire it is as quiet as the grave, although
John and Charlie are both working like shellfish building their
shells—laboriously, noiselessly and apparently movelessly. Kakoo
sometimes disturbs them but not more than a little draught. I broke
the stillness tonight by asking them what their work was. Their
voices answered fresh and proud: "Transcribing some letters of
George IV," and "Cataloguing my incunabula." If you know what
that is—I do.

Arlington Street   *September 25*

I naturally hoped the Grenadiers were battered out of all fight.
How can they again be bled? My cruellest fear is that you may be
thoughtless and flushed with past glory and risk all my life's hopes
to gild gold.

Arlington Street   *September 27*

I've just got a lovely letter from you before the battle. I am praying almost aloud that you are out again unscathed. It's a lovely
lovely morning, every tree still clothed and green, and the street will
be clear and brightly coloured when I go out. I have walked with
you on such mornings and once driven to Golders Green, and often
bought *brioches* for Fido's dainty breakfast in St James's Street.

I spoke too soon. Max has just rung me up to say the big English
attack is developing this morning, and incidentally that the Bul-
garians have asked for peace. I have a silly Steffie-like belief that if
I should control my fear (which I couldn't do) and think all well till
wrong is proved or strive to think of something else, as I do when
I think of Mother, that then I should lose my grasp of you that
tethers you to safety.

Arlington Street   *September 28*

Ivo, who I dined with last night, said a man called Menzies of the
Grenadiers said they all thought you should have a V.C. Claud

Russell had seen Jerry Villiers and spoken to him of you, and Jerry had said he could quite believe it—from the indifference you had always shown to your work, he thought it probable you would show the same to death.

Arlington Street *September 30*

I have got a great new money scheme. It dawned on me alone. I believe it's a flair. Capital must be scraped and planked on to the aviation passenger branch for after the war. It's Diana of the Crossway's husband and his railways over again, and steamships too. Beaverbrook shall do it for me. Scruples must fade—we must be happy. O my darling, are you safe? I only think of that, though I rattle on. See how my ideas bubble and squeak to-night. It's the stimulus they receive by greater hopes of your safety.

B.E.F. *September 25*

Tomorrow before dawn I fight a battle. I only fear death when I think of you, because you are all that I cannot bear to leave in life. Apart from you, I could be absolute. You must be brave and must remember that battles terribly disorganise the post. . . . Read no forebodings in the first pages. I have none.

B.E.F. *September 25*

A beautiful letter came from you in the dead of night. I think yours are the loveliest letters ever written and I hate to think of yours to me being lost by any misadventure. Light they could not see for many years, but after many years they might give light for ever. Should they ever fall again into your hands, you must give them to Alan, together with all your other ones at 88, and he should make a book of them. How I envy him the fun of annotations.

B.E.F. *September 27*

I have fought another battle and am none the worse. I haven't done anything to be puffed up about this time, you will be glad to hear, but we did what we had to do promptly and effectively and laid one of the cornerstones of a great battle. It was rather fun. We started in darkness after a wet night and there was a good deal of death about at first. Then the sun rose beautifully and the enemy fled in all directions, including ours, with their hands up, and one had a glorious victorious Ironside feeling of Let God Arise and let His Enemies be Scattered. And then they came back again over the hill and one was terrified and had a ghastly feeling of God is sunk and his enemies doing nicely. But we shot at them and back they went and God arose again. This happened three times. And now the battle has rolled away and I am tired, tired and wondering where I shall be tonight. I am so dirty. It was a shame to keep us three days in the line before fighting. The Germans hate the war even more than we do, thereby proving once more their superiority.

B.E.F.   *September 28*

We had a pleasant afternoon yesterday watching from high ground the battle rolling away in the distance and German prisoners marching towards us in battalions. Then in the evening we were relieved and came right back and had supper of sausages and spaghetti with plenty of wine. We were able to undress and sleep in comparative comfort, and this morning we washed and shaved which we hadn't done for four days. And with my buttered eggs I had three letters from my darling—one from the train and two from Wales. So you may imagine I am happy today, so happy that even Sidney [Herbert]'s dozen bottles of Madeira just arrived can hardly make me happier. Perhaps I should rather say content than happy, or hardly content but at ease—tired and safe and full of hope.

Exaggerated stories seem to be in circulation about me. I had a quite sickening one from Audrey congratulating me on being recommended for the V.C. You can imagine how she would handle such a theme. Of course you contradict such rumours.

Arlington Street   *October 1*

I'm on the cry again and Her Grace found me with crystallised cheeks. It's quite unreasonable but you must be lenient to great disappointment. I came in late and saw your letter on the hall table, brighter than the Bethlehem star. I thrust it into my breast and feeling it crackle was able to talk amicably about Eric and all sorts to Mother for forty minutes. I flew to my room and found it was a pre-battle letter—a dead pearl—and as I finished it disconsolate I saw Edward's darling eyes in a picture on my dressing-table and they frightened me with their tender pitying look.

Arlington Street   *October 2*

I am intoxicatedly happy to think of you safe, and your letters, all the day, are the cause. "Let God Arise," how good!

Venetia told me today she would open Breccles for your leave.

Arlington Street   *October 8*

You have made me feel so well and cured; as I walk down the streets high-headed and jubilant, people accost me with congratulation on your gain. Cardie and Bouch and Ralph for example. I felt last night that I had been a little damping over the whole flame and flare. It is ridiculous to act jealousy for the dead, yet I wrote in a tone of "Why should you have all the life and the fame and all the love, while they desiring more of these are dust?" It was out of a strange duty and faith, but what I really believe is that you must have everything and that you deserve the most.

May I put D.S.O. on the envelope? I do so like it.

B.E.F.   *October 1*

I am obsessed with the thought of Paris, tortured with fear lest anything should happen between now and the 9th to stop me going, tormented with impossible dreams of your meeting me there, constructing a thousand schemes to make your presence possible, harrowed with dread lest I should lose a letter addressed by you to the Ritz as I instructed.

Is Paris impossible? Cannot you rack your fertile brain, so cunning to contrive, so sure to execute? It would be the Austerlitz of your diplomacy.

B.E.F.   *October 3*

I wish it didn't make me so cross to be beaten at chess. A better loser at cards I've never met, but I can hardly be civil to whomever beats me at chess. When you beat me I pretend I'm not trying, and indeed how could I be expected to keep my eyes on the board?

B.E.F. *October 5*

I have just been sending home your letters—145 of them. I hated to part with them but it had to be done. They couldn't stand the war, bless their hearts. You see they were nearly always in damp places which is very bad for them. When I re-read them I often find that they have shut up again as though they had never been opened, like flowers that shut in darkness and only open to the sun. And then they cling to one another so that they can hardly be separated and grow limp and sad, and the marks of your little pencil grow fainter and fainter.

Life is strangely like a Shakespeare historical play these days with all its improbabilities.

Scene: A tent in Picardy. Soldiers playing cards. Enter a Messenger: "Bulgaria asks for peace."

Enter 2nd Messenger: "Bulgaria surrenders unconditionally."

Enter 3rd Messenger: "We have taken 10,000 prisoners."

Enter 4th Messenger: "The French have taken 20,000 prisoners."

Enter 5th Messenger: "An American Army is surrounded."

Enter 6th Messenger: "Turkey has made peace."

I suppose these are the spacious days which some people have sometimes wished for. Well enough in their way but I could have done without the space and should prefer a few of the people back who went to make the crowds.

Hotel Mirabeau, Rue de la Paix, Paris *October 7*

Carroll Carstairs and I left the war at daybreak yesterday and arrived at Amiens in time for lunch. It was delightful there—such a spirit of joy and victory abroad as made the eyes water. The streets full of parties of inhabitants returning, staggering under their household goods and carrying the canary in their right hand, all so happy to find their own house standing and that of their neighbour blown to hell. We had a gargantuan lunch and visited the cathedral which has been hardly in the least damaged. I met Sidney Herbert in the street, but he was with his Colonel and could only speak for five minutes. We arrived here at about half-past nine to find the Ritz and every other hotel crowded, so we came here which is really very nice and I can watch the Rue de la Paix from my first-floor windows. We had a little supper and a bottle of champagne in our sitting-room, played a game of cards and went peacefully to bed expecting to sleep for ages. But either the unaccustomed comfort of soft bed and linen sheets intervened or else the keen bright air of this beloved city woke me. At all events I could not sleep after seven but lay and read and breakfasted and was happier than any king that I have ever read of. My book was *Histoire Comique* of Anatole France. I had never heard of it and it's hardly worthy of him but quite worthy of me. When I at last got up and went out I was almost intoxicated with delight.

Perhaps my greatest pleasure has been my bath this morning. You have never been really dirty, so imagine what the joy must be when in that state to get into a bath of water which looks cleaner than what one is accustomed to drink.

We will come here when we are married and walk slowly about the sunny streets and linger for hours before the shop-windows, and you will enjoy everything that I enjoy, and I will enjoy you.

Hotel Ritz, Place Vendôme, Paris   *October 13*

As I was lying in my bath Carroll came in and said "The war is over." And really it would appear to be so and now we can be married and live happy ever after. Orpen spent the evening with us yesterday. O you silly baby to have believed his story of the Belgian spy. The lady in question is living in Paris and is Orpen's mistress. He says she was feeling a little tired the day he painted her. He deliberately invented the story in order to advertise the picture and got into some trouble with the War Office for doing so. I am so glad it isn't true. I had often thought of it since you told me.

Arlington Street   *October 11*

Such excitements since I wrote this morning. William (our dear ally) coming up met my eyes with a look of panic and appeal for several seconds, so unusual in a menial that I asked him if he was well. At ten he called Sister White down to His Grace's room and there raved at her madly—mad. Trembling and incoherently he tried to explain what he could not. He had dreamt of me, he said, and it had upset him terribly. He asked if he was a criminal? And if so what was his crime? He wanted to die before he did worse. It was due to the pictures he had seen as a little boy. He wanted to explain it to me and couldn't. Sister sent him to bed, quieted him a little and sent for the cook's husband to come and keep an eye on him. The whole story is like a lodging-house shocker. By one our beloved William, neglected for a few minutes by the cook's husband, had found a penknife in a drawer and forced its flimsy rust into his throat, narrowly missing the carotid, and after this he was borne away to a mental institution, and I feel really sad at the loss of him. He loved us both so much. Till now it has been a pointless story for you, but the interest begins and ends when I tell you that he went on after his throat was pierced murmuring "Duff Cooper, Duff Cooper, that little moustache. Has he really got the D.S.O., Sister? It's very fine, isn't it?" So that is why it has made such an impression on me. Poor man, it's real horror. The theories are many as to the cause of this defect. Is it sexual restraint? Or v. disease? He often raved "Women come to me but they don't want me." Is it fear of abnormality preying? I have nursed a similar case. I must go and see him tomorrow. Such a day for the servants. They are mad and totally disorganised with the stimulus of crime and tragedy, and the gold was gilded when news came that Marjorie's housemaid was on the Irish boat.*

Do you still love me, Duff? I dreamt last night that you returned, but your teeth were black and pointed like a dog's, and slightly blood-stained. I felt it to be the stain of the brutality of war (silly) and loved you less. A cruel dream.

Arlington Street   *October 12*

I don't know how to think of Peace and I am so certain we can hear the beating of its wings—the beating of your wings pluming for home. O dear, thank God for you—without your participation I could dread the war's end—the roll call and the cold blood's realisation of loss.

I send you a decoration of my own, found in old readings. Don't

* The S.S. *Leinster*, a passenger ship on her way from Dublin to Holyhead was sunk by a German submarine on the 10 October 1918.

let me for ever hear you brag brag bragging, or if it is to be my fate I must arm with some new eyes for my tail.

I had enclosed the following letter:

The fact is that Diana's dazzling Georgianism has licked up the fabric of the Pre-Messianic world, as flame licks up the stubble, so that the rate of obsolescence among all previous types can hardly be paralleled even in the province of naval architecture. She has telescoped time and shut up like an accordeon the inconsiderable ages which intervene between Olympus and Arlington Street. Because of her the daughters of many noble houses must bewail their virginity, bitterly regretting that they did not make hay before the sun shone. Theirs is the portion of weeds and outworn faces, and no man shall knock at their door till the Dustman calls to cart them away to the rubbish heap. Or do you think that, as there arose a Pre-Raphaelite school of painting, so there may some day arise a Pre-Artemid school of passion? I doubt it. ANON.

Arlington Street   *October 13*

The papers this morning intoxicated only. How disinterested the English are. I assure you that I walked out with an honest expectation of bunting and gaiety and of conductors asking their passengers their views, of more loungings at street-corners and civility from taximen, but both among the People and the Ritz the crowd wore the same look and talked as detachedly as they did when Paris was near being held by the enemy. I had to lunch with Their Graces and Wolkoff, but for all my stirrings of hope and optimism, he said nothing brightening except a funny confession, that I believe all the world would confess at Judgment Day, that after such a disaster as the *Leinster* one scours the casualty list with more hope than apprehension, for a name one knows.

I prophesy the laying down of the German arms, a super-Sedan, almost immediately, if only to disappoint the Foch schemes. Besides, what men will fight, feeling they may be the last to be killed, peace perhaps declared and the news not penetrated?

B.E.F. *October 18*

Amiens is rather depressing after Paris. The best rooms that we can get have neither windows nor doors, which compares so un-favourably with the Ritz. But there are beds and sheets. We are now waiting in the hotel where Orpen lives and we hope he will be able to lend us a motor tomorrow.

This is not a nice letter, darling, but I am feeling ever so little depressed and I am harried and hemmed in. I wish I shared your optimistic view of the war. I think people are intoxicated by victory and unless the old hope of revolution in Germany comes true I don't see how it can end for a year or two. Has Mr Wilson committed us to "unconditional surrender and no peace with the Hohenzollern"? If he has there is no hope but German revolution.

Arlington Street *October 14*

I have a confession tonight, my bird of the golden feather, for you are that. Leaving, you gave me a key, to be used only under stress and necessity. Tonight for the first time since April, dining with Bouch, Ivo,* Philip, Hugo and four strangers, we were in despair for an evening's entertainment. An empty house was found and lobsters packed from the Ritz, but it was 9.30, "too late for everything." I hesitated, darling, and disinterestedly, for I wanted none myself as it happened, I thought that you would like me to do a Christ and convert a dry situation into wine, and that wine the best, so I sent Ivo packing with the golden feather of 88, and he returned with four Binet 1914, which will be replaced with great relish and a tender touch tomorrow. You will be pleased, or I do not know you.

Arlington Street *October 15*

This is my last quite peaceful night. Tomorrow I shall start the old weary season of tormenting days and nights—fears for your body, sadness for your mind and brave spirits, too fine and elect to suffer the tired despair of the war.

* Ivo Grenfell, Lord Desborough's youngest son. His two elder brothers had both been killed.

Arlington Street   *October 19*

I had lunch with Dudley Coats today, and he depressed me about the war, and told me that Peter Broughton-Adderley was killed and that it would last some months. I feel near tears and despairing this evening, perhaps because I have not been to bed till 2 a.m. for so many nights that my nerves are feeble. Dudley told me you had lost £200 at Mr Dod, of all idiotic games. O darling, it isn't faithful of you. I ask no other whimsical boons. Do humour me there. Is it to be an obstacle to happiness all my life?

Arlington Street   *October 20*

After I wrote last night, half-crazed with sleep and longing to be in the dark and alone, the full horror of Her Grace's last lonely years seemed to stare at me, so I made her comfortable with lights and occupation by my fire, and read aloud to her till 2 a.m. Nights at home wear one down more than nights out. I read about eight Maupassants and enjoyed it very much. You had read them all to me, I think, *L'Inutile Beauté* and *Mouche*, and one about a woman too frightened to say goodbye to her son dying of smallpox, and going mad, illusioned always into thinking her face was pitted—and many others.

Arlington Street   *October 22*

No letter today and Peace fading into dimmer future. They think here that the last note was humility exemplified. Your leave will be my armistice. Does it loom?

Arlington Street   *October 24*

Today I sold produce and orchids and made a great quantity of money—£100 from Bouch, £25 from Max, £150 from Caillard. I was proud but then beaten with fatigue and despair as I read an evening paper proclaiming Wilson's impossible note and making it only possible for the Germans to die hard and honourably, where the alternative is the same with dishonour. British killed from today I consider murdered, and the overthrow lengthened out for three years. Then, worse, I read of the Third Army's part in yesterday's attacks and a famous Division's fine work, and I turned sick, remaining so till now, when returning from Lady Ridley's bud ball next door, partially calmed by darling Ivo, I find a letter which liberates my soul from hell. It announces my heaven. Write news of it every day. I don't want you to walk in on me unprepared. I must lose no flavour of anticipation. Ivo thinks he is going to France next week and speaks of it with an illumined King Arthur expression.

Your mother was so sweet and came with £1 to the Red Cross shop. I flung her in some partridges. She's so excited.

Arlington Street   *October 27*

This pneumonia plague is ferocious. Lovely Pamela Greer, née Fitzgerald, dead in three days and my poor Alan pretty bad, though so far not pneumonia. I have at last had a real qualm of perhaps being struck (since there are seven cases in the house).

I am very perturbed about Alan, seeing what a frail subject he is and already breathless with asthma. Life is a procession of differently clothed fears led by the greatest, that is always shadowing you, but on you there is a shaft of light too, and when as now sometimes it illumines you out of the shadow, these conditions thrust out all the minor terrors crowding round me.

Arlington Street   *October 28*

I had looked forward greatly to today, for it was to carry Mother off to Beaudesert, and without anticipating anything illicit, by this remove made possible, I knew that I should walk with a freer step and read over my fire with more delicious calm. I do not exaggerate when I tell you that the poor darling got into the railway carriage, packed and tucked herself into the evening papers (Austria's peace to preoccupy her) and tea and solitude, and on trying her temperature and finding it normal (she considers it feverish for *her*) bundled home again and found me, I'm thankful to say, poring over my army forms.

B.E.F.   *October 28*

They have just come and told me that I go on leave on the 1st. It comes from the Adjutant and is probably true though it sounds too good to be. I will send you every breath of rumour of news about it every hour, but if I am lucky I may outspeed my letters.

The Montagus opened their house in Norfolk for Duff's leave, and it was there that we heard of the Kaiser's abdication. Had Duff still been in France I would have exulted with the rest, but with him beside me and safe the Peace did not give me a compensating relief. After so much bitter loss it was unnatural to be jubilant. The dead were in our minds to the exclusion of the survivors. Back in London, the Armistice so prayed-for seemed a day of mourning. Duff went to bed with the Black Death—influenza that was to kill as many as had fallen in the war, while I with my mother and whatever dull friends could be found dined at the Ritz Hotel. I could not bear the carnival and slipped secretly away to St James's Street to moan with Duff on his fever bed, and from there to push my way disconsolately through the happy crowds to a house of sorrow where I remained till next day. The battle was over. Its toll made triumph heavy-hearted. My own battle had now to be fought. With Duff recovered and immediately demobilised by the Foreign Office, our resolve to marry could have no obstacle but one.

CHAPTER ELEVEN

The Happy Altar

IT seems strange looking back that Duff, the love of my life, my cause, should ever have spelt anathema to my mother. He had never failed in anything he had undertaken, he had won glory in the war, he was popular with his generation and most of his elders. He was cultured and could quote her two favourite poets, Meredith and Browning, *ad infinitum*. Some scales had dimmed her dreamy blue eyes that were not to fall from them for many a day.

True, he had no money and was only a Foreign Office clerk, but with his pay of £300 a year and my allowance of the same amount and his mother's allowance of £600 (which she could ill afford) it was not too black a prospect. Had he been taller, more like Apollo, had he been more flattering towards her, more winning in his ways and generally more debonair, could we both have been more demonstrative and openly proud of our attachment, the ordeal might have been avoided. But his position irked him and I discouraged him from coming to Arlington Street.

Because of my inborn devotion to my mother I found myself shamefully afraid to tell her of our irrevocable resolve. One night, tired of my cowardly procrastination, Viola Parsons offered to come to Arlington Street and tell her what I found impossible to tell.

The telling was more terrible than we had feared. My

mother, who should have been expectant, was incredulous. She could not accept the razing of her castle in the air. I could hear her screams and moans and a night nurse being called from the hospital below with sedatives to calm her. I felt a murderess and could do nothing but wait sleepless for the unhappy morning. I think both I and Duff coped with it badly. I should have told her I was desperately in love and thrown myself sobbing on her mercy. Instead some silly pride forbade me to admit that I loved Duff. She would beg me to say that I did. I could not frame the words. Could she not see for herself that it was not for his wealth or titles that I wanted him as my husband? For what then but love?

Duff talked to my mother at an Albert Hall Victory Ball, of all unlikely places, probably dressed in motley, and was advised to request an interview with my father. In his diary Duff wrote:

At twelve o'clock I went to see the Duke. There was something grotesquely old-fashioned about the solemn interview with the heavy father. He received me very civilly, listened to all that I had to say, complimented me on the way I had said it, added that he had always liked me, and concluded by saying that he could not possibly allow the marriage and preferred not to discuss it. I asked him if he could give me any reason for his attitude and he refused to. I asked, was it money? He practically said it was not. I asked whether he had heard anything against me. He said he had heard nothing. I tried to make him see the silly unreasonableness of his attitude and hinted that it could only drive one to take the law into one's own hands, but he would say nothing except "I am sorry I can say no more." We were both very polite and parted with every civility.

I was rebelliously intolerant of this intransigence and suggested elopement. Duff counselled patience and persuasion. Had they but seen into the future, seen this despised hero housing me in the gilded rooms of the Admiralty, sailing the seas in H.M.S. *Enchantress* and laying me to sleep in Pauline Borghese's eagle-crowned bed in our Paris Embassy, how happy and proud they would have been.

My sister Letty was my ally, so up to a point were my brother and my uncle Charlie Lindsay. The friends of course were encouraging, though some there were who thought Duff had chosen unwisely. After many unhappy bedside talks with my mother I from pity agreed to abandon the thought of marriage for six months. Separation was not insisted upon, so the old life before Duff's war began again. The hospital was still full of wounded and 88 St James's Street again a refuge from tribulation. On the top floor, looking down Pall Mall, we would meet and read and plan our future life. It might have been a happy phase had I not felt that the cruel wound inflicted on my mother must not be allowed to heal. Every month I had to probe and turn the knife and plunge her back into her grief. I did it with the greatest reluctance, for truth to tell I loved her again with almost all my heart.

By March, the six months passed, she begged for another delay. To this unkind move I played an ace that always wins. I agreed in cold sorrow to have a winter wedding, honeymoon in the rain, be wretched in the interim and only hope that one of us did not die before the marriage day and send remorse to break her peace for ever. Then came a complete reversal of the tussle, when I was insisting on a November wedding while my mother begged for one in June.

In April Duff again asked my father for my hand and again let him tell of both our interviews:

April 30. In the evening Diana had her interview with her father. I met her afterwards at the Ritz. They have given in completely and are willing for us to be married as soon as we wish. It seems too wonderful, and hard to realise. The Duke, she says, was perfect and gave away the whole case by saying to her after the interview, which lasted only about ten minutes, "Don't go upstairs for a little. I don't want your mother to think I gave in at once."

May 1. At 6.30 I went to see the Duke, fortified with whisky but feeling almost as nervous as on the occasion of our last interview. He was extremely charming, could not possibly have been nicer or made it easier. He said a word or two about settlements. . . . Our interview only lasted about twenty minutes, for half of which he succeeded in talking about other things such as the growth of Bolshevism and the future of the Territorials.

My five weeks of engagement were a little sad. My father chose June 2 for the wedding. He wanted to get away for Whitsuntide before the trains were too crowded. He was a generous father and meant me to have a fine trousseau. Dresses, hats, coats and linen were bought, but a little in the tone of "The life you have chosen needs durable unfrivolous clothes." Except from the friends there was little rejoicing, and my own spirits suffered from feeling myself to blame and from the Cassandra predictions and warnings of troubles unforeseen— doctors, dentists, bailiffs, *accouchements*, debts, disease, and being "brought home on a stretcher." (This last was to happen only too soon.) Sympathy for our inauspicious romance fired all those we knew and all our parents knew, and strangers and tradesmen, to load us with silver and gold and all it buys: fat cheques, jewels from the family, a motor from Lord Beaverbrook, furniture to fill a house and a library of books—from Maurice Baring the only copy of a specially edited anthology called *A Century of Phrases and Verses*. Duff's mother gave me her mother's gold-and-turquoise dressing-case that must surely have belonged to La Dame aux Camélias. Venetia sent frilled sheets and monogrammed linen that have lasted till now, and there was gold plate and silver, clocks and chandeliers, a bigger though not better gilt dressing-case from Lord Wimborne, a picture of Duff by Lavery and one of me by Shannon and another by McEvoy, statuettes by Frampton, Mackennal and Reid Dick, a Gainsborough drawing, cabinets and carpets and mirrors, cellars of wine, *objets de vertu*. There was hardly room in the big house to show what was enough to establish us for years to come in comfort, luxury and beauty. But my mother's face was sad.

It was in June, as I had always hoped it would be, that my father drove me to St Margaret's. Too early dressed in my "state" of palest gold lamé covered with a rare lace of lilies, on my head a crown of seed-pearl orange-blossom, in my hand a rose that Ellen Terry herself had brought me in the morning, I sat in the familiar morning-room, immobilised beneath a vast tulle veil like a clock beneath its globe of glass. At last the hour struck. Old Nixon packed us into the car saying "You'll be late" as he had said to every guest leaving Belvoir for the train, and I left my dear long-sheltering home with a high heart. There were wedding crowds surging as there are today in Parliament Square, and the wedding bells were crashing, and fatherly mounted police were imperceptibly controlling the jolly riot, but my father was rattled as the car got held up by smiling multitudes of well-wishers. Impatiently he thrust his tall body and top-hatted, eyeglassed head through the window protesting "What's all this about? We must get on. What in the name of heaven is it all about?" Beneath the church porch a man rushed up, for all the world like the soothsayer Artemidorus on the Ides of March. "Read this," he said menacingly, presenting me with a missive. My heart stopped. I stayed to read. It was only some fan's good wishes. My two sisters' children were waiting to carry my train, three angels in misty gold and white. The organ pealed and pealed again with the *Meistersinger* march as we passed through the wide west door where Viola and Alan's three children were scattering roses. St Margaret's bells were ringing as we left the happy altar to rejoicings at home and to all the fulfilment of our honeymoon. My mother was smiling. That day had no shadow. As I drove away among showering rose-petals I knew that I need never lie again.

Philip Sassoon had lent us his house at Lympne, and from there we crossed to France and so to Paris. We were rich with presents and cheques and stayed at the Ritz, and I liked being called Madame and wearing a wedding-ring and being happy all the time. We *"déjeunéd sur l'herbe,"* dined under trees and loved the French and the whole generous world. From Paris we went to Florence, where my old friend Ivor Wimborne had taken Berenson's famous villa, I Tatti. There I first saw fireflies in their millions. We were shy because we were so newly married and not alone. From Fiesole we motored to Rome, with a night at Orvieto, where we didn't know that "Orvieto sings," and ordered bad champagne. In Rome we lived in grandeur at the Grand Hotel (a wedding present from Marconi) and we bathed in the Specchio di Diana and planned to live there. Our destination was the heaven of Lord Grimthorpe's Villa Cimbrone on the mountain height above Ravello. Thirty years ago it was a day's journey from Naples. We drove, accompanied by dear faithful Wadey, for three hours in a bus and a few hours in a *fiacre*, and then a long climb, followed by our boxes on bowed peasant shoulders. The house, set in its vast hanging gardens of lemons and olives and statues and quotations from Omar Khayyam carved on stone seats, seemed all that mortal lovers could demand. With too much zeal we ran down the two miles of hill and steps to the sea, bathed, lay rocking in a boat in the June sun and came back in the evening glow to our dinner cooked by the butler who was also Mayor of Ravello. He gave us a fish curled like a scythe holding a branch of honeysuckle in its poor gills, and wine made on the estate that fizzed a little and intoxicated a lot.

The next day, crippled by stiffness and raw from sunburn, I could move only on a donkey, and on its back the Mayor led me into the churches and round the altars. We could not bear it to end and thought foolishly that the return would be less prosaic, and also less hot, if we took a ship from Naples to Marseilles. Green as saplings we took berths in the ship that sailed on the day that suited us. It turned out to be a Rumanian troopship packed past its plimsoll line with soldiers. A violent Mediterranean storm blew up as we left. The troops were laid all over the decks and passages and were sick to a man. It was a dreadful journey, but at Marseilles the guns were banging away, not for war but for peace, which that day was declared.

In London we had no roof to our heads. We hesitated to return to the charity of Arlington Street. A close friend, Barbara McLaren (shortly to marry the famous Freyberg V.C.), lent us the beautiful house she had built in Westminster. It was from there that we pushed our way to the Peace procession in Pall Mall. I remember only Marshal Foch and the magnificent marching of the giant Americans who carried green wreaths. I think I cannot have looked at the English regiments. The Grenadiers especially must have inclined me to close my eyes.

Fireworks that night in Hyde Park drew us to dinner in Green Street. The hosts were Norman and Marion Holden, new friends who attracted us and who were to become loved neighbours in Sussex. It was drizzling a little when the first rocket screeched, so I put on some man's thick coat and rushed with the rest of the dinner-party to the lead roof. The sky was in-laid with fiery particles. The chimney-pots interfering a little with my vision, I must needs in the dark jump on to a slight elevation, the better to see. O fatal step! on to glass and through glass down-a-down two floors, with time enough, as Alice had, to see shelves passing before the thud that was to break my thigh. There I lay, a broken toy, on the floor of the linen cupboard. Through the round hole in the skylight glass I saw my hat, too big to follow my body. Soon Duff was on his knees by my side and above were the frightened faces looking through and down, fearful of asking me how I fared. I fared all right. It was curious to be so calm and collected, even capable of enjoying my efficiency and power. I knew first by a reassuring wriggle that my back was not broken, next that my femur was. My myrmidons I sent in all directions and they all obeyed my orders. It was Peace Night and traffic was virtu-ally off the streets. The doctors to a man seemed to be out celebrating. Our own old Dr Hood, living in the same street, did not answer his telephone.

The guests scattered on different missions, one to the nearest chemist to fetch chloroform (I knew that moving me would be horribly painful and that a self-administered whiff would tide me over), another to St George's Hospital to borrow a splint. Viola agreed to break the news to my mother. I told her to say "Diana has broken her leg *again*." Another friend had the task of finding my hero, Sir Arbuthnot Lane. A new nephew called Hirsch found a doctor on his own and brought him to me triumphantly. This feat caused me my only qualm, for, coming into the linen cupboard, he covered his face with his hands and said "Poor girl, poor girl." The planning worked like a clock. My mother arrived. Lane applied the splint. The chloroformed handkerchief numbed the pain of descent to a bedroom. Morphia quick—goodnight all—no one need worry.

Next day Lane set my thigh and again I was to lie, this time my leg hoisted high into the air with suspensions and extensions, for six weeks in a drawing-room of the Holdens'. It was August. The hosts left London and me in possession, my bed dolled up traditionally in a silly fantasy of four spotted muslin curtains rising to a centre of tricolour ostrich feathers, designed, I imagine, to disguise my high-flying leg. But there was much less frivolity and nonsense, no balloons or budgerigars, no officers in khaki or Prime Ministers or hilarity. I was a staid married woman, happy though broken, and Duff would be with me for an hour at lunch and from seven until the morphia was allowed to work. Morphia was nothing new or sinister or in the least menacing to me. In hospital I had given patients injections by the score. The restricted allowance for sufferers was already widening in the hospital world. It was buyable without prescription at any chemist in the early days of the war (a tube of quarter-grains was always sent in our war parcels of brandy, handkerchiefs, pencils and pocket classics) and I had come, in the days of my first broken leg, to treat the drug as a friend and then as a staunch partner in times of stress. I had welcomed it as a giver of Chinese courage and stimulus and ultimately dreamless sleep, and not as a knock-out drop. So, desperately uncomfortable as I was, on hardest planks, leg in air and no means of altering my position in bed, I would claim my daily "shot" at an hour that corresponded with Duff's time off, that I might be gay and stimulated for the happiest hours. He had learnt to drive Lord Beaverbrook's car very badly. I would recognise the frenzied hooting and jams of brakes and gears as he drove into Green Street. Sister Manley of the Rutland Hospital was my nurse. She cosseted and loved us both.

It was too good—too good to be good for me, I thought, so I sent for a mesmerist to save me from the doctor's warning of addiction. Well-famed he was, with a hundred cures to his credit. Like most young people I had been fascinated by hypnotism, and now was my moment to test its efficiency in calming those hideous sleepless nights. The good magician came to tell me my lids were getting heavy and to work with faith and tirelessness. How could I disappoint? Of course I closed my eyelids, of course I breathed heavily, of course I let him tiptoe out of the room before I called for my giggling nurse to give me a dose of the real stuff. Henceforward we kept two charts, one for the dedicated hypnotist: "natural eight-hour sleep" and another for the doctor: "$\frac{3}{4}$ gr. morphine at 10 p.m., nine hours' sleep."

I remember it as a happy time, but everything was happy. I swallowed my pride in returning to Arlington Street on a stretcher. Back I came to the golden drawing-room with my husband, my nurse, my morphia and a silly kitten called Kitty Marlow which we had bought on our one "day out" at Marlow before my fall. My parents were at Belvoir and Mrs Seed from the lodge cooked for us. I soon graduated to a wheel-chair. Duff, dressed in a black cloak-coat, white silk scarf and top hat, would wheel me round London. I would be in my trousseau "best," diademed in seed-pearls, for parties. Both of us would be mackintoshed for rain. Immediately after the war taxis were scarce and together we would wheel all over London to dinners, to plays, and pride ourselves on arriving first. The quartet I had loved at Chirk, which included Désiré Defauw and Lionel Tertis, came to play for me, and Olga Lynn would sing. Artur Rubinstein too would play us the things we clamoured for—Chopin and Albéniz. Once he hired a hearse to transport me in my chair to a concert in Hampstead. It was

too far for Duff to push me. Besides, Duff never really liked
music: he preferred silence. We did some entertaining. Max
Beaverbrook and Edwin Montagu and Winston dined to make
up a difference, and Iris Tree returned from America with her
charming husband Curtis Moffat.

In my chair on Saturdays and Sundays we went house-
hunting, chiefly in Bloomsbury, which I had always fancied for
its Georgian houses and tree-shaded gardens, and there in
Gower Street we found one. My mother not only approved
but longed to get her creative hands on to plans for improve-
ments. Already she was realising that a daughter dependent
and poor gave her more scope for help and invention than the
others who lived secure in their married estates. In my eyes the
house was beyond compare. It had particularly beautiful Adam
chimney-pieces and rounded corners to the large-windowed
rooms. A wall knocked down left a spacious hall. There was
a dining-room on the ground floor giving on to a strip of
garden with four forest plane-trees. The polished stone stairs
had a classic ironwork banister. There was a drawing-room
whose three sash-windows looked on to the street—one
eighteenth-century row reflecting the opposite houses. On the
garden side was a library lined with books, designed with
broken pediments by my mother. Above were two more
floors. But what gave the house a unique character was that
we were able to crash through to the first floor of the house
next door, and there I had my bedroom and a drawing-room-
sized bathroom. Eight years later when my son was born we
crashed through again into the house beyond and made a bedroom and sitting-room for Duff.

The furniture and books and linen and silver were distributed about. The fat cheques bought beds and brooms. I had
my dear Wade, and Duff his Napoleonic manservant Holbrook.

A housemaid and cook were hired, also a "tweeny." Our rent was £90 a year, with £100 added for the extra floor. The lease of fifty years had cost £750, which included the decorating and the fixtures. We had what was considered the minimum of servants, five for the two of us, and we had £1300 a year. My mother helped me to paint my huge bathroom. We took a tracing of a Chinese paper at Belvoir and together on ladders we painted the white trees and birds and cages and butterflies on a pale green ground. It had a marble perspectived balustrade and, as at Belvoir, a marbled dado. The bath was hidden in a lidded coffer marbled to match. There was a large sofa, a pretty fireplace and gilded looking-glasses. The Dame aux Camélias gold-and-turquoise bottles and brushes and boxes lay on the Chinese Chippendale table, while the handsomer, less-loved dressing-set looked too big and too grand for the bedroom. All the floors were carpeted white to the walls. I felt a queen in a fairy story and could not ask for more. "What a quarter, Violet, what a quarter though!" Lady Scarbrough exclaimed to my mother, hands raised in horror. But hers were the only ones not raised in admiration.

Never were two people as happy, but we must not rest on our laurels. Duff had always had political ambitions, but for him to leave the Foreign Office needed money. Money had to be spun from somewhere even for the life we were living. Max Beaverbrook had been helpful and had commissioned four articles for his new *Sunday Express*. Duff had written them for me. I had agreed to be editor of a paper called *Femina* that was short-lived, but I was only a figurehead and had no hand in its death. I felt a fortune was to be made in America if I had the nerve to seek it. But what would Duff do while I worked for it in Hollywood? He could write his projected book on Talleyrand, but then could he write? I never had enough faith in myself or in those I loved. I could not believe in his powers of oratory which he assured me he had, nor in his pen to write anything but jokes and poems and letters of love. Still we talked a lot about "The Plan" and meanwhile kept our eyes and ears open for opportunity.

Mine saw and heard a man who arrived one ill-starred day. His name was well known because his brother was successful and respected. He suggested to my delight that I should be director of a company he was floating to distil English roses into essence. What could be more alluring? I accepted gladly and said I thought £200 a year would be splendid pay. Who else did I know who would like to be a director? "Viola Tree, of course. She lives next door." Viola gleefully said yes. Poor ignorant fools, the pair of us! Occasionally the gentleman would blow in to tell me everything was booming to a start, and his colleagues had suggested that I might like to be chairman at an extra £500 a year. Can a duck swim? Of course I would. Once he drew from his pocket some samples of scent-bottles and sprays and left me to count my unhatched ducklings.

He never called again. In his place came a policeman with a subpoena, an order to be in court as witness in the case of a man obtaining money under false pretences. Irish blood fears the police. I flew to the telephone to warn Viola, but the law had us in its arms, and trembling with fear of it we sought out Hutchie * to stand and watch for us. It was quite humiliating. In court the prisoner's appearance had changed from a man-about-town to that of an old lag, collarless and unshaved, who could not have deceived a child of four. How much money had I put into the company? None. How did I

---

* St John Hutchinson, the eminent criminal lawyer.

imagine I could be a director without shares? I didn't know. How had I been educated? At home. Confused and ashamed after this pi-jaw from the magistrate, I left the court resolving to be more careful, while the poor culprit was led away to the cells.

We lived above our means and were never in debt. This marvellous achievement was due to a reconciled and loving family, good friends, treats, foreign holidays, Paris jaunts, dresses without bills (first Ospovat, later Molyneux, faithful till our retirement, Chanel and Patou). Blind to my fantastic luck in these worldly ways, I did not consider it wonderful. Clothes were only trappings, and useful for our treats, but I could have managed perfectly with my needle and a fashion paper.

We were asked to stay at Cap Ferrat. From the smart hotel where we were lodged we would sneak out in shame (I can't think why) in the dead of night to the Sporting Club in Monte Carlo. There we were delightfully dogged by good fortune. We won at *chemin-de-fer* at every session. I can see us returning, still on tiptoe, at dawn to kneel beside our bed and count the paper gains. They came to close on £200. Deauville next —twice we went there invited by the hospitable well-wisher Lord Wimborne. It was a little too smart for me, but not for Duff, who could revel better than I could and play with more zest. I liked sitting under the apple-laden trees sipping cider and bathing with Lord Beaverbrook in the cold unattractive sea, and was even proud to be a nurse to the host, badly concussed by a polo accident. Leeches were prescribed. Guy's had discarded leeches, but, being unwilling to boast of English advance, I had a shot at making them ingest and regurgitate his blood with success. The old doctor was pleased. He was a tired old man who prescribed my patient some patent tranquillising bromide. I read its wrapping of directions—*mode d'emploi.* It told me to give *le malade une cuillière à soupe* at bed-time. His brother and Duff, after a meal silent in homage to Death's advent, had both separately left the house, ostensibly for a breath of air. They met at a party on Solly Joel's yacht, while I alone in the house, beneath a shaded light, was measuring out the drops and coaxing the poor man to swallow them. At earliest dawn he was dreadfully calm, and re-reading the medical folder in fear, I felt certain that the *cuillière à soupe* meant a teaspoon and not the large ladleful that I had administered. My blood froze with dread of manslaughter—worse, murder—for he might leave me a legacy. The motive would be plain. His pulse I could hardly feel. Quick, a looking-glass! It clouded still beneath his failing breath. I rang and rang the bell until a sleepy valet appeared, whom I told to run full speed and tell the doctor that His Lordship's pulse was about fifty, so come at once. Holding the testing looking-glass in one hand, searching for a pulse with the other, I waited beneath the noose's shadow for half an hour, only then to hear that the doctor would not displace himself and that he advised me not to be anxious. With morning came a nurse from Paris, and I handed over my patient with my guilt untold.

His brother and Duff had spent my gruesome night happily in the Casino. I never was very happy in casinos. Today I am desperate, alone and in search. Once at Deauville I lost Duff among the dancers and gamblers. Asking everyone vainly if they had seen him, I requisitioned a Rolls-Royce to take me back to the villa, and finding there an unlaid-on bed, I felt sure that Duff had been knuckle-dusted and robbed of his winnings. Running back to question the crowds again, I could see that they thought me in the throes of suspicious jealousy. "Fools," I said; "it's not adultery I mind, it's assassination!"

CHAPTER TWELVE

The Plan

A FORTUNE had to be made, and the next opportunity was a very handsome offer from a film director called J. Stuart Blackton. He was said to be the first man to put a story on the screen. Up till then it had been documentary, street scenes, some reels of the Delhi Durbar, and budding slapstick. But Hollywood had risen above Mr Blackton and he had come to England ("there the men are as mad as he") to try again with my help. He made me a preposterously big offer for two films, to which I, as usual, said "Snap." There was no deflecting him from his plans, which I could see needed adjustments that were never made. But what did it matter? It was exceedingly exciting and amusing and anachronistic and profitable.

The first film, called *The Glorious Adventure*, was set in the golden days of good King Charles. It was made in a new colour process called Prizma. The crowds and countryside were not up to much, but the close-ups we thought wonderfully faithful to flesh-tints and really artistic. My lover Gerald Lawrence, the juvenile lead, must have been twenty-five years older than me, as I remembered him in important parts at Her Majesty's when I was five. Victor McLagen made his debut as the jailbird villain. He had been a champion heavyweight in his native Australia, and here he was with his big pugnacious face for me to punch in defence of my honour. I lay *on* not *in* my Stuart four-poster bed, my fist clenched for the fray, but his tough jaw hurt my knuckles too much for that scene to carry conviction. He carried me through the Fire of London into the crypt of Old St Paul's, and the melting lead from the burning roof rose higher and higher to engulf us both. Somehow I was rescued and restored to my elderly lover, and it all ended happily and silently as it had begun.

The second film was less propitious. I was cast for Queen Elizabeth and in spite of a red wig and shaved eyebrows my full young face could not give a suggestion of her fleshless aquilinity. *The Virgin Queen* was shot at Beaulieu in the New Forest. I took a nasty little house there with Wade, and Duff came for week-ends. I learnt patience, which is an all-important virtue if one is immobilised in farthingales and ruffs and collars like tennis racquets. Bewigged and caked in a yellow mask of paint, I would wait for three days running for an English sun that never shone with the rays we needed. I loved laughing with the cast in the village pub and motoring in the dark through the too-lonely forest, where wild ponies flitted across one's way like ghosts, to meet Duff at Southampton on Saturday nights. I had little hope or faith or charity for *The Virgin Queen* with all its grotesque anachronisms, but I delighted in it as an inartistic lark.

The results were only fair, though they were fair enough to be stepping-stones to my next venture—a glorious adventure indeed. Out of the blue came the most unexpected of offers, one that I received as "The Plan" ready-made. Thirteen years before I had seen Max Reinhardt's magnificent wordless spectacle given in Olympia, a miracle play laid in the Middle Ages. The miraculous statue of the Madonna, the Nun, the convent, the crowds, the Powers of Evil and Good, the bells, the dancing children, Death in skeleton guise, all the symbols and all humanity were there for Reinhardt's genius to assemble. It was C. B. Cochran's enterprise and was not a popular success for Olympian reasons. The hall was bespoken for a motor show before *The Miracle* had time to overcome the public's surprise. Too late Lord Northcliffe, through the *Daily Mail*, ordered headlines to boom it, and articles and pictures and appeals to the gods of Olympia to prolong its life. But to an end it came and was only a memory till in 1923 Mr Otto Kahn, Reinhardt and a remarkable impresario called Morris Gest agreed to recreate the pantomime in New York.

Why I was ever chosen to play the Virgin remains a mystery and a miracle. Morris Gest, who got confused between truth and falsehood, used to give an imitation of Reinhardt jumping three feet off the Broadway pavement when my name was suggested, but Reinhardt had not followed the English *Tatler* and *Sketch* and had doubtless never heard of me, nor was he impressed by daughters of dukes. Morris Gest was; and Reinhardt, knowing his impresario's genius for publicity, did not veto the idea. After seeing my raw efforts in the film, the offer was made to me and I was asked to suggest a salary. I remember rushing into a telephone-box at some theatre where the proposition was being made, trembling with excitement and fear and dread and hope, to ring Gerald du Maurier for advice. He fixed on £300 a week. I felt faint. George Grossmith, for I was negotiating with him, looked pale himself when I told him. Followed the anticlimax of "I'll cable and let you know the answer" and silence for weeks, silence that was broken by the news that the scheme was abandoned and with it went "The Plan." Very sad (I remember crying out of the window into a dark night), I was quick to recover, for the alteration had its compensations. America seemed a vast place in which to be alone and, best of all, I would not have to divorce myself from Duff.

I should have liked to have had a child. That I did not was a cloud in my bright sky. A wicked and famous doctor had told me to abandon hope. Another alarming one had advised an operation. The third good and experienced old *accoucheur* pooh-poohed the others and advised a tonic-cure at Luz St Sauveur, where the Empress Eugénie's prayers for a Prince Imperial had been answered. Fortified by its baths, she gave this little town in the Pyrenees a frail bridge over the deep gorge, in gratitude for the birth of her son. There I thought I would go, and Duff and I would drive down together in a car I had had made for our needs. It was a cheap little machine, but boasted a Rolls bonnet. Moreover the back of the front seat let down to meet the back seat and formed with a thick rubber mattress (made to order) a luxurious bed for two. The capriciousness of lilos was not yet to be bought. Square like a real mattress, ours smelt of rubber and was blown up by a resisting concertina. The equipment included sleeping-bags (linen-lined), a case of cooking utensils, a petrol-air lamp and a primus stove—everything that I loved and that my poor Duff hated. Off we set, disappointment at "The Plan's" collapse forgotten, into the spring weather, happy pilgrims in search of a child. Never once did we sleep *à la belle étoile* nor even in my snug kennel-car. The weather favoured Duff's choice, and beyond eating our luncheon once or twice in fields of Pyrenean narcissi, we sheltered in the inns of France. Duff's poem recording this voyage evokes it poignantly:

> Lest we forget, by any chance,
> The happy days we spent together,
> Travelling through the fields of France
> In sunshine and in cloudy weather.

TRAVEL DIARY

Lest we forget the ruined keep
    That Richard set above the Seine,
And how we climbed that castle steep,
    You, I and Berners in the rain.

How Berners left us for Montmartre,
    And how we took the road once more,
And didn't care to stop at Chartres,
    Because we'd seen it once before.

How, where another Diane lived,
    And where I rather think she died,
With promises and bribes we strived,
    And strived in vain to get inside.

At Châteaudun and at Vendôme
    We stopped and stared; then on again,
Until we reached in cold and gloom
    The capital of fair Touraine.

We went, intending not to go,
    To Amboise, having lost our way.
They took us in at Chenonceaux,
    They shut us out at Valençay.

Limoges we saw, but liked it not,
    We saw and loved Rocamadour,
For there we felt the sunshine hot,
    The thing we had been longing for.

Saint Antonin! the small hotel
    Down by the river, where the band
Played in the darkness, till we fell
    Asleep together, hand in hand.

THE PLAN

Though other things may be forgot
　　In the bleak days of life's December,
That happy night, that lovely spot,
　　We shall, oh shall we not remember?

Our hosts there who were kind and good
　　Shall be remembered, and so shall be
The devils who refused us food
　　In most inhospitable Albi.

We climbed La Montagne Noire with ease,
　　Whence looking on the plain below,
We cried "We're in the Pyrenees,"
　　Which we were not—but didn't know.

We coasted down, we seemed to fly,
　　And ere the sun to bed had gone,
We saw against the evening sky
　　The battlements of Carcassonne.

At Foix we saw a drunken man
　　Who'd lost his leg and lost his wife,
And been in prison for a span
　　For taking of his colonel's life.

And there we bought red wine and cheese
　　And feasted in a field of green,
Surrounded by the Pyrenees,
　　And happy as a king and queen.

The joy of Luchon! and the fun
　　Of waking up at break of day,
Climbing the hillside in the sun
　　And picking wild flowers on the way.

TRAVEL DIARY

Breakfast at the Hôtel Bordeaux,
  And then the stern and steep ascent,
We cooled the heated car with snow,
  And down the other side we went.

At Lourdes we watched the pilgrims pray,
  And saw the holy waters stir,
No miracles were worked that day,
  So we went on to Saint Sauveur.

I saw where you were bound to stay,
  The doctor who should make you strong,
And then it rained the livelong day,
  From matins until evensong.

Next day we travelled back to Pau,
  Forlorn we were, my love, forlorn.
It didn't cheer us much to know
  Where Henry of Navarre was born.

Our thoughts were turned to fleeting joy,
  And time's all-conquering attacks—
We drank a bottle of "the Boy," *
  And said a sad farewell at Dax.

Luz was a gloomy little place and the cure filled one hour of the day, but unselfish friends came to solace me, the last of whom was Katharine Asquith. She and I were never parted from Belloc's book and his Pyrenean injunctions. We read and wrote and talked and made expeditions. The first was to Burgos, where the armed Spanish police forced us to pay twice for our fares. Another was on foot twenty kilometres over the Cirque de Gavarnie into the Val d'Arazas, which is a poor man's Grand Canyon. Over snow we trudged in great elation

* Champagne.

and slept in a cabin and returned next day triumphant wrecks. We dressed like palmers in wide straw hats with hoods beneath them to protect us from sun and wind. Then a last memorable trip to Lourdes, where the Blessed Virgin heard and in time answered both our prayers, mine for a child, Katharine's for a conversion. We came home together, this time sleeping nightly beneath the stars. My mother was writing and tele-graphing daily to remind us of the dangers of wolves in France. We saw some or thought we did—grey whining wraiths that frightened us, though less than the *garde-chasse* who could move us on when the camp was made. We lived on milk and potatoes to make us slim and pure, and we had the strength to send back our first gourmet's luncheon at the best Bordeaux restaurant, it being uneatable.

Reunited in Gower Street, happiness refound, sun shining through the shutters. London was dancing in its season. Duff sweated away at the Foreign Office. He had become secretary to Ronald McNeill, the Under-Secretary for Foreign Affairs who had once thrown a book at Winston's head across the floor of the House. This post brought us another £100 a year to the good. My one-time patron Lord Curzon was Foreign Secretary and was apt to have his knife into Duff. It is true that we had toyed with an idea of taking for a song and as an investment the great *piano nobile* of the Palazzo Labia in Venice. The rumour got into some gossip column and enraged Lord Cur-zon, who complained that Duff was having too much leave. This not being true, the permanent head of the Foreign Office defended him. The dear Lord Curzon replied, "It is not so much his ordinary leave to which I object as his ability while performing his duties to enjoy an amount of social relaxation unclaimed by his fellow-workers." ("Utterly meaningless drivel," wrote Duff in his diary.)

Among our intimates were Belloc and Maurice Baring and Hutchie and his family, and a new concerto in three movements, Dr Ethel Smyth. Maurice Baring must have brought us to the notice and to the great affection of Hilaire Belloc, perhaps with Winston Churchill the man nearest to genius I have known, "one of the most complex, contradictory and brilliant characters ever to thunder, rumble, flash and explode across this astonishing world of ours." He was to dedicate to Duff his great Ode on Wine and to write me some beautiful sonnets. He was the "Captain Good" in life as well as the minstrel, the story-teller, the soothsayer, the foundation and the flush of the feast. St John Hutchinson, our Hutchie, was indispensable and for some reason bracketed with Alan Parsons as "the Boys." He looked like a Caldecott picture and was a companion as lovable and funny as one could find in life or legend. Maurice Baring lived in a minute flat in Gray's Inn, giving luncheon parties (cooked by the Embassy Club) for Ethel Smyth and us and H. G. Wells and Arnold Bennett and Squire and other writers, and lots of sailors and beautiful women. Ethel remained a perpetual dawn to me. She grew almost stone-deaf and lived to a great age and to the very end she surprised. Sargent's drawing shows her truly. She wore an unmoored tricorne on her wild, wild hair, through which a quick gesture of her hand would pass, oblivious of the hat, to make it rock like a ship in a storm. She thought a lot about her clothes and was ambitious for them, but they disappointed her sadly. To hear Ethel draw blood out of the piano while shouting "*Ah, ça ira, ça ira, ça ira, les aristos à la lanterne*" was to make you hold your head in your hands for fear of losing it.

It must have been in these years that Chaliapin returned, not to Covent Garden but to concerts in the Albert Hall, to make his gramophone records and *ballader un peu* in Gower Street.

One night especially I remember he brought a Russian quartet of men singers. I lit the green grass and plane-trees of the garden with projected light from the house-top (unusual then). Moonlight and sunlight we could turn on, also quite an effective snowstorm for the Russian choruses. We cannot have been more than twenty close friends supping in this London backyard magically transformed by light and laughter into a poor man's Parnassus where Chaliapin with his choir sang both high and low, with laughter for *The Flea*, with heavy groan for *Ich grolle nicht*, where Belloc quoted his ballads and sang in a red glow *Auprès de ma blonde* and other marching songs of the French Army, and Viola danced the nymph in the blue moonshine while Maurice, an agile satyr, pursued and lost her. The back windows of the other houses opened and those too of the cheerful chemist opposite. The frowning Irvingite church in Gordon Square (the last apostle dead) was lost in darkness. What can the neighbours have thought? They were chiefly occupants of boarding-houses. They never told us to "have done" for sleep's sake, and I fear we never gave them any thought or sympathy.

Next glorious morning a letter arrived from America to say *The Miracle* was after all to be put on and announcing the arrival of Morris Gest in London on his way to Reinhardt's Salzburg palace. "The Plan" rebuilt itself into airy castles. Came too a letter signed "R. Kommer von Czernowitz," dated from Leopoldskron, Salzburg, inviting us both to stay with Professor Reinhardt in August. There was something in that first letter from my dearest friend that allayed fears and promised fulfilment of one's wishes. We had taken, with three or four others, a floor of a palace in Venice for a fortnight. It was a cheap holiday in 1923. Three couples paid £100 a month between them. You found someone else to take it for two weeks and for £50 you lived for a fortnight in the splendour of wide *salas* hung with Doges in carved frames. We agreed to stay with Reinhardt on the way. Before leaving I had an appointment to meet Morris Gest at the Savoy Hotel. He noticed my tremblings and lost the respect for my rank which had prompted him to engage me. He told me to take off my hat and gloves and hold up my skirts. I became human merchandise. Luckily I got bought—at least I said "yes," signed something provisional that I did not read and got a two-dollar bill thrust into my breast for luck. Later I realised that it was on approval that I went to Austria.

In the hullabaloo of departure, with the new life of fame and fortune ahead (holiday packing for the summer still had something of nursery days, since it came but once a year and demanded months of designing and economising and synchronising), I forgot to dread Leopoldskron, but once in the train puffing towards Salzburg my nerve began to flutter and fail. I infected Duff, who having bragged of being fluent in German was not looking forward to my finding him tongue-tied. Millicent Duchess of Sutherland was pacing up and down the train corridor. She also appeared to be in trepidation. She said she was going up to the top of the Geistberg "to think things out."

At Munich we both panicked and resolved, unless we were pulled out of the train, to go straight through to Venice. But pulled out we were by the funniest, most fantastical, spherical figure in *Lederhosen* and sky-blue silver-buttoned jacket, shirt open on a fat child's neck, round nose, round dark velvet eyes, thick semi-circular eyebrows and ruthlessly shaved round head, who, immediately recognising his unknown prey, had us out and into an open *fiacre* in a trice. He brought letters of encouragement from my mother (she always wrote ahead to welcome me) and special shoulders for all my burdens, wings

for my feet and heart. His name was Rudolf Kommer. I can
see him sitting on the box looking back at his two charges,
pointing out the characteristics and monuments of his beloved
Salzburg and at the same time giving us a clear précis of the
situation. It amounted to this; that the Professor would like
to see us at tea (it was about 2 p.m.) or would we rather wait
for dinner? That there was to be chamber music that evening
in the castle, and that the Sitwells and Lord Berners were in
town. Should he ask them? Should he find the Duchess of
Sutherland, who had escaped us, and invite her? That Frau
Helene Timmig was the hostess and that Reinhardt was unfamiliar with any language but his own. That we must wait
in Salzburg for the arrival of Einar Nilson, the arranger of
Humperdinck's *Miracle* music, that he was expected daily, and
that nothing in the nature of rehearsal could be started without
him. That it always rained, that we should be completely free,
and that everything else should be organised and shaped to fit
our pleasure and desires. I felt sure that Kommer would design
even the weather through some link with the elements.

By this time we had arrived at the famous Palace of the
Prince-Archbishop and were being shown by retainers to our
room. It was very large and, like the rest of the Palace and
most things Austrian, spacious and fresh as a dairy. There was
a bath, in a room nearly as big as our bedroom, that required a
fire to be lit beneath it if one wanted it hot. Tea with the shy
Professor under a pillared porch looking towards the lake was
fairly paralysing. Duff's German, as I suspected, was unheard.
Mine was worse. Kommer translated our social banalities. I
felt my every movement was being analysed, criticised and condemned. I felt fat and unspiritual and unsuitable and stupid.
It didn't last long—one trembling cup of tea to be drunk and
a dry biscuit to be nibbled, and the ordeal ended.

In the evening the presence of so many English helped, as did the candle-lit chamber music. The Sitwells were there with young Willie Walton, a name to become famous but then unknown to me. "They murdered Willie's work," said Osbert. "They played it last night. The cello spike stuck in the join of the stage boards. The cellist was brought to the ground. They murdered Willie's work." The Duchess had been tracked and captured and brought in. We felt ourselves on the stage and under the manager's eye. Once out of the *mise-en-scène* came the freedom actors feel in the greenroom and *coulisses*.

I cannot remember how many days we stayed. Kommer shone through the rain. We went on pelting picnics. One in particular I see. On a lake stood a villa full of charming smiling people in dirndls and *Lederhosen*. The dew of the morning, it seemed to me, was upon them. The sparkle of the lake, the crystalline purity of the high mountains were above them. Young and old they dived and darted like trout through the water. They gambolled, they ate ravenously of fresh bread and yellow butter, crisp green salad and all things wholesome. They turned out to be morphia-maniacs, every one of them, and their playful dog died of eating some stray heroin pellets with his dinner.

At long last Nilson arrived and the fateful hour struck when I must be tried out by Reinhardt. I partially masked my nerves by dressing up. It was impossible, I felt, to get outside oneself in everyday dress, so I tied my head in a pair of chiffon drawers and safety-pinned my skirt into a longer one, and patched and pulled and pinned and improvised my garments into a disguise. The Professor must have found it hard not to laugh, but he had learnt his psychology from Freud and himself had suffered a great deal from inhibitions. He told me later that as a young actor he had been unable to play a part without wearing a beard. My drawers and pins were my beard, and no doubt he divined it.

First the story of the play was told to me in his spell-binding voice. Kommer was there to translate, though I understood most of it and was naturally moved to quiet tears. Those tears, so normal to me, stood me in wonderful stead. The English are unemotional, therefore I must be an artist. So Reinhardt reasoned. Nilson then went to the piano and played the themes, while my motifs and movements were directed by Reinhardt. The statue must wake from stone, turn to flesh, and the living Virgin must break from her cerements, descend from her niche, lay down her jewelled crown and gather up in all humility the veil, scapula and cord of the fugitive Nun. She must dress herself in this livery—her own—and fastening the rosary to her cord must look at the crucifix with heart-rending compassion. I had no confidence. Who could have enough belief in herself to interpret so beautiful and spiritual a part? But Reinhardt had experience of raw material and living, willing material, and I could see he was satisfied. So when he said *"Sie könnte vielleicht auch die Nonne spielen"* I knew that I had not been found wanting.

The search for a Nun was in full swing. Potential nuns flitted through the passages and came to meals and died away like chords of music. I knew that my chord was to linger and reverberate for a long time. So to Venice we went, gay with relief, and for a few weeks forgot "The Plan" and the imminent separation, and came back to London and the Foreign Office to hear the strangest stories, reported chiefly by Lord Berners, who had remained some weeks at Salzburg. Maria Carmi had preceded me at Leopoldskron and had told them all that they would be mad to engage, for the part she had created in *The Miracle*, one who was drugged to the teeth, rarely sober, and totally unreliable. After my departure Morris Gest had swept in, grinning with clever mischievous ideas. Had anything been found in my room? Empty gin-bottles, hypodermics, compromising letters? No. Then his choice was a good choice and Maria Carmi must be engaged to act the Madonna as well as Diana Manners. It would stop her mouth and also stimulate interest in the elaborate publicity which was being prepared for American headlines during the long delays of rehearsal and preparation. The play's opening had been set for Christmas week at the Century Theatre, New York. I was to arrive in November. On hearing these things I heard also a knell to "The Plan." I could not see myself going to a new continent, to new people, to a new profession, being separated for six months from my husband, and having with me in the same yoke a woman older, more experienced both in life and on the stage, neither respecting truth nor fearing slander and bent on suppressing a menacing rival.

Mr Otto Kahn, a man I was attached to and trusted completely, was, in admiration of Reinhardt, financing *The Miracle*. To him I wrote confessing my fears. I expect Kommer drafted this *cri de coeur*. He certainly answered it, as he came to do all the letters he wrote for me. As usual he dealt with the impediments and left me a smooth path to tread. Things that the lady was supposed to have said, she had also written. He had the letter in his possession, so she would say no more. Besides, he was there to protect me. What more did I need? Confidence returned. The Plan had taken the shape of a shining road leading upwards to the Vision Splendid.